Vietnam – The Teenage Wasteland

Story of a Hippie in War

Tom Martiniano

Copyright © 2012 Tom Martiniano

All Rights Reserved

ISBN – 13: 978-1478350842
IBSN 10: 1478350249

To all combat veterans – a very special breed of person. Because of the combat soldier and all of their sacrifices, life in America is a lot easier for all of us.

And to all combat veterans everywhere including all of our past foes, they too knew what it was like to experience the horrors of war. I know they hated it as much as we did.

INTRODUCTION

"No event in American history is more misunderstood than the Vietnam War. It was misreported then, and it is misremembered now."
— Richard M. Nixon, 1985

Whether it was to fight the spread of communism as textbooks say or to gain control of the lucrative opium trade in the Golden Triangle (as more progressive scholars claim), American involvement in Vietnam was one of the most controversial events in United States history.

First one foot in, then the other, our involvement in Vietnam escalated from an innocent "advisory role" to an "aggressor role" until the fighting became a disaster for both America and Vietnam that wasted the lives of fifty-eight thousand Americans and more than three million Vietnamese, creating ill-will, bad public relations and loss of face for the United States.

Over a period of two hundred years the United States grew to become the greatest power on Earth, a power that proved itself victorious time and time again – defeat did not exist as a word in the American vocabulary. But, for the first time in American history victory was beyond its reach in Vietnam. And it was not a good feeling; in fact it was downright embarrassing.

The failure, apparently, was that the South Vietnamese were unable to carry out the war on their own. The US tried "Vietnamization", an attempt to turn the war over to the Vietnamese where it belonged, but the program bogged and the US ended up carrying the load which pitted it against its Cold War foes.

President John F. Kennedy formed a relationship with the South Vietnamese President, Ngo Dinh Diem, with a view to avoiding heavy US involvement, but those efforts were dashed when Diem was brutally murdered. JFK had no interest in Vietnam and planned to limit and unwind US involvement there. However, just two weeks after Diem's death, President Kennedy was also assassinated. With those two key political leaders gone, chaos was bound to turn up sooner or later in South-East Asia, and it did in the form of Lyndon Baines Johnson who quickly escalated the "conflict" to all-out war.

At the time, American citizens did not understand why their country was involved in the war. The PR line from the Johnson Administration was that we were fighting abroad to keep the "domino theory" from expanding communism in Asia. But did the United States really or truly care if Vietnam, with no visible, valuable export, fell into the hands of communists?

The Gulf of Tonkin incident on August 4, 1964, in which U.S. destroyers were attacked by North Vietnamese torpedo boats, gave Lyndon Johnson and his advisers the excuse to order immediate air attacks on North Vietnam in retaliation.

Lyndon Johnson asked for a mandate for future military action and got it. The war escalated from there despite the fact that a declaration of war was never officially approved or given, only "implied."

During the mid-sixties the two opposing forces sparred but gradually, step by step, became formidable foes. The NVA and VC were successful on many occasions with their guerrilla war tactics while US forces utilized their superior weapons technology and air support.

The turning point of the war came during the Tet Offensive in 1968. While it was a defeat for the North

Vietnamese it made it obvious to the world that the resolve of the Communist forces was stronger than the USA's commitment. And perhaps more importantly, Tet made the viciousness of the war very apparent to the American people who were now able to witness the carnage on the evening news as they sat down to eat dinner.

Due to the growing media coverage the conflict became known as "The TV War". Some Americans became outraged when they saw the devastation with their own eyes while others began to rally and demonstrate against US involvement in Vietnam. Internally, the country began to turn against itself as the argument over the Vietnam War caused the largest rift in American society since the Civil War. This was due in part to the fact that the casualties in 1968 were the highest annual losses of the war. The American people were stunned at the year's toll of 14,000 US soldiers killed. And as if to pour salt on the open wound of mounting disagreement, the US commander in Vietnam, General Westmoreland, brazenly asked that 200,000 more American soldiers be sent. This request, along with what they witnessed on television, made many Americans reluctant to believe that the Tet Offensive had been, as was claimed, a glorious American victory.

Unlike many other major conflicts, as the Vietnam War progressed the reasons for fighting became less and less defined. Initially, many soldiers in Vietnam held to the principle used by American soldiers before them: duty and honor. During WWII, for example, soldiers went by the principle that it was simply their duty to serve their country but in the Vietnam War a number of factors muddied the waters.

When the draft came into play in the 1960s the American teen was given a nasty choice: go to war and get killed, or blow to Canada or Sweden — never to see friends or family again. It was a felony to dodge the draft; one's future would be forever blemished should he follow core beliefs that this was not a legal war and so refuse duty. And pressure was applied by parents too. WW II had ended but twenty five years earlier, many fathers who had served while fighting the Nazis or The Empire of Japan demanded their sons "defend the United States", thus encouraging them to accept the draft. American teenagers succumbed to the dual pressure from government and elders. Eighty-nine percent of draftees accepted it, went into the infantry and onto the battlefield.

Once the troops arrived in Vietnam they asked their superior officers the purpose of the conflict only to find out there wasn't one. They were merely told: "Kill the enemy, stupid, that's your purpose." But the USA was not at war and the draftees had no axe to grind with the Vietnamese. Despite the no-war, American soldiers knew one thing for sure; they were in a combat situation, people were trying to kill them.

And the Vietnam War was, in reality, not a war. It was a "policing action". A point of view many US soldiers agreed with was voiced by one veteran: "We are basically cops walking around in the open hoping the NVA and VC will attack us so we can attack back, throwing our entire inventory of ordnance at them." And they did. The military complex was more than willing and able to try out all the shiny new weapons they had developed over the preceding Cold War years; weapons such as the F-111 Super Sonic Bomber, the B-52 bomber (which had been in service all through the Cold War and never dropped one bomb in anger until Vietnam). New ordnance such as the Smart Bomb and laser-guided bombs were tested and developed in this time period. The new mini-gun and the new Vulcan Cannons for jet fighters were tried and tested there too. You name it;

Vietnam gave military leaders and armament companies tons of important information about the effect of their munitions that were only heretofore tested under dummy conditions. A record 6.5 million tons of bombs were dropped on Vietnam; more than any other single war or conflict up to that time.

And the grunts in the field got whatever weapon they wanted and were gladly given them to use just for the asking. To the absolute glee and gratification of the manufacturers, American soldiers killed hundreds of thousands of Asians with their modern devices. However, despite all those fantastic new weapons, the tenacious enemy just came back harder and stronger every time.

By the end of the 1960's something unprecedented in our nation's history began to happen on the home front : Opposition to the war became popular, even fashionable and turned into open protest and then riot in the streets and on campuses. And the target of the growing animosity became our own soldiers even though many of them had been forced by draft into the conflict and the rest (professional soldiers) ordered into battle! Even some high profile Americans gave aid and support to the enemy of America – the North Vietnamese.

The Battle of Hamburger Hill in 1969 alarmed Americans so much that it became the catalyst for emboldened liberals to step into the fray. Led by true congressional liberals like Ted Kennedy, severe criticism was cast not just on the tactics but on the actual mental competency of the military leadership. This caused a row in the Senate that almost resulted in the resignation of the entire Joint Chiefs of Staff.

To stay focused on the task at hand, soldiers in Vietnam had to turn a blind eye to the noise and distractions back home. Losing focus was fatal as the North Vietnamese stepped up their efforts yet again. GIs had their hands full; they were literally fighting for their lives on a daily basis.

Facing such aggression from the North Vietnamese while ham-strung by tactics they were ordered to use led to mass mutiny in the field where US soldiers demanded they be allowed to finish off the enemy as they were taught to do in training. However, Washington insisted on keeping their role a "policing action" whilst attempting a futile transfer of the war to the South Vietnamese, who were not interested, were tired of twenty-five years of conflict and wanted no more of it. Meanwhile, the American GI, caught in the middle, was pummeled, pounded and sent home in a box.

If they were lucky enough to come close to the end of their tour, American soldiers were more than ready to return home and get back to "the real world", as they put it. But none were ready for what they encountered upon their arrival. Protesters stood at airports with signs decrying veterans as "baby killers" and "murderers". Returning Vietnam veterans were spat on, ridiculed and humiliated for having accepted the draft and having served their country.

Strangely, some of the animosity shown to the returning soldiers was caused by false testimony and accusations from anti-war organizations such as the VVAW (Vietnam Veterans Against the War). Those so-called veterans created and nurtured an environment of hatred, disrespect, and hostility towards all men in uniform. Men who were never deployed to Vietnam but who wore their GI uniforms in public were openly chastised. At that time, even men who paid the ultimate price and sacrificed their lives for their country were not honored or commemorated but instead defiled. There were few signs of appreciation in the USA, unlike when the Vietnam veteran's fathers had returned home from WWII as heroes with parades thrown amid the adulation.

Yet the combat in Vietnam was just as real as any war before it. The dying was certainly just as real, the sacrifices and the pain of war were very real for those who fought in it. The amount of combat the American soldier experienced in one year was unprecedented. The statistics of the Vietnam War are not well known and have been kept secret for decades but Vietnam was one of the harshest combat experiences in our country's history.

As a comparison: during WWII the average combat soldier spent forty days out of a year in actual combat. No doubt the combat in WWII was fierce, but each battle lasted anywhere between 2 days and 2 weeks — but then there would be a lull in the action for the soldiers, sometimes for months. And there were forward lines one could withdraw from: one could go back to the rear area behind the front lines and be safe. As for statistics on kills per infantry soldier, the average WW II soldier killed two enemy soldiers.

In Vietnam the statistics were much different. Most US soldiers spent an average of 240 days in combat out of the 365 days they were there. The average combat soldier in Vietnam killed fifteen enemy soldiers while one out of every nine American infantry soldiers died. Four out of ten infantry men were permanently disabled. Seven out of ten were wounded in one way or another.

To give real hard statistics: in WW II the vaunted 101st Airborne Division lost 1,766 men KIA. In Vietnam the same 101st Airborne Division lost 4,011 men KIA.

These were outrageous statistics never before seen in the annals of American combat. The soldiers that came out of the Vietnam War, particularly the infantry soldiers, were more battle-weary than their fathers and their grandfathers had been in WWI, WWII or the Korean War. Testing done on Vietnam War combat soldiers found their adrenaline glands active twenty-four hours a day, seven days a week. It is no wonder their adrenals were so out of control, the soldiers had lived in the battlefield, vigilant and ready to fight twenty four hours a day, seven days a week for nearly a year. Many didn't even take their boots off at night for fear of having to get out of harm's way in a hurry — which was the case frequently.

Similarly, jet fighter and helicopter pilots flew several missions per day, staying in their cockpits for up to eighteen hours a day, seven days per week supporting ground troops and knocking out enemy installations round the clock. These pilots were worn to a frazzle because of the constant and unending sorties that they flew.

So when the soldiers finally arrived home fresh from the killing fields of Vietnam they were spent physically and mentally. And, unlike their forefathers, they were flown straight from the combat zone to the USA without time to rest or gather their thoughts and emotions. There was no buffer -- they just travelled from a foreign hostile environment to a home hostile environment within 24 hours and had to cope with the unexpected social viewpoints of war protestors, their friends and families. During WW II, soldiers returned to the States on ships and had several weeks to gather themselves. Plus, they were excited to arrive home, straight into the welcome arms of warm, loving Americans applauding them for their sacrifice.

Yet despite all their experiences, the resilient Vietnam combat veteran demonstrated incredible statistics upon reintegrating into civilian life. Eighty five percent of all Vietnam vets made successful transitions into civilian life and a Vietnam vet's personal income has been eighteen percent higher than those of non-vets of the same age. Many Vietnam vets were successful despite all they had gone through. The reason it is believed is that these vets knew they had overcome and beat unprecedented odds in surviving the war. Additionally, they knew they had been fighting not for the salvation of the United States against enemy oppression (as had been the case in earlier American wars) but for the survival of one another. They quickly learned that they were in a killing zone that had no real purpose and just wanted to make it home alive and help others make it home. So when they did make it home, many vets used the opportunity became industrious and worked to make a better world for themselves, their friends and their families.

The war in South-East Asia was grueling and harsh. The return home was anguishing and there was no chance for the soldiers to tell their tales. After all, who wanted to hear about triumphs in a war that everyone was against? But there are stories to tell and they are just as riveting and heroic as the best of WW II or Korean War tales.

In this book we bring you a big fat slice of the Vietnam War. Within its pages you will experience what it was like from the perspective of a combat soldier, the story of one man, a drafted "peace-nik" who slowly became a warrior. As you turn the pages you will experience what he experienced in a war that became a teenage wasteland.

This book is different. It seeks to answer every question anyone has ever had about Vietnam while allowing the reader to fully experience the way it was through the eyes of a combat soldier.

As with all stories of human endeavor there are valuable lessons to be learned. I consider myself a student of history and particularly the part played by leadership. I would not swap what I learned in the pages of this book for all the texts I have read on what constitutes leadership or the lack of it.

Haydn James
Editor

INSIGNIA

Emblem for the 101st Airborne
"Screaming eagles"

"CIB" or Combat Infantry Badge
This is what the Army gives you once you have been in combat.

CMOH or Congressional Medal of Honor

23rd Infantry "Americal Division" Emblem

An Army Division is composed of anwhere from 10,000 men to 25,000 men. It is composed of several Brigades. A Division is usually led by a General.

NOMENCLATURE

An Army **Brigade** is composed of 3,000 to 5,000 men. It is made up of several Battalions. A Brigade is usually led by a Colonel.

An Army **Battalion** is composed of around 500 men. It is composed of several companies. A Battalion is usually led by a Lt Colonel.

An Army **Company** is composed of approximately 100 men. There are 4 or more Platoons per company. A Company is usually led by a Captain.

A **Platoon** is composed of 2-3 squads. A platoon has around 20-25 men. A platoon is led by a Lieutenant. A squad is led by a Seargent.

PART ONE

QUESTIONS & ANSWERS

Vietnam – The Teenage Wasteland

1

THE NIGHTMARES

It's an odd, distant kind of feeling. I'm buried under heavy dirt. It's almost smothering but I can see a smattering of calm blue sky and that gives me a somewhat peaceful, almost serene feeling, like "thank God I finally have peace" as I slip deeper into the warm, cozy fuzziness of it. I know for some reason I shouldn't be going there… but what the hell, the serenity is enticing, drawing me into its safe, warm bosom and I'm getting lost in it…very tired…I should just let go…. let go…..

Alert! A little voice in my head tells me serious danger is nearby as I teeter between the warm-cozy place and the real world of pain and confusion.

Suddenly, I'm slammed back to the real world by the thunderous sound of a jet flying directly overhead, real low. Huh? I'm not near an airport…then I hear something more startling, automatic gunfire. Confused, tired, very tired, need sleep – but… danger close! Real close! Move it mister! I tell myself. MOVE YOUR BODY AND GET THE HELL OUT OF HERE NOW!!

I still feel held down by heavy dirt but when panic takes over I jerk my body into action and the weight falls away. I start to sense the sticky, hot humidity and the familiarity of the oppressive heat brings me back. I sit up, still dazed and wince as I see bullets hit around me. I know what that is!

Instinct takes over. I jump up and run. Bullets kick up dirt all around me as if to urge me forward. I look down and see I have an M-16 in my hand – oh yeah, now I remember. I look ahead and see my friends urgently waving me toward the river bed. I feel like I'm running in slow motion. I need to get to my friends. I run harder but to my horror I'm not going any faster. The harder I try to run the slower I go, and now bullets are hitting real close. Danger is right on top of me. Run! RUN! I order myself.

Making some progress now, getting closer, I'm sweating profusely and I feel giddy as I near the safety of my friends, like you feel if you run out of a totally dark room with the uncontrollable urge to scream. I let escape a silly giggle as I see my friends near. As I arrive, I recognize my friend, John French. He looks at me oddly, as though there's something terribly wrong with me, but wait – I thought he was killed days ago. Oh my God I must be dead! I am dead!! I scream, "NO…!"

This is the point I wake up in a cold sweat still screaming "NO!" and jerk my body in all directions, as if fighting to get back into it. Then I sit up straight, panting.

My wife soothes me and asks me if I'm okay. I look at her and am glad to see her because it means I'm in a safe place, not "back there". I tell her it was another nightmare and she asks me, like she always does, if there is anything she can do. I say no like I always do and get up and go into the bathroom.

I feel embarrassed as I sit there in the dark. I really don't want to be the stereotypical combat veteran who has screaming nightmares. But I was and I wasn't able to get rid of them. They didn't disable me or anything; they just came and scared the hell out of me and my wife, mainly her, actually. I know they really concerned her.

I sat on the toilet in the safety of the dark bathroom and chilled out while I convinced myself that everyone had nightmares. So what's the big deal? But I knew better than that. After years the nightmares were just as fresh and raw as

Vietnam – The Teenage Wasteland

when I first had them. And that wasn't the only nightmare I had. I had three of them – all different and distinct. I used to have four but one finally went away – the worst one – the one where I was doing a second tour in Vietnam and was on a patrol when we were ambushed. Everyone was getting shot and falling down around me. I had no chance of fighting back. I was totally overwhelmed and confused. I finally got hit by several bullets; it was the last thing that happened except the feeling of being hopelessly alone as I spiraled down a dark, bottomless tunnel. That one really affected me and when I woke from it I would be totally disoriented for quite a while. I had it every night no matter what – every dammed night. I tried to stave it off by not eating certain foods before I went to bed but that really didn't help. It showed up right on time, couldn't stop it. But like I said, that was the one that eventually disappeared.

I didn't mind the nightmares. Not really. Sounds odd I know but the only thing that bothered me was that it freaked out my wife and made me a bit of a stranger to her. I'm on my third spouse now. Not because of the nightmares, just because of the usual things that cause marriages to break up…or maybe it was the nightmares. I really don't know. As an aside, I did lose one girlfriend who found out I was a Vietnam veteran. She moved out of the house the day after she found out. She asked me if I was in the infantry and if I personally killed people. I said yes and when I got home from work the following evening she was packed and gone.

I sat in the bathroom and mused as I remembered that I had that one particular nightmare every night whether I needed it or not. It went on every night for seven years. It reached the point where I actually got so disoriented from it that I had to ask my wife if I did more than one tour in Vietnam. She looked closely into my eyes and I saw the pity and her concern. She assured me I had only done one tour there. I knew it was true but at that stage I was not fully convinced.

Life goes on. The next morning I'd be back to normal and go about my business, the previous night's nightmares forgotten. I always managed to make it through another boring, nothing happening day. But the daytime became as troublesome as the night because of another monster that plagued me: there was no longer any danger in my life. How the hell can anyone live without some danger? Danger is a drug. In the day-to-day motions I went through to make a living there was a huge, empty hole. Danger was a wonderful drug and I was addicted to it. It's nothing you can kick in a week because it is so potently addictive. I've never done heroin but I bet danger beats it all to hell.

I've always liked action and found that action was especially good when it contained danger.

Danger meant the possibility of death. Death is the highest stake. To brush with death and survive is to be alive, and for me, the only way to feel alive was to be in danger or close proximity to death. Being in a combat zone gave me that ever-present feeling of danger. I was never so alive. It was a drug and I became a junkie for it.

When I got back from Vietnam I was happy to be home but on the other hand there was something missing: It was *danger* that was missing. I missed danger right away; I missed the smell of it, the taste of it and the rush of it. I missed it horribly.

But I wasn't the type of person, nor am I the type of person who wants to make danger in the environment just so they can get their fix – I'm not that selfish. When you summon danger it involves other people who don't necessarily want to experience it. So I kept it cool and keep it cool. I don't need it that bad. I just have that hollow feeling and live life as it is. I have what I wished for – peace – so I accept and appreciate it.

I finally got rid of all of the nightmares and the angst of missing danger.

It's funny how therapeutic life is. I have turned into a story teller. I remember in Vietnam us guys used to say: "well,

Vietnam – The Teenage Wasteland

there's one you can tell your grandchildren!" But it takes too long to get grandchildren, and hell, they won't be ready for these stories for another ten years. My kids never really cared for them anyway, but acquaintances did.

Over the years I met a lot of people and made lots of friends. I do believe I'm a gregarious person – I like people. They eventually find out I'm a vet and right away they get interested and want to know about my times in Vietnam. I've told my stories to people a thousand times in the last thirty five years. It helps more than hurts. Only a few have sat in judgment of me – at least to my face.

I found that people are curious. As soon as they find out I've been in combat they're eager to learn all about it. They ask me a lot of questions and I try to answer them to the best of my ability. I know people want to know because this war was different and caused a lot of curiosity. So I finally wrote it all down for you. It will answer all of your questions, not only about Vietnam, but about war itself and what our boys currently go through and compromise for your benefit.

Here it is.

2

WHAT WAS IT LIKE?

I've been asked, over the years, "what was it like in Vietnam?" When people learn I was in actual combat they ask me all sorts of questions but what they really want to know is, "what was it like?"

The word "like" is used to give a comparative. The reason a lot of people ask me for such a comparative is because they want to put themselves in the same shoes. They're not necessarily interested in my exploits; they want to compare my answers to their own experience, to see if they would have measured up or withstood the trauma and excitement of combat. They want to know if they would have cut the mustard and made it.

Some (very few) come out and ask me very blunt questions. "What was it like?" is a safe option used by the more cautious, in case I might be offended at being asked direct questions, while others think "maybe he's crazy and I should avoid asking him questions at all". Some take me out for a beer and figure they have to soften me up before asking the questions. But regardless, what I've found is there's a great amount of interest in the Vietnam War.

People are kind of amazed that a normal guy like me killed other living beings. What the good majority of people really wanted to know was how can I have killed another person yet stand there in front of them, acting like any other normal person? I have seen people just marvel at the fact that I have killed, but if I hadn't told them I was a combat vet they would

Vietnam – The Teenage Wasteland

have never guessed it in a million years. I marvel at the fact that they marvel.

So when people ask, "what was it like there?" they're asking because they want to put themselves in my place to see if they have the moxie to do the things I did.

I answer with short anecdotes or long stories. Either way, people are always amazed. And to tell the truth, as time went on, I became amazed too. I thought that everyone had experienced that sort of thing in their lives. It never occurred to me that people had not. And so I found out, few people have seen or done the things I have.

I know some people don't believe half the things I tell them, but they do like to hear it.

So, after many years I decided to write it down. In addition to telling the overall story, I've broken it into different aspects of what it was like being a combat vet in Vietnam so you get the actual feel, the real taste and the total experience of it.

3

WHAT WAS THE WEATHER LIKE?

This is a question I'm asked quite often. You've all seen war movies about Vietnam and got the idea it is wet and hot there. But you have not the slightest idea how hot it gets there. Think *tropics* in the summer time on steroids and you'll have only a near-idea of how hot it gets there.

It actually wouldn't have been that bad but we lived in the bush and often carried 120 pounds of stuff on our backs, especially right after being re-supplied. In that frickin' heat that's a lot to carry.

People go, "no way, no one could carry that much." Okay, well I am here to tell you it *was* that much and we *did* carry it and we carried it all over the place.

Our back packs were not something you hear a lot about but I think it's important you know what mules we were.

I remember one day, right after re-supply, I looked at my overstuffed rucksack, put it on and wished I could be beamed right into the living room of my parents' house while they watched Lawrence Welk, just so they could see the sacrifice I was undertaking to "preserve their freedom". I'm sure they would have appreciated it more, just seeing the amount of crap I had to carry.

Vietnam – The Teenage Wasteland

So check this out – let's add it up: I carried a radio, and the handset, speaker box and that all weighed in at thirty five pounds. Eight hundred and eighty rounds of .223 ammo for my M-16. That's close to 20 pounds. (I liked a lot of ammo because, to me, it was much more important than food when you're in an environment where everyone is trying to kill you. So, enthusiastically, I carried twice as much as anyone else).

I remember when I was first outfitted by the Supply Sergeant. He asked me how much ammo I wanted. I never, ever thought about it prior to being asked. I asked him how much everyone else carried and he told me that most everyone carried four hundred and forty rounds of .223, four hand grenades and one Claymore mine. I thought I'd run across a little secret (that I could have as much ammo as I wanted). I maintained a poker face but inside I was elated that I could have whatever kind of ammo I wanted and in any amount I wanted it.

I immediately told the Supply Sergeant to double the amount of .223 ammo. He thought I was crazy because that was a lot of additional weight. I didn't care; I knew I was in a battle zone where people shoot at other people and try to take their lives, and I figured if I had a lot of ammo I could possibly last longer and come out a winner. It made sense to me! It took six months for that philosophy to pay off but it actually saved my life in the end.

So, in addition to the radio, handset and speaker box, I had all of that .223 ammo, 4 hand grenades that weighed 2 pounds each = 8 pounds. A week's supply of food is 15 pounds. An M-16 rifle is 8.2 pounds, loaded. A Poncho = 2 pounds. Water is very important and weighed 9 pounds. Bayonet and entrenching tool = 5 more pounds. Everyone had to carry 100 rounds of machine gun ammo = 11 pounds (radio men did not have to carry machine gun ammo, also called M-60 ammo). Spare socks, extra shirt, a towel, camera, two cans of beer, 2 cans of Pepsi or 7-Up put you right up there in terms of weight, and if you were real lucky you carried 2 pounds of C4 explosive so you could cook your food at night.

Add it up:

Radio = 35 lbs.
Ammo = 20 lbs.
4 smoke grenades = 8 lbs.
Food = 15 lbs.
M-16 = 8.2 lbs.
Poncho = 2 lbs.
Water = 9 lbs.
Entrenching tool = 4 lbs.
Bayonet = 1 lb.
Spare battery = 2 lbs.
Helmet = 3 lbs.
11 Magazines = .5 lbs.
Spare clothes = 2 lbs.
C-4 = 2 lbs.
Other drinks = 2 lbs.
Medical supplies = 1 lbs.
Claymore mine or rocket = 3.5 lbs.
Total = 120.2 lbs.

I'm not a big guy. At that time I weighed a little over 125 lbs. So add to the above the wet clothes and boots I was wearing, my camera, mosquito repellant, Zippo lighter, salt tabs, bandages and whatever else I got my hands on. It was a lot of weight and was ridiculous when I first started to carry that much but, like anything else, you get used to it.

Just before re-supply (once per week) the load could get down to 90 pounds. I used to get mixed emotions about being re-supplied because while I was hungry and needed the new gear or other things, it also meant another twenty to thirty pounds to lug around.

A lot of guys worked at getting rid of what they considered to be "excess weight". After re-supply they would dump some

Vietnam – The Teenage Wasteland

of their food on the trail, or dump their Claymore mine or grenades, just to get rid of some of the weight. This was beyond stupid because all it did was give food and ammo to the enemy which made them more able to kill us.

Then, just prior to re-supply, these same guys would act like leeches and come around begging for food or cigarettes or beer or something. I personally would never give in to them and when I saw them begging others I'd chase them off. When we were ambushed by the NVA using our Claymore mines or American grenades, I would find them and let them know it was their stuff they dumped on the trail that killed and injured Americans.

One time I caught a guy who had a Claymore mine one night and the next night no longer had it. I slapped him around until he cried for his mommy.

You couldn't miss the guys that dumped their supplies on the trail because they were always trying to borrow something. Whenever I identified a major mooch I put the word out to everyone in the company that if they tried to mooch so much as a cigarette, to let me know. I was on a big campaign to halt the bullshit of throwing stuff away.

I remember one guy who was one of the biggest mooches in the company. He refused to be supplied with more than one grenade and 240 rounds of ammo. One day we were engaged with a company-sized unit of NVA and were in a major fire fight. The mooch came up to me and begged for some ammo. He had the audacity to explain how I always had a lot of ammo so I had some extra to give away.

I told him that yes, it was correct that I had a lot of ammo and the reason I did was because I carried it for a lot of hard miles. "Guess what?" I told him. "I'm not going to hump ammo all around this country for your sorry ass so get away from me, fool."

He continued to hammer me for ammo because he was totally out and the bullets coming our way were intensifying.

I asked him to show me his wallet. He produced it and there was $236 in it. I snatched all his money and gave him one magazine of ammo – less than twenty rounds.

He was pissed, but there was nothing he could do about it.

He came back ten minutes later for more ammo, and I told him to go to hell. He told me that I had taken $236 from him and I should give him as much ammo as he needed. I again told him to go to hell and he got really pissed at me and tried to make me into a criminal and all that, but I refused to budge. Then he told me he was going to kill me. I screamed at him "how is that possible if you had no bullets??" I asked him if he even had his bayonet and at that he stomped in the dirt, frustrated.

I finally gave him one bullet. I told him it was for him should we get overrun. He could put himself out of his misery.

He was wounded a half hour later, enough to get him sent home. To me, it was a shame. He should have understood the circumstances he was in and carried his share of the load. Truth be told, with him gone, it was one less weak link in our chain and we were stronger because of it.

A long story short, I was not going to be someone else's mule. I had enough of my own stuff to carry in the sweltering heat.

We had a little fun with the rucksacks when we got up in the morning. We'd get the word about moving out so started to pack our rucksacks, putting everything in the little pouches and sacks.

And this is a must -- to balance the dammed thing, because when we are hauling 120 pounds on our back it had to balance. If it was off as much as a pound on either side our back was killing us by the end of the day. We learned to balance the pack the next day: The pain reminded you.

When we were packed and ready to move out we would lay the rucksack on the ground and put it on while lying down, synched up and, tighten the shoulder straps and told our buddy

Vietnam – The Teenage Wasteland

standing nearby to help us up. We put our legs in the air and brought them down fast, rocking our body forward while shooting out our right hand to our buddy. He grabbed our forearm and pulled us up. Once we were up on our feet we bent over and adjusted the pack so it was "comfortable". Then we helped our buddy with his pack the same way.

After a bit, everyone was up and ready to hump twelve klicks in 110 degree heat. Nothing like it. (A "klick" is a kilometer which is 0.62137 of a mile).

I added the subject of the rucksack to this section so you get an idea of what weight had to do with the heat.

When the sun came up in the morning it was better than any alarm clock because it woke you up the minute it broke the horizon. The blast furnace was on and there was just no sleeping after that. So you got up, got something to eat real fast and when the word came to get ready to move on out, you packed up your stuff up and got ready to go.

We usually stayed on high ground overnight because high ground is more defensible than low ground. So in the morning when we moved out we went downhill. That was absolutely the best way to start the day because you didn't want to start out going uphill with all that weight on.

Even though we were going downhill, the first part of the day was the worst. The first kilometer was a killer but we'd press on and, just like an athlete, we'd get into the rhythm of it, get our second wind and keep moving on, one foot after the other. After an hour or so we'd feel good, like we could go all day.

Around 12 o'clock in the afternoon the heat became overwhelming so we usually took an hour or two break to let the oppressive sun have its time frying everything in sight. We sat in the shade, caught up on sleep or just lazed, or talked with buddies quietly, and basically chilled. I think that is where the term "chill" comes from because we were trying to stay cool and not sweat. Good luck on that. Then after an hour or two of chillin', we were off again.

I think the enemy did the same thing because we rarely got into a fight during the midday hours. It was just too hot to fight.

Sometimes we walked in the open for a length of time, under the sun with sweat running off you by the gallon. When I reached for my canteen which was sitting in the open on my rucksack, the water in the canteen was too hot to drink. It burnt my lips. But we had to drink, so we drank a lot of hot water.

Speaking of water, clean water was hard to come by. We got water from streams or rivers. Each day we sent a "water patrol" out to get our canteens filled. A patrol gathered up all the company's canteens, went to a stream and filled them all. Sometimes the enemy waited near the stream and ambushed the water patrol and the canteens were left behind. We'd have to get new ones flown in so we didn't die of thirst and then go find another place to fill our canteens or fight for the rights to that watering hole and reclaim our canteens.

The water had to be treated in order to kill all of the microbes and bacteria. The way it was treated was with iodine tablets. We put the tablets in the canteen to kill any and all microbes that caused hepatitis, dysentery, or just plain made you sick. The iodine was pretty bad tasting; like chalk, so sometimes we would trust that a stream didn't have bacteria in it, and we'd skip the tablet. I did this on several occasions and half the time I got dysentery. Nothing like walking along and having the shits all of a sudden and have to run into the bushes to take an emergency dump.

We found out that bandages, which everyone had to carry, came in real handy in the heat. If you were in the sun for any length of time (and we were often in the sun from early morning to late afternoon) your helmet (which was made of steel) became so hot that temperatures under it reached well over two hundred degrees. That level of intense heat literally fried our brains. So we wet our bandages and put them on our

Vietnam – The Teenage Wasteland

heads, under the helmet as insulation to keep our brains from being cooked. It worked great.

The humidity was stifling. I was never dry once in the whole year I was there…. never. Always wet. The dew saturated me at night and by the time the sun came up I started melting again, sweat just poured off me.

And it rained almost every day. The good news about the rain is that your clothes got a good and much needed wash. But the rain was warm so it didn't cool you off. And when the rain ended the sun usually came back out and the heat and humidity worse than ever, almost suffocating. But as rain was a constant over there it was another thing you just got used to.

There is a line from the movie *Forrest Gump* that perfectly sums up the whole rain thing. Forrest said: "there was little bitty rain and then there was great big fat rain. The rain came down hard then it came down sideways, and sometimes it came up from the ground." That is beautifully fitting and wonderfully descriptive.

The monsoons started in late fall and it would just pour rain on a daily basis. The monsoon went from November to March. It was always wet – and muddy. There was mud everywhere. It got into your clothes, your rifle, your eyes, your food – everywhere.

One night in January we were operating around LZ Cork in the mountains (LZ stands for landing zone). We got word just before nightfall, just as we were settling in on a little hill, that a typhoon was coming to shore by midnight and they expected a lot of flooding. The C.O. decided to relocate us to a higher place so we moved to even higher ground.

The rain that night was biblical. It rained so hard we were almost washed off of the side of the hill. I clung to a tree for an hour as torrents of water ran down the hill. Then a churning river formed right under me so I moved to another tree. I hung on to that one for three more hours. I was absolutely freaked that I was going to get washed down the mountain and be lost forever. I had never experienced anything like that before and haven't since.

When dawn finally broke the rain had subsided to just a shower. We looked out at the valley below and were all overwhelmed at the sight. The valley was now a gigantic lake about twenty square miles in size. It was one of the most amazing sights I have ever seen. Battalion sure knew what they were doing when they advised us to move. It saved our asses.

We sat there the rest of the day and waited for the valley to drain which it did by the end of the day, leaving behind nothing but mud.

Because it was so wet, fungus thrived. Our feet had to be taken care of because they were always wet from either water or sweat. Athlete's foot was easy to get. But this was not the kind of athlete's foot you get from the shower room floor in school. This was a different, stubborn strain.

And most of us had what was known as "Gook Sores" which were open ulcers somewhere on the skin. I had about five of them. One of them was a huge sore on my left forearm. It was there from the first month until I left the country. Nothing got rid of it. The medics all told me it would go away when I got home. It did, but it left a good scar.

Salt was a big deal. Everyone had salt tablets and we ate them like candy. It was the first time in my life that when I took salt and sucked on it, it tasted like candy. The medic told me that if it tasted sweet it meant you really needed it.

We had a "salt drill" which was a drill for someone about to die from heat prostration. One of our responsibilities was to watch the guy behind us while we were humping from one destination to another. We turned around and looked into the eyes of the man behind. If he seemed alert and looked at you then he was fine. Anything else you'd query with, "how's it going, buddy"? If you got anything less than "fine" or "okay" or "bite me" you queried him a little more.

Vietnam – The Teenage Wasteland

One day the guy behind me had an odd look in his eyes. I asked him how it was going and he said something like "being a bug is nasty". I yelled out "salt drill", dropped my rucksack and threw him to the ground. We had only two minutes to get salt into him.

The body runs out of salt from sweating heavily for long periods, and when it does the brain calls for all blood to go to the stomach in order to get access to the rest of the salt in the blood. That causes blood to vacate the brain and is usually followed by convulsions and then death. In two minutes he would be in convulsions.

Four guys sat on his limbs while another mixed a saline solution and another held his nose so he had to inhale through his mouth and in went the saline solution.

It never ceased to amaze me how fast the saline solution stopped the convulsions and the glazed look. In ten minutes the person who had been just two minutes from brain death was up and walking around again, getting told every fifteen minutes to make sure he had enough salt in him.

I rarely peed. Most of the liquid in my body came out through my pores. I peed about ever third day and even then it would be just a trickle.

One other thing about sweating is that when you sweat that much liquid out of your pores you flush the body of vital nutrients. The C-rations were supposed to contain vitamins and minerals to support the body but they contained barely enough nutrients to keep up with everything that was lost through sweating out gallons of water. As a result, we sweated out the vitamins and nutrients we badly needed, especially calcium. Because there was no calcium in our diets, my teeth literally started falling out of my mouth. The calcium just left my body and my teeth all suddenly went south. After I got out of the Army I had tons of trouble with my teeth. It was not until I got onto a calcium-magnesium rich diet that I got my deteriorating teeth under control.

Oddly enough, the coldest I have ever been was in Vietnam. During January of 1969 we were in the mountains at the five thousand foot mark, and it was cold up there during the night – the temperature would go down into the mid-forties. Also it was raining the whole time because it was monsoon season. We didn't have blankets so when it went down to forty-two degrees at night it was a shivering, bone-piercing cold.

We slept under a poncho and worked it out that three guys slept together at night, shivering under the poncho. The reason for three sleeping together was for body heat. We climbed under the poncho and hugged each other; actually spooning like little faggots, and took turns each night for the middle spot. It was great to get that middle spot, your front and back was warm during the whole night. This is something most of us did not tell anyone later because it's embarrassing. How do you tell people that you slept, hugging another guy all night long – spooning? Oh, my god!

In the morning we got up and every bone in my body ached because of the cold. It took a while to loosen up and be able to move at all.

Two guys actually snapped and went berserk during that period. They couldn't take being wet and cold all the time so went over the edge. We had to ship them out never to be seen again.

The indigents of South-East Asia are small in size and I generally found them in bad health. This, to me, was because of the environment. I have met a lot of Vietnamese that grew up here in the States and they are normal size. Hell, I even saw one professional Vietnamese football player who was a six-foot, five inch, two hundred and eighty pound lineman for the Dallas Cowboys. That South-East Asian environment must stunt human growth. Dunno, but seems like it to me.

In the final analysis, the weather over there was oppressive. I was never comfortable. The only time we got a respite was when we climbed into a helicopter and flew at

Vietnam – The Teenage Wasteland

three thousand feet. The air was a bit cooler up there and for a short time you felt like you were in San Diego. But it only lasted twenty to thirty minutes.

4

HOW WAS THE TERRAIN?

Unfortunately we were located way up north in "I-Corps" where the ground is not flat. In fact, we spent most of our time roaming the mountains. It was rough going up those mountains in that heat with all that weight. One slip and it was down, down, down, and I mean hard.

Seeing that it rained a lot, the going was really difficult — mud everywhere as earlier described. We moved along trails that led to different hilltop villages and when it rained the trails got pretty slick and that meant a lot of spills.

One day, we were trying to surprise an element of NVA on the side of a mountain. The Captain didn't want to use the trails because it was likely the NVA were monitoring them. He decided the best course of action was to go up and over the back side of the mountain and surprise them. That meant mountain climbing.

We stopped at the base of a beautiful waterfall that was about a hundred and fifty feet high. We all took baths under the falls – half of us pulling guard duty while the other half bathed, and then we switched around so the other half could bathe. It was satisfyingly refreshing.

Vietnam – The Teenage Wasteland

The next morning all hundred and ten of us set out up the side of the mountain. Unfortunately, it started to rain. Then it poured.

After a hundred feet or so the mountain terrain became a straight vertical climb. Ropes and D-rings had to be used for safety. Around forty guys started the climb before me and then it was my turn but by then the trail upward had turned into a quagmire of running, gooped-up mud.

I was climbing for about an hour, my D-ring attached to a rope, using bush after bush as handholds, trying not to break the branches for the poor guys climbing up behind me, when we suddenly stopped. As things ground to a halt the guys up ahead were left hanging on the side of a near-vertical slope. At that point I made a huge mistake and decided to look down. I freaked out. That waterfall was way down there and very small. I realized that if I fell I would tumble near vertically for a hundred feet. I held on tight to the branch of a large bush for ten minutes as we all hung fire but then it started to come out of the ground. Guys below were yelling for us to move out. We, in turn, started yelling to the guys above us to move out who passed the demand up the line. Finally, things started moving again.

After another half-hour of climbing without the use of a rope – and I never looked down again – I got to a point where there was another rope dangling down. I put my D-ring on it and started to haul myself up. It was grueling. The rope was wet and muddy and I was exhausted, but had to move on.

I climbed another fifty feet or so on the rope when my footing gave way and down I went. I slid twenty feet before I could synch the rope in the D-ring and stop my decent, and I did but not before I took out four other guys who were all hanging on to me for dear life, all of them punching and verbally abusing me. I finally got my footing back and off I went again.

We finally made it to the top. To me, it was a real miracle no one got badly hurt or killed. We never learned, in any of our training, how to climb mountains or use a rope to climb. But the Captain felt we should just be able to do it. And we did, just like it was an everyday thing. Amazing.

Humping along on the flat ground was sometimes pleasurable because it was the only time you got to daydream. Everyone daydreamed about being home, driving around, getting drunk, getting laid, getting high, having fun, being with their wives or their kids, whatever. This is what we all did when we humped on flat land. No one said so much as a word. We just walked, and walked and walked. And we daydreamed while we walked – for hours on end. It was actually a pretty peaceful stretch of time.

I would always start out thinking about the stinking situation I found myself in and the stupid Army and how bad it all was, but after a while I realized how useless it was to be thinking about that, and so would start thinking about fun things. So after a while of humping along on the trail I was gone from that god-forsaken place and in a place I wanted to be. There were times when I even fell asleep walking along. No kidding. The trail would take a turn but I continued straight on and ended up in the bushes wondering how I got there.

But when the reverie was rudely broken by automatic gunfire we were all jolted from our little personal paradises back to hell in less than a nano-second.

The scenery was absolutely wonderful. Vietnam is, in my opinion, the most beautiful place on the planet. High rolling hills carpeted with triple-canopy jungle amidst steaming valleys often usurped for rice paddies. That was the scenery we enjoyed, everywhere.

I have seen rice paddies terraced up the side of hills in geometric symmetry that would take your breath away. Everything was green, green, green and gorgeous.

Vietnam – The Teenage Wasteland

I have been in the darkest of jungles where it was so dark you could hardly see even though it was sunny topside. And whenever I lit a cigarette with my Zippo lighter, the flame from the lighter was six inches high from the abundance of oxygen. Then my cigarette lasted just three puffs before it was gone.

Ever been in a rain forest with giant bamboo as far as the eye can see? No? Then you are missing something magnificent.

The foliage is amazing. The plants are very hearty. I don't believe there is a chance in hell you could kill any of those plants. When we had to cut through the jungle, guys took turns on the machete, having to wrap their hands in bandages to keep from being cut too badly (I still have scars on my hands from the foliage cutting me up) while others worked at sharpening replacement machetes because the cutting edge on the ones being used dulled so quickly. Sometimes we only made forty feet an hour with two guys cutting steadily with machetes.

One time, we got lost on a recon mission into Laos. We had to cross mountains to get to our destination but they were full of iron. The iron caused our compasses to go crazy; the needles in them just spun and spun giving us no direction. To make it worse it was the monsoon season and the clouds were right down on the mountains putting us in major fog from morning to night. So we got lost.

At night I climbed a tree to find the setting sun (so as to find west), but the cloud cover was so thick the sky was uniformly dark three hundred and sixty degrees around.

We used our machetes to cut through the jungle to get to where we were going, but when we tried to retrace our steps and double back, we found that the undergrowth had already grown back and our trail disappeared as a result. We were hopelessly lost in Laos.

We asked Battalion to send a chopper out to us to guide us back but the request was denied because we were in Laos and we weren't supposed to be there.

The Captain had the idea of having artillery rounds fired on the border every twenty minutes. We called the Arty (artillery) boys and they started shelling the border. We headed for the sound, and of course it got quieter as we went on. So we headed back and they got louder and then quieter. We realized we were going north and south. So we headed ninety degrees to our left but the rounds sounded quieter, of course. Naturally, it was the fourth and final direction we headed in that ultimately led us back to the border. And we got there none too soon because we'd been out of food for those four days and were famished. Battalion sent us a chopper with hot spaghetti. What a treat!

All told, I would live in a place like that. I thought it a wonderful, magical place. No picture ever taken has come close to capturing its true beauty.

5

WHAT KIND OF ANIMALS WERE THERE?

Because of the war, the constant pounding of artillery and air strikes, there were not that many animals around. They mostly split for Laos long before I got there. But make no mistake, there were still enough animals around to make things more than "interesting".

Monkeys were abundant. We walked a trail one day in the rain forest where large monkeys flew high above, jumping from tree to tree yelling and taunting us. They looked a lot like Chimpanzees but they were some other breed. I knew they wanted us to leave their rain forest. They inherently knew we were dangerous. And it turned out the monkeys were right. They kept putting themselves in harm's way. If they would have just hidden it would've been better for them.

The poor point man killed three of them that day because the monkeys kept jumping out onto the trail in front of him, yelling. He didn't mean to shoot them but on point your reflexes had to be fast or you were dead. So when an ape appeared suddenly, running at him, the poor thing got drilled. And because monkeys were being shot the rest of them got really pissed. It reached a point where we had to stop and let things calm down. There must have been two hundred of them all flying above, yelling monkey profanity, throwing rocks and tree limbs at us to the point where the noise was deafening.

While we were looking up in fascination at the monkeys they all suddenly took off swinging from branch to branch and disappeared. A minute later real trouble showed up. I saw the jungle move off to my flank. The trees were bending as if a silent tank was moving through the jungle. An invisible creature was coming right at us. We all brought up our rifles but couldn't see anything and there was no sound except the snapping of branches.

All of a sudden, a bright orange Orangutan showed up in the middle of swirling, snapping branches about eighty feet from us, up in the trees, twelve feet off of the ground. He came right at us and then stopped about thirty feet away, looked at us and started shaking trees with his hands and feet, basically spazzing out and screaming at the top of his lungs. Then he started hissing at us.

John Minor started to take aim at him but I pushed his rifle barrel down to the ground.

He looked at me like "what's your problem?"

I told him in hushed tones, "if you end up wounding him, he'll come over here and beat all our asses, and take away your M-16, shove it up your ass and empty the magazine in it."

John nodded in agreement and we all took our rifles off the creature.

The Orangutan was beautiful and huge too, around five feet tall and as orange as you can get. He finally stopped his screaming and in a show of force broke all the tree limbs he had in his hands and feet and then looked at us threateningly. He then turned around and took off through the trees the same way he had come. We were all relieved because he really did scare us. I mean, he scared the shit out of me, and I'm sure he scared everyone else.

The only other scary, big animal I saw was a Boa Constrictor that was draped around a tree, hanging right over the trail, swaying back and forth, scanning the path with his infrared sensors. We all walked around it. He was a big boy, brown, white and tan and around thirty feet long.

Speaking of snakes: I really do hate them. I think they're vile. We were briefed about the "Three Step Viper" which was a mamba that was very common in our area. They were called the "Three Step Viper" because if they bit you, you took three steps and then cardiac arrest set in.

I went a month without seeing one and that was just fine with me. I had forgotten about them. But one day we were on a trail, I was just trooping along, doing the usual day dreaming and suddenly out from a bush came the bright green snake. Before I could do anything he struck at me, hitting me on my left leg.

My heart went up into my throat and I almost vomited right there and then. To my absolute horror he came at me again. In a panic, I pulled my machete from my rucksack and swung at him, cutting off his head. I screamed insanely as I hacked him into little bitty pieces. I remember hacking madly and screaming (I don't know what) and then finally I realized that I had not gone into cardiac arrest and was not dead and so stopped. The guys around me were looking at me like I was insane.

The medic came running up, looked me over and then had me drop my drawers, looked at where the snake struck me and announced I was not bitten. I didn't understand why I was not bitten. I didn't say I wasn't grateful, I just didn't understand.

Good old Doc Johnson picked up the snakes head and opened its mouth and showed me that a viper cannot open its mouth like a rattle snake can; it can only open it a bit. So it has to be able to bite you on the hand or foot. I then remembered that the snake did not go for me right away, he was looking for a place he could get a bite into me and not seeing one, decided to keep on striking at me until he did. Fuck him. I lopped off his head before he had a chance to find something good to bite on.

I was rattled the rest of the day. The guys razzed me for a couple of days about how I went berserk, chopping up that snake, screaming insanely, but I was unfazed. I'd like to see how they would have acted if the same thing had happened to them.

I killed seven of those bastards the whole time I was there. My second encounter with the viper was about two weeks later. We were on a trail in the lowlands when the captain called for a lunch break. I was pretty tired and just sort of plopped down where I was. With more than a hundred pounds on your back, when you decide to go down the process is irreversible. As I was going down, I saw I was going to end up in a bush, a dead bush and that's where vipers hang out. Before I hit the ground I had my hand on the hilt of my machete and sure enough, a viper squirted out from under me. I lopped his head off and then chopped him into little pieces, but this time silently.

They sure were pretty snakes though, dark green on top which faded to bright lemon yellow on their underbelly. I always wanted to paint my car like that, someday.

The first American I ever saw killed was by wildlife. We were walking in some low lands. I a few men back from the point man and we were all a standard forty meters apart. We were close to the end of our patrol when suddenly the point man stopped and aimed his rifle off to the right. I looked to the right and saw what he was aiming at: A big, four-foot round bag hanging from a tree. I thought "what the hell is that?" He shot the bag and it exploded in a cloud of dust.

After the dust from the explosion wafted away a shimmering essence took its place. The shimmering essence was around five thousand bees all in a perfectly round ball. The ball all of a sudden flew toward the point man and lit on him. He tried to run but I think the sheer weight of all those bees took him down. And they all stung him. He was screaming and rolling around and they stayed on him until he lay still.

There was absolutely nothing any of us could do except stand stock still and watch in horror. Finally, the bees gathered in a ball again and hovered five feet above him. The hair on the nape of my neck stood straight up as I realized the ball of bees was looking at us! They hung there for a good two minutes looking at the rest of us knowing there was nothing we could do if they decided to come after us and then suddenly they took off in search of a new home.

We ran up to the point man and found he was dead and lifeless except for an occasional involuntary twitch. I was horrified looking at a life just wasted like that. And how in the hell did the bees know it was him? He's the only one they went for.

It was stupid to lose a GI like that. I mean, what do you write to his parents? "Dear Mr. and Mrs. Smith. Your son was killed because he was an ignorant asshole: he blew up a bee's nest and they killed him for it." That would be one hell of a letter to write. Different wording, but …

I got bit by all kinds of things, scorpions, bees, and other little bugs. But that place had one little critter that was the biggest pain in the ass and bothersome and became public enemy number two on my list. And that critter, as small as it was, caused me to come as close to death as I got over there. It was the lowly, small but ubiquitous leech.

A leech is a little thing – anywhere from one to two inches long and an eighth of an inch in diameter. They are dark brown in color, almost black. They are indestructible. You can stomp on them and it doesn't hurt them at all. You can grind them between rocks – nothing. You can hit them with a hammer on a rock and it doesn't faze them. But put a little salt or acid on them, and they go up in a foamy fizz.

They live everywhere. There are billions of them. The ones in the rivers and rice paddies are much bigger. They range anywhere from four to six inches long.

Leeches find YOU. They seem to be able to smell humans because you could be sitting down and look around and see about six of them making a bee-line towards you.

They crawl on your body to where they find a nice warm vein to tap into. Then they squirt a little numbing agent into you so you can't feel them cutting a hole through your skin and vein, lock their jaws inside the epidermis and let your blood pressure feed them. They also squirt an anti-coagulant so the blood flows unimpeded for twenty-four hours.

When fully glutted on your blood they are an ugly dark brown sack about an inch in diameter and they then just kind of rupture and that is the end of their life. The funny thing about them is they live just for that one big feast, but it's also the end of their life. That's how weird they are.

And you cannot just pull them off, because if you do and their head detaches and stays in your skin you get a serious infection. If they get on you, you have to put salt or mosquito repellant on them, and they just fall off. If they're on your legs you just simply piss on them and they fall right off.

I used to have to deal with them on my body at least three times per week. But one day they almost killed me.

Battalion command told us they had intelligence on a prisoner of war camp that had American prisoners. They sent us an "expatriated NVA soldier" who was going to lead us to the camp. He led us on a wild goose chase for three days before we got wise to him.

Finally, the Captain asked him to show on the map where the POW camp was.

He pointed to a place far away.

Captain pointed to another place.

He said, "maybe".

Captain pointed to another.

He said, "maybe".

Captain pointed to another in the opposite direction.

He said, "no!"

The Captain said, "That's the place for sure".

Vietnam – The Teenage Wasteland

We tied up the NVA soldier, put a guard on him and set off.

When we arrived at the POW camp it was pouring rain. The Captain was on point and I was on his flank. We saw a bamboo fence. An NVA guard saw us and opened fire. We returned fire.

The Captain yelled at me to chop the fence down with gunfire. I opened up on the fence on full automatic but watched in horror as the bullets just bounced off the tough bamboo. I had no idea bamboo would stop an M-16 bullet but it sure did.

The Captain shouldered his rifle and pulled out his machete. He told me to cover him.

I advanced to the fence but slipped on a rock and went down hard, rolling downhill and into a bush. I went down so hard the hand guards on my rifle came off. I picked them up and put them in my pocket and then ran up to the fence, pushed my rifle barrel through the bamboo and started shooting at targets of opportunity.

The Captain finally made it through the fence and I followed with Holloway on my heels. Both me and Holloway were shooting prison guards as we breached the fence. The guards who stayed to fight died at the hands of the Captain, Donnie Holloway and me.

We went to find the prisoners and found them in caged pits in the ground. They had all been shot in the head. There were seven of them. One of them, a black dude, was still alive. We got a chopper in and got the dead prisoners and the wounded guy out. I just now realized that we never found out if the black dude made it or not. We searched the rest of the place and made sure there were no other prisoners.

An hour after the initial attack I sat down on a camp bench and took my helmet off. Someone pointed and said I had leeches on my head. I felt around and found seven of them on my head. The medic came up to me all concerned and told me to take off my clothes. We found twenty-four leeches on me. I must have gotten them when I fell down and rolled into the bushes.

We got them all off but now the problem was that I had twenty four holes in me and was losing blood, fast. A hole or two is not a problem but when you have twenty four you lose a lot of blood. The anti-coagulant leeches inject into their host lasts for about 24 hours – so I had about 23 hours of bleeding to go. It was too late to get me on a chopper because it was now dark. So for the rest of the night ten guys had to hold compresses on me while we waited for the wounds to coagulate and close.

By the next day I had stopped bleeding but I was so weak from blood loss that we had to wait there another day before we could move out. Man, what a way to go. "Dear Mr. and Mrs. M – your son died in Vietnam because he was sucked dry by leeches." No, I did not want to go out that way.

Leeches are the pits but they stand no contest to the number one public enemy; the all-time heavy-weight pain in the ass, killer in some cases, nearly invisible, but constant irritant, the ubiquitous, lowly but omnipresent *mosquito*.

Mosquitoes are more than abundant in Vietnam. When they come out at night there must be thirty billion of them per square foot and they are all starving for my blood.

This was the "other war" over there, the war of man against the mosquito. It was an every-day battle, but you don't win against them. There is no way to defeat that enemy. Even if you totally nuked the entire area with an atom bomb there would still be mosquitoes – and leeches too, come to think of it.

We were all told that mosquitoes carry malaria and that malaria is a killer. So we had that to contend with amongst all the other things trying to kill you.

To combat malaria we had to take medicine. We had to take one big fat orange horse pill once per day and one little one, once per week. I asked if it would stop malaria and was told that it would not, but the pills would make malaria a lot

Vietnam – The Teenage Wasteland

less intense. Great. And it was a court martial offense if you got malaria and it was found you were not taking the pills.

You don't want malaria. It's nasty. I finally did catch it and it was the sickest I've ever been. I caught it in late April when we were going into the mountains. I decided to stop taking my medicine because I noticed it made me feel weird. Two weeks later I woke up in the morning with a 104.5 degree fever. There is nothing like shivering and freezing to death in 110 degree heat. It was very painful. I was sorry then and I'm sorry now that I quit taking those pills because I've had a few malaria relapses and they are not fun.

Nonetheless, mosquitoes were still the bane of our existence. They were invented by a very evil spirit. God couldn't have invented them because they have no excuse that I can find for their existence. They contribute nothing to anything. And did I tell you I hate them?

When I first got over there and in the field I put mosquito repellant all over me. It was horrible, toxic stuff. It did keep the skeeters away, but if you got any of it in your mouth you tasted a horrible oily, chemical all night long. If you got it in your eyes it almost melted them and the pain was intense. It left your skin greasy, and it smothered you. So when I put it on at night I put it everywhere except my lips and my eyes. One morning I woke up and my eyes were swollen shut and my lips were twice the size of Mick Jagger's – only because I didn't put the repellant on my lips and eyelids. It took an hour before I could open my eyes.

At night, you covered yourself up with anything you could find and you could hear them buzzing around all night, looking for a way in to get your blood. You listened to them coming for you and it drove you a little batty. But after a while you tuned them out and then they didn't get to you, mentally.

I have a real problem with mosquitoes to this day. I will not go to a climate that has them. San Diego, which is where I am now, doesn't have mosquitoes and that's just fine with me.

Vietnam had its nasty critters and I don't miss them.

Vietnam – The Teenage Wasteland

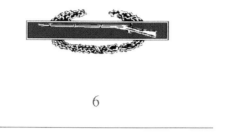

6

FOOD

This is one of the sorest subjects about life in a combat zone. George Washington once said that an army travels on its stomach. This proved true from my experience.

Our main staple was "C-Rations", canned foods that came to us in cartons that contained a main meal like "Ham and Eggs, Chopped". They always had those official names: "Ham and Eggs, Chopped". Why "Chopped?" That's the military for you. Who gives a rat's ass if the ham and eggs are chopped and stuffed into a little can? It should have read: "Ham and Eggs: Stuffed in Can." And the friggin' eggs were powdered and the ham was… well let's just say it didn't taste like ham, that's for sure. It was barely palatable. In fact, it was horrible.

Other choices were "Ham and Lima Beans." That was also horrible. Then there was "Chicken, Boned" which was one of the worst things mankind ever put in a can. It didn't taste like chicken. We used to make fun of it telling each other it was "Boned Cat" or "Boned Horse Hoofs".

"Pork and Beans" was the only meal that actually tasted good. I have seen fist fights over "Pork and Beans". It was the only meal any of us liked.

With each meal came other stuff. Pork and beans came with a roll that was in a can and fruit cake in a can which was okay, as well as fruit cocktail in a can, which was pretty good, then a little flat can of peanut butter. In other meals you would find a little flat can of jelly. But the peanut butter and jelly never came together in the same meal. How dumb is that? These meals were all boxed up into one container which also included a little 10-pack of Marlboro cigarettes, a little roll of toilet paper, a packet of cocoa mix, a packet of coffee and a packet of cream and sugar, salt and pepper packets and "Matches, Waterproof" (they actually worked!).

I never found a GI who liked the C-rations. Everyone complained about them.

Later, I tried K-rations which are also called MREs or "Meals, Ready to Eat" (Why not "REMs" – "Ready to Eat Meals"?). They were dehydrated meals like Chile Con Carne, Chicken a-la King or Turkey and Rice. They actually tasted pretty good. However, they were dangerous to the infantry in Vietnam. Here's why: you had to boil water and pour it into the MRE bag. You stirred the water into the meal and it got pretty solid, like dry, lumpy oatmeal. So you put more water in and stirred it around but it got dry again. So you added more water, stirred, and it got solid again. I used to think "where the hell is all of that water going?" I sometimes thought I was putting more water in the bag than the bag could hold. Finally, I got a pretty good consistency and ate the meal. But for the rest of the day I was dying of thirst because those MREs robbed all the moisture from every source in your body. We were already drinking half gallon of water per day due to the heat. The MREs stepped it up to almost a gallon. So I dumped them and went back to the dreadful C-rations.

One good thing the C-rations caused was "care packages". Because the C-rations sucked in taste, and because we had to eat, we would send home for hot sauce and other spices we used to drown out the taste of the rations. But when we sent our requests home, we also asked; "while you're at it could you send me a ___ and a couple of __?" These turned into what we called "care packages" coined from the packages that were sent by "Care USA" to third-world countries in the mid-60's.

Vietnam – The Teenage Wasteland

I asked my mom to send me three cans of Mandarin orange slices in syrup. I loved those. Also had her send pear slices in a can and Hormel Chile and stuff like that. I scarfed that stuff up.

I got a care package from home once in which my mom had included a small 8-inch salami that hit the spot! So I told her to send me a larger one. She sent a two and a half foot long salami that was sooo good. I ate a little of it when it came and tied the rest of it to the outside of my rucksack. As I walked down the trail guys snuck up behind me and cut slices off it. In one day I lost a foot of it.

The next time I got salami I tied it to my sack and then kept an eye open for robbers but it lasted less than a day, because at the end of that day we got into a fire-fight and it was literally shot off of my rucksack leaving me only a two inch piece. I went back to locate the rest of it but was unable to find it. I knew that someone had found it and kept the fact a secret.

I got seven care packages the whole time I was there. I stopped ordering them from home when my last one came off the chopper busted open and raided. The only thing left was one can of hot sauce and one can of mandarin orange slices. It pissed me off that people in the rear stole from the infantry.

Once in a while we would get hot meals flown out to us on choppers. It all depended on if we were in a hot-area or not. If things were quiet for a while the Captain would give an okay to have hot meals flown out to us. We got anything from spaghetti and meatballs, to meatloaf to sliced ham and potatoes. It was a real treat.

The DOD (Department of Defense) had a great idea for Thanksgiving 1968: they were going to serve turkey, mashed potatoes, gravy, stuffing, relish and apple pie to everyone in Vietnam – including the infantry troops in the field. They choreographed the whole evolution of cooking the food in San Francisco, flying it across the Pacific in hot containers and sending it out to the field on choppers. All of the companies in our battalion had to find a safe place to hunker down and cut an LZ for the choppers to land and deliver the food.

It was a disaster. The logistics worked out excellently, but as soon as we started dishing out the food we got a call not to eat it but to throw it away because guys were getting sick from it. About half of the company had already started eating. They got really sick. Good intention. Nice try but the NVA could have won the war that day because most of the infantry was sick from food poisoning.

One day John Minor and I, along with three other fellows were out on a look-see patrol and at midday we came across a slow-moving river that was about thirty feet wide. It made a nice turn and at the bend a big tree hung over the water casting a shadow. I thought there had to be some big fat fish there. I told John to send some guys downriver to stand across the stream. I then tossed a grenade into the stream, right on that shaded bend. After it blew there were around ten big, fat fish floating downstream on the surface for the guys to collect.

Some of the fish were around a foot long. I asked John if he thought they were edible but he didn't know. So we took our catch to a local village and showed them off there. One man in the village offered to trade us a chicken for just two of them which was a good trade for us and confirmed the fish were edible. That day we feasted on cooked up fish and chicken. We stuffed ourselves.

We arrived back to the company late because of our little cook-out and Lt. Waltz wanted to know why. We told him we got lost. Later, one of the guys that had been out with us spilled the beans to his friend and the officers all found out that our "recon mission" turned into a Bar-B-Q. They were pissed that we didn't bring any back to share with them. Piss on that, I was happily stuffed for once!

Cooking food was made possible by the fantastic discovery of plastic explosives, namely C-4. To cook C-Rations you had to punch a hole in the can you were about to cook. Then take

Vietnam – The Teenage Wasteland

some C-4, make a line of it by rolling it in your palms, spiral the C-4 around the can, light it and watch it burn at 1700 degrees. It scorched part of the meal but it also heated the food inside for you.

It did the trick but you had to be careful because C-4 will explode while it is burning if it is hit. We used to make "grenades" out of C-4 by rolling it in a ball like a snowball, stuffed rocks in it and any other solid object we could find, light it on fire and throw it. It would explode with twice the force of a regular hand grenade and fling the rocks and other solid objects in all directions: much more effective than a standard-issue M-2A hand grenade.

So when cooking, you had to be careful. Sometimes a can that was being cooked with C-4 fell over or was knocked over and exploded with the force of an M-80, and you'd get hurt from can fragments. Sometimes guys would forget to punch a hole in the can while cooking and it would explode sending scalding, boiling hot pieces of "Chicken, Boneless" in all directions.

After my fifth month of eating only the crap the Army had to offer I started eating fresh rice daily and stopped eating C-rations. I used all my spices and made some pretty decent rice meals. I ate some of the canned fruit cocktail and peanut butter but my main staple was rice. I lost weight, getting down to about 120 lbs. but I was healthy and had plenty of energy.

Food was such a problem for all of us. We occasionally found coconut trees or banana trees, but they were scarce and when we did find them the fruit was not ripe.

Next time I go to war I'm going to take a chef with me and make sure I have plenty of money so I can order the right foods – because the Army sure screws up on the food.

7

WAS IT HARD WORK?

Yes, yes, oh yes it was! It was crazy hard work from the time I got there until the day I left, a year later. I can safely say it was the most grueling, hard, physical work I've ever done and it wore me down to a nub.

First of all, when you're in the bush you walk everywhere. You walk mile after mile after long mile under a dazzling hot sun in the highest humidity there is only to arrive some place completely exhausted. Then you had to dig a "standard military foxhole", four feet deep, four feet long and two feet wide and hunker down completely burned out only to get woken up twice in the night for guard duty. Then you had to rise the moment the sun came up.

In most "night loggers" you had four guys to a position or a fox hole. So you dug your fox hole, put trip flares in front of your position, put a claymore mine out in front as well and then pulled your share of guard duty during the night and hoped that nothing happened so you had some semblance of a night's sleep.

I have dug more holes than anyone in the world (except other infantry from Vietnam). I have dug in soft ground, dug in shale, dug in rocky ground, dug in mud – you name it, I've dug it.

I calculated one day that I displaced with my standard military "entrenching tool" alone, thirty thousand cubic yards

Vietnam – The Teenage Wasteland

of dirt. Hence the term: "can you dig it?" My answer, since Vietnam was "yes I can – always".

We did not sleep in the foxhole at night. We slept on the ground next to the hole. The hole was used if and when we were attacked, in which case you jumped into the hole with the other three guys at your position to fend off the attack from there.

To get our "beds" ready for the night, we found a nice piece of earth, got out our entrenching tools and started scraping the ground, carving out a nice, comfortable sleeping position. You scraped away at it and then lay in it. Finding some lumps you got up and scrape away again, tried it again and eventually, you had the perfect bed.

When it was time to go to sleep you used the bottom part of your rucksack as a pillow and covered yourself with the rain poncho, pulled your helmet over your head and looked up at the stars and the next thing you knew it was morning. Had many a night's sleep like that. Wonderful.

In the spring and fall months it became dark at around seven o'clock at night and the sun came up at five o'clock in the morning. That gave ten hours of darkness which is ten hours of guarding time at each position of the perimeter. There were four people per position so a guard shift was two hours and thirty minutes long. That meant you got all of about six and a half hours sleep per night, if you were lucky and if nothing happened.

In the dead of summer it was worse because it stayed light until nine o'clock and the sun was up at four thirty – seven and a half hours. So with guard shift a little less than two hours you got under five hours sleep per night, and again that was if nothing happened during the night.

These figures take into account going to sleep anywhere from thirty to sixty minutes after the sun went down, then another half hour to get back to sleep after guard shift.

Winter wasn't as bad. The sun went down by six o'clock at night and was up at six in the morning. That is 12 hours guard duty per four men. But we usually didn't do all three hours at once. We did two, one-and-a-half hour shifts, which was a pain in the ass because it meant you were woken up twice during the night for your two shifts. It took half an hour to get back to sleep each time so that left seven-and-a-half hours of sleep. It was better but winter only lasted a few months. The rest of the time we were bone-tired.

Guard duty at night was the absolute mental stress test of all time. Once per month there was a full moon. The full moon lasted a week, for all intents, and it was bright. I read many a book under a full moon. I read the entirety of "Catch-22" under a full moon.

There were nights though, under the full moon, when I'd be sitting there, tired as hell, expecting an attack, looking out into the shadows. I'd see things that played on my mind like never before. I took LSD after Vietnam but swear I hallucinated more under a full moon than I ever did on acid. Many times I sat in a frozen position in my foxhole for a couple of hours looking at the same dammed trees and swore I saw shit moving. But the last thing anyone wants to do at night is shoot a rifle or blow a claymore mine because that gave away your position. So if you shot at a target at night it had better be a real one or you put the whole company at risk. Not only that but it'd wake everyone up and they wouldn't get back to sleep for another hour or more and they would be real pissed at me.

No matter how long I was there, those moon-filled nights were beyond stressful. I can't tell you how many times I had my rifle on full automatic with the "target" in my sights, finger on the trigger, just a pound of pressure away from pulling it, only to spend a long time talking myself out of it. It would go on for an hour sometimes: "I know that's a god dammed gook out there sneaking up on us with a twenty pound satchel charge. I can see him, but then, whatever it is hasn't moved for fifteen minutes so maybe it's not a gook." It is really stressful, *trippin' under a full moon*. Nothing like it.

Vietnam – The Teenage Wasteland

When I woke up the next guy for his turn at guard duty, he'd ask me how everything was. I'd tell him: "It's quiet out there, nothing going on." That was only because I didn't want to start him tripping right away - let him settle into his own trips. If there was something real out there he'd pick it up. It was best not to say anything otherwise it'd start him out alarmed and then his trips would be twice as bad as mine right from the get go and he'd blow a claymore or shoot and that would be one hour less sleep for me and I didn't want to do that to myself by getting my buddy started out with my trips.

But just imagine twenty guys on the perimeter line pulling guard duty at the same time, sitting there hallucinating; sweating it out like I was. And the miracle of it all was that usually no one shot.

I know other guys tripped because I've asked a lot of guys about it and they all went through the same thing I did, just sitting there trippin' under a full moon, trippin' away, battling with their minds, arguing with themselves…, and it went on for hours. Vets reading this right now are laughing their asses off.

But one night the NVA really did get by the guards. I woke up one night around two in the morning because I heard a twig snap and I just plain felt something weird going on. I was lying on my back and when I opened my eyes I looked up and saw the black silhouettes of seven NVA against the star fields in the sky. At first I thought it was a nightmare, but there is this one thing: I never have a sense of smell in my dreams, and that is how I distinguish dreams from reality: smell. And I could smell the night just then. There were NVA soldiers right in the middle of our perimeter with classic pith helmets, the outline of AK-47s against the stars, along with the smell of the night in the jungle. I knew this was for real and my skin crawled. I forced my body into disciplined motion as I slowly reached for my weapon and then slipped it on automatic. I open fired immediately – right at those silhouettes ten feet away from me. The NVA were lit up by the strobe-light flashes of my rifle and those of several other GI's M-16s. The fire-power blasting away at those ghostly apparitions showed them in strobe-light motion – running into each other like Keystone Cops.

When all was said and done, all seven lay dead in the middle of our perimeter. It was a miracle that none of us shot each other while we were at it. But the bigger question stood: how did they get by the perimeter guards?

I think the NVA had gotten lost, and I think all of a sudden they realized they were all smack-dab in the center of snoring, stinky Americans, and silently they freaked out. I think that is what actually woke me up. I am a hard sleeper but you can wake me up easily by trying to be quiet around me. I go on full alert if someone tip-toes around me when I'm sleeping. It means someone doesn't want me to hear them and that means danger.

The good times at night were when there was no moon and good cloud cover. It got so dark you couldn't see your hand in front of your face. No one moved in the night when it was that dark. It was time to daydream under the no-moon night conditions as there was nothing to see. One could just entertain oneself while easily keeping your ears open. It was a lot less stressful than trying to use our eyes under that full moon, that's for sure. We only had our ears to depend on, and they did not hallucinate. There are seventy million bits of input with sight and only three thousand bits of input for sound. So sounds are crystal clear and the categories of different sounds are not as cluttered as sight input.

I would say in the year I was in the bush, we had action in the middle of the night maybe twenty times. Various things happened but they most always resulted in casualties on our side, most always.

One night I dreamt that I was sleeping and we were under mortar attack. I dreamt that I was paralyzed with fear and continued to lie on the ground where I was, sleeping. I dreamt that a mortar landed three feet from my head.

Vietnam – The Teenage Wasteland

I finally woke up as Donnie Holloway dragged me into a foxhole. I landed with a thump in the hole and looked up at Donnie.

"What the hell, man?" I fussed at him.

"We're under mortar attack," he said.

"Oh, shit, I thought I was dreaming that."

"No man, that was the real thing and one landed right next to you."

After the attack subsided, I went back to where I was lying and there was a small crater in the ground ten feet from my head. In the crater was the tail fin from a mortar. Luckily, the ground was a little soft where the mortar round landed. They usually explode upward so the chances of getting hit by shrapnel when lying down are slim, plus the soft ground allowed it to go deeper before exploding – saving me from getting hit.

It scared me that I incorporated current happenings into my dreams. Not good.

Every fourth week we would have to "pull security" and guard the firebase. A firebase is a hill in your Area of Operation (AO) that has cannons on it. It's also called a Landing Zone or LZ, and they have names like "LZ Cork" or "LZ Baldy" etc.

The cannons are 155 millimeter and there are four of them. They can shoot twenty miles accurately and have a good sized shell that can do a lot of damage. Then there are four 105 millimeter cannons that shoot about ten miles. Although the shell is a lot smaller they can still do a lot of damage. Then there are the 4.2 inch mortars. They have a range of eight miles and are pretty good. Then there are the 80 millimeter mortars with a 2 mile range, used for close-in support. Usually, there is a 106 recoilless rifle, a quad-fifty (four of the fifty caliber machine guns operating on one platform), rockets and all sorts of defense stuff dreamed up by the wildest of imaginations.

Battalion Command post is also on the hill. The office of the Battalion Commander is called TOC (Tactical Operations Command). Battalion Command runs the five companies in the field designated as Alpha Company (my company), Bravo, Charley, Delta and Echo. One of these companies runs security for the Hill for a week and then rotates back to the hill after four weeks away.

Being on the hill for security had its pluses and minuses. The Hill is not necessarily a picnic. I actually preferred being in the bush than on that Hill. The reasons are plenty. First of all, on the Hill you are a sitting target for rockets, mortars, sapper attacks and army officers. The military bullshit kicks in a lot more on the Hill because there are high ranking officers present. So you have the spit and polish routine going on a little more.

The officers are told to keep us busy so for the most part we were fixing barbed-wire fences, bunkers and all sorts of do-nothing crap. Mainly, we filled sand bags. We were constantly filling sand bags to re-enforce the bunkers.

At night we pulled guard duty on the Hill. This was almost fun because we had more sophisticated equipment on the Hill. We had Starlight Scopes which allowed us to see quite clearly at night with the use of only amplified star light. Every time we checked one out we were told "be careful with that thing, it cost Uncle Sam twenty-five thousand dollars." They were expensive but they worked well.

One night I was on a bunker line at LZ Professional and I was entertaining myself looking though Starlight Scope, tracking a sapper in a loin cloth with twenty five pounds of satchel charge on him and he was heading in my direction. I watched him in amusement for an hour as he picked his way through five rows of concertina wire. He was good, moved slowly and deliberately and made no noise what-so-ever. I hated to pull the trigger on him because he was so good. I watched and watched and then he crawled right up to where I

Vietnam – The Teenage Wasteland

wanted him to be and silently said goodbye to him as I tripped a Claymore mine he was right next to.

The Claymore set off his satchel charge, there was a tremendous explosion that woke up the entire Hill. The flash totally washed out my scope for five minutes but when the picture came back there was a two foot deep crater where the sapper had been but no sign of him at all. The total of thirty pounds of exotic explosive surely vaporized him. I'm sure he is still there to this day working his way through the concertina wire, not knowing he was vaporized. Somebody should talk to him and set him free.

Snipers also tried to get at us on the Hill. NVA snipers were good. They could make those long shots. So every now and then a sniper would claim someone on the Hill.

When we first got to LZ Professional we learned what life was really like on and the around the Hill. Our company, Alpha was the first of our battalion to get choppered to the Hill. We replaced the remnants of another battalion on that Hill that had been decimated down to fifty men (out of five hundred). That really sobered us up.

The last company in our battalion was sent straight out to the bush. At first I was glad my company wasn't going into the bush, but the gladness was soon replaced by terror. Within an hour it started raining mortars to the tune of one every second. It went on for three days and nights. Going to the shitter was a matter of taking your life in your hands.

After the second day, guys were sticking their hands and legs outside the bunkers in hopes of catching some shrapnel to get them sent to the hospital for some respite.

We lost a couple of guys and around twenty were wounded in those three days. The constant bombing crushed moral, which was the goal of the bombing. It was kind of like "welcome to our neighborhood, boys, and we just want to let you know there are a whole bunch of us out here, and we have a lot of ammo and we can keep you fellas under our thumb all we want." It really worked. We all wanted to go out to the bush where we had the ability to break contact and get out of harm's way. On the Hill there was no such option. I realized we could break contact out in the bush, but up on the Hill we were sitting ducks.

I decided that if I was going to be up on the hill I'd better find a better way to defend myself, so I got myself a fifty caliber machine gun and put in on my bunker. A "fifty" is an anti-aircraft gun that shoots a half-inch diameter slug as far as five miles, faster than any other bullet can travel. Its designation is M-2 Machine Gun and is nicknamed "Ma". Its bullets can penetrate tanks, go through twelve inches of steel, and it can fire high explosive rounds. I wanted the gun to spook the NVA a bit – a show of force, as it were.

I got the gun the next day, and it was a rusted relic that had not been used since WW II. It took a lot of work to get that gun working, using a file, emery cloth, and a brass hammer, but I did get it running by the end of the day. We fired off some practice rounds to make sure it worked and retired to the inside of the bunker to hunker down for the night. The sun was just going down.

The bad guys must have been watching me set up the gun. We had been in the bunker for ten minutes when I heard a "boom" out in the valley in front of my position. We all looked at each other like "what was that?" Then we heard the unmistakable whooshing of a Chinese B-40 rocket as it plowed into the hillside right below our bunker with a thundering explosion.

We ran outside and I saw the telltale sign of smoke wafting up from a spot two miles away, straight in front of me. I gave the command to man the gun. I was the shooter. I had a spotter and there was an assistant gunner whose job it was to make sure ammo fed to the gun. It was a standard three-man machine-gun team.

I grabbed the charging handle and cranked a round into the receiver. I aimed at the smoke two miles away and opened up with a rhythmic cadence of shoot five rounds, stop, shoot five

Vietnam – The Teenage Wasteland

rounds, stop, and so on. You had to do it that way or you burn out the barrel rifling, a disaster when you really need it.

I got twenty rounds out when I saw an explosion where I was shooting. My heart leapt a little in hope that I had caused a secondary explosion, but that hope was quickly dashed when I saw in my sights a little black dot with an orange halo around it getting bigger and bigger. That I knew was a rocket coming right at me. I lamely tried to shoot it down, but it kept coming.

Directly in front of my bunker is what we called an RPG fence. It's a fence to keep rockets from hitting one's bunker. If they hit the fence they blow up there and only the shrapnel comes through. You don't want rockets directly hitting your bunker because they can penetrate and shred everything on the inside. The fence stops that.

The rocket was coming right at us and would be on top of us very soon. I left gun and dove for the bunker. The rocket went right over the bunker and landed harmlessly on the other side of the hill but I knew they now had us bracketed.

The NVA guys that shoot rockets are old farts that have the 'art' of rocketeering down cold. They dig a round hole in the ground about three feet deep. They take a half round bamboo stalk that is about six inches in diameter and use that as a launch pad. They lean it on the perimeter of the hole and adjust distance by raising or lowering the bamboo. If the rocket they launched is too short, they raise the bamboo and so forth.

Now they just needed to lower the bamboo a tad, and they would be right on my fence. The rocket would destroy the fence and the next round would be on the bunker itself. I needed to knock the rocket launcher out <u>now</u>.

I got back up and started hammering with my fifty, laying rounds into where the launcher was two miles away. Then I saw another blast and another black dot with the orange halo. Shit, I was going to be in pain in six seconds. I tried to shoot it down and at the last second dumped the gun and hit the deck.

The rocket hit the fence and a large piece of shrapnel hit a sandbag in front of me and threw me off the top of the bunker. It knocked the wind out of me but I jumped back onto the bunker and opened up again with the gun. This time I just held the trigger down and hoped for the best. I was laying the rounds all around that launch site. I could see them hitting out there. I could also see my barrel was turning red and I told my assistant to pour oil on it. Big mistake – the wind was blowing in my direction and the hot oil burnt my face and hands.

All of a sudden, I saw another explosion out there and my heart sank. But this one was a little different – I saw a rocket fly through the air, straight up from the launch area – kind of twirling 'round and 'round, and then I saw another snaking along the ground. Then I saw another one snake along the ground followed by a huge explosion. We all jumped up and cheered as we saw the rest of the rockets they had stockpiled blow up. There must have been another twenty-five of them.

I was elated. I knew I was going to get my first Bronze Star for Gallantry. Instead, I was in the Colonel's office ten minutes later being chewed out for shooting the fifty without clearance. It turns out I had Bravo Company pinned down because they were four hundred meters my side of the rocketeers and were moving into position to get them for us. They were in a wooded area and my big bullets were breaking branches above them.

I wounded two guys in Bravo with flying lumber. One had a broken arm and the other got a mild concussion from a flying tree limb. They were really pissed at me. I got in some trouble but I know that I saved the Hill a lot of damage and probably lives. Nevertheless, that didn't help my promotion which was later turned down.

I was always glad to get off the Hill. In addition to being a sitting target for the NVA we were also basically slaves for the rest of the units up there. We had to do all the garbage details, clean out the shithouses and all of that. And the spit

Vietnam – The Teenage Wasteland

and polish was abrasive so it was largely a royal pain in the ass being on the hill.

When I was down South in the 1st of the 20th in Duc Pho province, I walked point. Duc Pho Province was famous for booby-traps. I walked point a lot and found booby-traps almost every time.

No one taught me this, but I had the idea that booby traps worked well because no one spotted what was "not supposed to be there." So I was looking for something that was not supposed to exist. That meant that as I walked, I looked for odd or strange or out-of-place things – anything incongruous, and I found them. Don't ask me how I learned this, but it was good and workable pattern, thank God.

One day I was teaching another guy how to find them. His name was Fred. He was going to replace me so I was training him. We were walking down a well-worn trail. In the middle of the trail was a rock. What does a tired and hot GI do when he sees a rock? He kicks it out of the way. But what I saw was something that was not supposed to be there…a rock on a well-worn trail. I stopped and told all behind me to move back a hundred meters. I took off my rucksack, got on my hands and knees and searched under the rock with my bayonet. Sure enough there was a "Bouncing Betty" waiting for me there. A Bouncing Betty is a land mine that comes up to head height and then blows up – taking your head off. If it's a good one it kills a couple of other people too. I put some C-4 plastic explosive next to the rock and detonated the mine.

I refreshed Fred: "So you see that? The rock is on a well-worn trail. It is not supposed to be there. But it was, so that means someone put it there. So if someone put it there, it was put there for a reason. And that reason is suspect. So we look. Got it?"

He nodded.

Later that day I let Fred take over point after he convinced me he was onto how the job worked. We walked on and after a few hours we came across a point on the trail where a large stand of bamboo had been cut down and laid across the trail. There was a new trail going around to the right and Fred headed in that direction.

"Where are you going?" I quizzed him.

"Uh, the bamboo is lying across the trail; you can't cross bamboo without getting tangled up, so go around. Right?"

"Wrong, liver-lips. You are putting us all in danger."

"Why is that?" he defended himself.

I pointed to the bamboo. "How do you suppose that bamboo got cut down?"

"I dunno," he said, lamely.

"Well, let me ask you this: do you suppose an artillery round exploded there and cut it down?"

He looked. No sign of an explosion. "Ah, no."

"Did Americans cut it down?"

He was getting frustrated. "I don't know."

"Look, I'm trying to get you to think with this. Okay?"

He nodded. "Okay, the bamboo looks like it has been cut down."

"Good. So now the natural thing for us to do is…"

He smiled. "… go around it. I get it. So you think there's something waiting for us on this new trail. Right?"

I started taking off my back pack. "I don't think – I know. C'mon, let's go have us a good look."

We both took off our packs. I proceeded ahead of him on my hands and knees, probing with my bayonet. For some reason I was real wary of this one. That they cut down the bamboo for us was a little extra more work than the bad guys usually put into booby traps so to me that meant they had an extra surprise for us. I was very cautious as I probed ahead.

I had only gone twenty meters or so when I came across vegetation covering the trail. My heart raced as my probing bayonet disappeared down through the vegetation and into a hole beneath. I pulled my bayonet back slowly and then ever

Vietnam – The Teenage Wasteland

so cautiously removed the vegetation covering the hole in the ground.

It took me ten minutes to uncover a pit about five feet long, three feet wide and four feet deep. In the pit were sharpened spears. This was the bungee-pit, a camouflaged hole that a GI falls into and skewers himself. But this one was a little different. What got my attention was a trip-wire going across the pit.

Fred was right up there with me. He whistled. "Holy shit, man. What do you suppose this is all about?"

With that, he started following the wire. It went back to the trail and back another fifteen meters. Fred was on the case. He found the wire disappeared into another pit on the side of the trail. In that pit was an unexploded five hundred pound bomb one of our jets had dropped. It was a dud that had not been recovered.

I pushed my helmet back and whistled to myself. "At this point Fred, I would order the rest of the company to go back four or five hundred meters. Tell them we have a five hundred pound bomb here, possibly more stuff too. Tell them to stay on the trail and not to move off it. Follow only our footsteps back. Got it?"

He nodded and took off.

While he was gone, I studied the bomb's trip mechanism. It was an American hand grenade that one of my "friends" had thrown away. The grenade was stuffed into the nose of the bomb where the bomb's fuse used to be. The wire was attached to the pin of the grenade.

I whistled. It would have worked and it would've killed a lot of us.

But you don't stop there. You check out everything and I got real thorough about this one. I saw weeds that had been placed over the tail end of the bomb and carefully removed them and saw something that really disturbed me. There were batteries back there and a mechanism with wires coming off it. This was the most elaborate booby trap I'd ever seen.

Fred came back and told me the Captain said to blow it and let's get out of here.

"Not so fast, Fred. What do you make of this? Study the entire bomb."

He looked at the firing mechanism for the bomb and then looked at its tail. Then he saw the batteries, with wires that went back down the trail we were on. He followed the wires back another five meters and found a Bouncing Betty. A wire was coming out of that one and went back further down the trail. Then another one ten meters back and then another. Fred went back a hundred and fifty meters and found ten more Bouncing Betties placed alongside the trail.

We were at this for about an hour and uncovered everything that was set for us. I finally decided that we were not going to even try to diffuse all of it but would do a controlled trip of the whole thing.

I looked around one more time to see if I could find anything else, and it seemed like we'd found everything. We had a bungee-pit with a trip wire. That would have gotten the point man. Then we had a five hundred pound bomb in a pit. That would have taken out the whole first platoon. Then we had ten large Bouncing Betties that would have taken out another platoon. All-in-all, it was a well thought out booby-trap, the most dangerous I had ever seen. It would have killed 40 to 50 men.

It was time to quit admiring it and blow it.

I used Claymore mine wire, which is pretty long, and tied it to the trip wire in the pit. I also tied it to the grenade that acted as the fuse to the 500 pound bomb.

You usually use two detonators when you explode something large so you have a back-up in case the primary detonator fails. You don't want to have to go back to this kind of set up only to have it go off in your face. For extra safety I put an extra charge of C-4 right on top of the grenade with a fifteen minute fuse, just in case. I really did not want to come back to it.

Vietnam – The Teenage Wasteland

We crawled back with the trip-wire to a safe position. The Captain was with us now and was more than interested in the way we were blowing it. He agreed to trip it rather than try to disarm it or blow it.

I was finally ready and announced on the radio, "fire in the hole". I waited ten seconds and yanked on the wire. A deafening explosion followed by ten more blasts rocked all of us. Shrapnel was flying all over the place and the area turned into a cloudy brownish-gray Los Angeles-type of atmosphere.

It was gone. I'm sure the guys who designed this killing zone were not too far away because they were waiting to see the results of their handy work. The day however was going to be a huge disappointment to them.

Even though they were good and I respected their work, I wanted to find them and kill them before they could build more of them. This particular booby trap was set up to kill half of a company and maybe more. It was deadly.

Fred came to see me that night and told me he would never have spotted that booby trap and would have accidentally tripped it and killed a lot of folks. He told me that he was sure he would have missed the Bouncing Betties. He told me he was sorry but that he was not cut out for this type of work and bowed out gracefully. I agreed and we shook hands and he went back to being a rifleman in his platoon.

But I was still stuck with the job and wanted to get rid of it. On the other hand, I didn't want to give it to a guy who would kill half the company so needed to find someone with smarts enough to do the job.

Two weeks later I noticed I was getting palsied from fear. I had found more traps and stuff to blow up and it was starting to get to me, handling all of those explosives.

One day in February, we were on LZ Cork, waiting for deployment. The Captain came and got me. There was a lot of old ordnance (unexploded artillery) and stuff that had been lying around and needed to be blown. I was the ordnance man so I had to take it all and blow it.

There was an old bomb crater on the side of the hill right in front of my bunker, two hundred meters down the hillside, and I decided to use it as the place to blow the ammo.

I went around to all the artillery and mortar units and got whatever ammo they figured was useless or dangerous and took it down to the crater. I then lined the bottom of the crater with around two hundred pounds of C-4 and put all the ordnance on top of it. Then I put a further three hundred pounds of C-4 on top.

No one checked this out and everyone stayed away from me while I was doing it. I never stopped to do basic math to find out how big of an explosion I was about to make.

I finally finished it off and ran two electric detonating wires back to my bunker. I was about to blow it and called around to all positions and told everyone to get inside their bunkers in fifteen minutes. Everyone hid. The Hill came to a standstill. I finally did a countdown on the radio from twenty-five to zero and pushed the plungers.

I didn't hear any sound at all. All I knew was that the bunker wall hit me in the face. I got a bloody nose from it. They say that if you are near a big explosion and can't hear it, it's because you're in the middle of it.

After the ash and smoke cleared I got up to see the damage. Part of my bunker had piled into the doorway. I had to move sandbags to get out. I then got a call on the radio that the Colonel wanted to see me right away. I have to admit that I had a nagging thought in the back of my head that I'd had enough ordnance in the crater to make a small mushroom cloud.

I went to see the colonel. He was outside his bunker and the first thing I noticed was soup in his hair, on his face and on the front of his uniform. He had a spoon in his hand.

He looked at me. "Do you mind looking in my canteen cup and telling me what is in there?"

I walked over to his canteen cup, which was on a burner and looked in it. There, in his soup, right there, was the fuse

Vietnam – The Teenage Wasteland

for an 82 millimeter mortar. I knew, right then and there, that this was going to be a real bad day for me.

"Ah…that is a mortar fuse, Sir."

"And why is there a mortar fuse in my soup?" He asked sarcastically.

"Uh, because Sir, it came from the explosion."

"And if there's a mortar fuse in my soup, that means there is other ordnance lying around my hill. Am I right?"

I was stunned at the thought. "Uh, not sure, Sir."

His radio man came outside. "Sir, I am getting reports of artillery and mortar rounds all around the perimeter and they are fizzing and smoking."

The Colonel looked at me, raised an eyebrow and told his radioman to call around the Hill and keep everyone inside while Tom cleans up the mess.

I told him I would handle it and took off. To my horror I saw sparking, fizzing, smoking, squashed ordnance lying around everywhere.

I ran down to the crater and saw rounds lying all over the place, some on fire some just sparking and smoking. There was a large 155 mm round lying right in front of me, snapping and sparkling. I ran away as fast as I could and had gone fifteen feet when I hit the dirt. It went off ten seconds later. I got up, ran to my bunker and gathered up the rest of the C-4. I had another twenty pounds or so.

I ran over to the motor pool and found a quarter inch steel plate that was about three feet by three feet. I took it with me. I found a smoking mortar round right in the middle of an open area inside the perimeter. I knew that if they were hot or smoking a sneeze could set them off. I took a piece of C-4, put a blasting cap in it, lit it and put it next to the mortar round. I put up the steel plate as a shield and backed off. The C-4 blew, but it just knocked the round twenty feet away. I did it again and it knocked the round away again.

Guys were watching from their bunkers, laughing and cajoling me. The Colonel's radio man found me and told me I needed to move faster because the whole hill was shut down.

Seeing that twenty minutes had passed since the blast, I figured if anything was going to blow it would have blown by now, so I stood up and picked up the mortar round by its fins and ran down to the crater. I threw it in. Then I found another and threw it in. I did the same with every other round I could find, including the fuse in the Colonel's canteen cup. I policed up about forty rounds from all over the perimeter. It took me an hour and a half. I finally got it all down there and called an all-clear.

I sat down with my Captain and tried to figure out what went wrong. He asked me why I didn't just put the ordnance in the crater and put the C-4 on top of it and blow it. I told him I wanted to put the ordnance in between the C-4 and smash it between the blasts. He laughed at me and told me there's too much of a blast that way; it just blew everything out of the crater. He was right – obviously.

The next day I went down to the crater, which was now three times bigger than it used to be, and put all of the ordnance in the bottom of it. Then I put a hundred pounds of C-4 on top of it. I blew it and it all went up.

That night I noticed my hands really shaking and it was almost permanent. I was palsied. I had to get rid of the job.

That night a new guy came into the company, assigned to my bunker. He was energetic and enthusiastic. He was asking when we were going to get into action and had a sort of false bravado, but he wanted action so I asked him if he liked to blow things up. He said he sure did. In fact he was hoping to get a job in which he could do just that. The other guys and I exchanged glances. I asked him if he'd like to be the ordnance man for the company. He lit up like a Christmas tree and begged for the job.

The next day he got it, I taught him everything I knew. He was good. He could think with it and he took to the job with aplomb. After teaching him the ropes I turned it all over to him. My hands stopped shaking.

So yes, it was hard work. Harder than you can imagine.

8

WHAT WERE THE PEOPLE LIKE?

This subject breaks down into several categories: officers, draftees and people who joined, including the South Vietnamese, the North Vietnamese and the Viet Cong.

The North Vietnamese soldiers (NVA) were highly trained and disciplined. They were tough and dedicated. I respected them a lot. When you engaged them in a fire-fight it was fierce. They humped their ammo a lot further than we did and because they didn't have helicopters to bring in fresh supplies they conserved ammo and shot to kill. The NVA were well trained and worthy opponents. We used to call them "Mister Charley."

The NVA were brainwashed to believe that Americans were "giants" and so decadent that if they were captured; their souls would never go to Nirvana. Such indoctrination was carried out so they resisted the temptation to come over to our side. One captured NVA told me that GI meant "Guy Intelligent". I thought it funny, but for him and the rest of the NVA, it worked and caused them to fight us more fiercely.

The Viet Cong, or VC or Victor Charley were just a bunch of hoodlums. Supposedly, they were South Vietnamese sympathetic to the North. But personally, I think they were hired thugs just put there to be the fly in the ointment. They rarely did damage to us. For the most part, they were hit and

Vietnam – The Teenage Wasteland

run terrorists. A lot of them had jobs during the day and were "weekend warriors who mainly attacked on weekends.

Americans arrived in all sorts of shapes and sizes. The officers were, for the most part, competent individuals. But a lot of them arrived with dumb attitudes and (sadly) most were insufficiently trained or poorly trained on how to fight in that sort of environment.

Officers were a rare commodity in the Vietnam infantry. It was not often that an infantry company had a full complement of officers. There were just not enough officers. In my opinion that was only because there were too many in the rear areas. You almost tripped over officers in the rear. Officers generally had high IQs so many decided to specialize in a non-infantry status, keeping distance between themselves and the on-the-ground action.

The only reason a real infantry officer was in the infantry was to become genuinely experienced in and with the infantry but not enough did that.

The plus side of being an officer in the infantry was that one could get promoted faster. But after all was said and done, there weren't many of them.

The West Point grads were the worst because they came over with fixed ideas on how things should go. They thought they knew what they were doing, only to get themselves killed. ROTC officers, for unknown reasons, were the best. I think it was because they were real people and had more of a street sense about them that allowed them to survive.

But when you had a good officer, he was very good. Like Dave Waltz – he was a gem. We had a few others that were good but Dave really stood out.

The sergeants were usually good. The ones that came up through the ranks were the best. The ones that arrived in country after sarge-ing around in the USA were okay, but they clung too much to their ideas of spit and polish and lacked a certain sense in jungle warfare.

The regular foot soldiers who joined the Army to go to Vietnam were the real troublesome guys. Look at the idea of someone joining the Army Infantry just to go to Vietnam. Well, they definitely had something wrong with them. That is all I'm going to say on that subject.

In my estimation we draftees were good. We fought hard to get through and get each other through and back home. Once we received our draft papers we had a choice, go to Vietnam and fight or go to Canada and never see loved ones again. So when we got to Nam we fought hard to survive and get back home to those that mattered. Kinda like one plus one equals two. We knew the way home was to carve a big hole in Vietnam and make it back. So we did, for the most part. We had no other agenda. Just make it through the year, survive, deal out as much damage to the bad guys as possible and get home.

The villagers were hard working people who did not want to be stuck in the middle of anything. They were apolitical. You had to have a lot of understanding for their situation. Americans searching a village one day found both American and North Vietnamese flags because the villagers knew that the next day the NVA would search the same village. The villagers just wanted to be left alone.

The kids in Vietnam were a trip. In larger towns and villages the kids were professional beggars and thieves. If you happened to walk into one of their villages you emptied your pockets first because the kids surrounded you, and before you knew what was happening, their hands were in your pockets – all of them. If there was nothing in your pockets they hit or kicked you. Their little hands were like quick, little snakes, rummaging around in your pockets and pulling out anything they could get hold of.

The kids in the far out villages were shy, but very curious. I always tried to save chocolate or sugar for them because when you gave them something sweet it was a new experience. The looks on their faces was just too precious.

Vietnam – The Teenage Wasteland

In the larger villages there was a lot of corruption. Another guy and I were giving kids chocolate one day. There was a rather large crowd around us, maybe forty kids, all vying to get a piece of chocolate. A Vietnamese teenager on a Honda 250 motorcycle came plowing through the crowd of younger kids on his bike, running over several and hurting them.

The teen on the bike was what we called a cowboy. They were teens that wore cowboy hats, cowboy boots, blue jeans and so on. They had a lot of money, somehow.

This one particular fellow just came plowing through the crowd yelling "Yehaaaaaww". I stuck out my arm and clothes-lined him. He fell off and jumped up and went into a Kung Fu pose, squaring off to me.

I handed my rifle to my buddy and as soon as I did the cowboy was on me, punching and kicking at the same time. I think he hit and kicked me around forty times per second. It shocked me at first. I thought I was going to get the shit kicked out of me because he was apparently a pro, well trained at Kung Fu. But I finally realized something about the guy. He weighed all of eighty-five pounds and when he hit me, there wasn't much behind the punch at all. I decided to put an end to it and punched him right in the forehead with a good ol' fashioned Detroit "thump between the horns" and he went down like a sack of hammers – out like a light. I took his motor cycle and dumped it in a rice paddy with the throttle wide open.

The indigents of Vietnam are called Montagnards. They're like our American Indians. They, for the most part, don't want anything to do with the war and try to stay out of harm's way. They are peaceful, hardworking people that just live off the land with what they have.

We were scaling a mountain of about six thousand feet in September of 1969 and got about two thirds of the way up when we broke for a rest. It was around noon, so we decided to have lunch. I was sitting, cooking my lunch when I looked at the terrain around us. I could see sort of a ridge in the ground that ran off to the left and then to the right as you looked at the top of the hill. I sat and studied it for a bit and decided I was going to check it out.

I pulled out my entrenching tool and started to dig. The captain asked me what I was doing and I showed him the ridge. He laughed and asked me if I had too much energy or something.

Undaunted, I furiously dug down about three feet when I hit rock. Jessie Spencer got interested in what I was doing and helped me dig around the rock. We dug on one side of it and found out it was not a rock, but a bunch of rocks. We dug a little further and found out the rocks were neatly stacked into a stone wall. I knew it, a stone wall under three feet of earth. It must have been real old. Like hundreds or thousands of years old. What a find. I was elated. I started thinking about the civilization that used to live in that place -- there must have been untold amounts of gold and other riches under all that dirt.

The Captain told me to mark it on the map and get ready to move out, and that I could report it to MAC-V later and someone would make the archeological find at some point in the future.

I always wanted to go back there and find out what else was under the three feet of dirt. I bet there's a real find there.

We moved on up to the top of the mountain and the Captain and I walked right into a small village of about fifty Montangards. They had tree cover over the village so it could not be seen from the air.

The people froze. We froze too. We just looked at each other for more than a minute. I realized they were primitives and had not seen Americans before. I looked around at the people and it seemed like they didn't know whether to shit or git. I looked around some more and saw that they'd gone down to the valley and collected up all sorts of military junk that had fallen from the skies, like expended rocket launchers, shrapnel from bombs, empty gas canisters from jets.

Vietnam – The Teenage Wasteland

I moved a little further into the village and the people kind of backed up. I realized that I must look hideous with my helmet and back pack on. I guessed I looked like some sort of monster. I took my helmet off and all of the villagers gasped. Then I took my backpack off and then my shirt and I stood before them with just my pants, a t-shirt and my rifle. They started to warm to me a little. One man stepped forward and touched me. He must have been the village leader. He was smiling as he touched my mustache. He got curious about my rifle and tried to touch it but I wouldn't let him. He backed off and was a little taken back that I got serious about the rifle. So I smiled at him again and showed him my bayonet. He lit up like a spotlight. I offered it to him and he snatched it out of my hand. Then he ran off with it and showed it to other men in the village. He then ran into his hut and came out with a real primitive crossbow with several darts. He proudly handed it to me. I thanked him by bowing,

The children figured it was safe by now and came forward and touched my hair and mustache. They gleefully giggled and kept touching me all over. A few other guys from the company came forward and stripped off their gear.

We spent an hour and a half playing with the kids and showing the natives our gear. It was a magical time. It was like we had crossed over into another time or something. Finally the guys, sans their bayonets, were loaded with all sorts of goodies – like knives made out of bomb fragments, or cross bows like the one I had been given, and we left the village. The people were actually sad to see us go and wished us well.

Mostly, the villagers were good people. They didn't want to be involved in war. They just wanted to be left alone.

One thing that struck me as odd was that all the people of South Vietnam had bad teeth. They had to chew Betel Nuts, which had a Novocain of some kind in it. I suppose they chewed the nut to take away their teeth pain. The only thing was that the nut, or what it grew on, was red in color and it stained their mouths red, so when they smiled at us or talked to us, they had bloody mouths and teeth which made them look like horrid Banshees or something evil. Wasn't quite sure what that whole thing was about.

A lot of times in the field we came across villagers and they freaked out. They had reason to because we often searched their village, and I am sad to say we were not gentle about it. They stored stuff in wicker rice barrels and when we searched we just turned the barrels over to look in them. I am sorry for the messes we left behind and would like to make it up to those villagers someday.

The South Vietnamese Army (ARVN – Army of the Republic of Vietnam) was a disaster. We tried with those people, but their hearts just were not in it.

We used to go on "drafting missions." We surrounded a village before sun up and caught the local men as they tried to run out of the village and back to the hills where they hid during the day. We caught them and "drafted" them into the Army.

Once, we did this for three weeks straight. It was one of the best times I had in the country. We parked on the beach of the South China Sea after we did our "drafting." We left the village after putting the new recruits on a chopper, then walked the six or seven kilometers down to the beach and found a nice place to hang for the rest of the day. We took turns swimming in the Sea and standing guard. Then we'd go to sleep at eight o'clock, get up at three in the morning and hump for a few more kilometers, surround another unsuspecting village and do our conscripting number.

One day we got a call that a company of South Vietnamese had killed their captain. We rushed to the scene and surrounded them. We had orders to do nothing because a new captain was coming. They were mainly lying on the ground, flipping us the bird or making fun of us, or pointing their weapons at us and taunting us. They were a rag-tag bunch.

Vietnam – The Teenage Wasteland

The new captain showed up in a helicopter thirty minutes later. He was a short, little guy who was as spirited as a cock-rooster. He walked briskly up to the company of which he was now in command, ignored us and looked them over. He walked up to a soldier laying on the ground with a radio in his back pack. He asked the soldier if he was the CO's radio man. The soldier smiled at the captain and said something smart to him that got the others laughing. The Captain pulled out his Colt .45 and shot the radio man between the eyes.

He went over to another man who was slow standing up and shot him in the face. He then ordered another man to fetch the radio from the dead RTO and put it on. Then he got everyone else off the ground and into formation, screaming out orders, whacking people with the barrel of his pistol.

At one point another soldier got defiant with him and asked the new Captain if he was going to shoot him too. The captain said nothing, just shot him in the face.

After ten minutes of this he had the whole company of eighty ARVN soldiers at attention. Then he marched them off smartly into the west.

I was pretty impressed. There were three bodies lying in the dirt and to tell the truth I was grossed out that the Captain shot those men, but I thought about it the rest of the day and realized he probably shot the guys who killed the previous CO and had no choice but to take the actions he took to get the men under control. But then again, he had to sleep at some point…

Working with the ARVN was NEVER fun. We were working with them one day, sweeping a valley. There was a company of them and our company. That night we parked on separate hills; theirs just two kilometers away. Around ten o'clock that night we heard them pop a couple of mortar rounds. They landed right in our perimeter. We could hear them laughing. So I called an artillery strike on them. That stopped their laughing. The next day they told us we called the arty strike on them and that three of their men were wounded.

I just shrugged my shoulders and acted confused. We got rid of them that very same day.

Vietnam – The Teenage Wasteland

9

WHAT ABOUT DRUGS?

This too is a very sore point. I've read and heard all about people getting into drugs in Vietnam. I don't know who those people were. I think it must have been the guys in the rear areas.

I was a dope-smoking' hippie before I got drafted. In that regard I was a little more than a weekend warrior. I got high as often as possible. But when I was in basic training at Fort Dix, NJ, I was not allowed to even smoke cigarettes, so I dried up pretty well. I would have quit smoking all together, but I started up on cigarettes again when I found out I was going to Vietnam.

I got high only one time in the field. It was after we shot a dink that had a pack of cigarettes on him which was actually marijuana. I saved the one joint and when we got back to LZ Cork, I toked up one night. It was a funny time too, because it was when we had a stupid milk-drinker, four-eyed idiot of a Captain.

We were on top of the bunkers, stoned, when someone called and said the Captain was doing bunker inspections. We waited for him to come around in his jeep.

He finally came and started toward our bunker. It was pretty dark out and you had to use flashlights to get around. As the Captain approached I did a very standard: "Halt, who goes there?"

"Captain Rousch," he responded,

I got a wild idea to humiliate him while also doing everything right. "Put your ID card on the ground and step back five paces. Do it now!" I ordered.

He was a little taken aback. "Uh, this is your Captain. You don't need to do that."

I hung in there. "I don't know who you are, Sir. I'll tell you again, take out your ID card, place it on the ground and step back five paces. Do it now!"

He argued with me. "Alright, knock it off, you know who this is."

I fired a burst in the air on full automatic. "Whoever you are you are violating security measures, I suggest you get down on the ground now and put your hands behind your head or I will shoot you where you stand." I fired another burst in the air to prove I was not fucking around.

Captain Rousch threw himself on the ground and put his hands behind his head.

I had my bunker-mate check his wallet and pull his ID card. I read it in dramatic fashion and then shouldered my rifle. "Okay Captain, I was not sure it was you. We get pretty jumpy out here at night, you know."

The Captain got up and came up to me with his flashlight shining in my face. He was pissed. "You are in trouble mister. I'm going to have you Court-Marshaled for your antics here. You got me soldier?"

I smiled and said, "For what, following security procedures? Go for it, Captain. I didn't recognize you and neither could any of the other guys. You shined your flashlight in our faces to blind us, so I thought you had to be enemy, Sir."

He immediately took his flashlight out of my face and looked around at the rest of the guys who just looked back at him, all witnesses to what had happened. He gave a little whine and spun on his heels and took off.

We all had a big laugh and told the story over and over again for days. But after it was over, I decided that what I did

Vietnam – The Teenage Wasteland

was pretty risky. I decided to never smoke dope in the field again.

The best story I have about drugs was when I was with the 1st of the 46th and Dave Waltz was my platoon leader. I was his radio man. We had a fellow by the name of Leroy Jones, from Detroit, Michigan. He was a tall, lanky black dude who was as serious as a heart attack. He never talked to anyone and kept to himself. He was also spectacular at walking point. He loved walking point and he did a good job of it. He busted up ambushes about three times a week.

Command wanted to know what he did to do such a stellar job of walking point. Lt Waltz had me walk right behind him for a couple of days and observe him, so I could pass it on to David, the Captain and then on to Command.

I told Leroy I wanted him to teach me how to walk point and he said he would be glad to.

The first day we moved out and I followed him. We were about two hours out of camp when suddenly he stopped on the trail. He froze like a deer in someone's headlights and then, ever-so-slowly, melted back into cover. As soon as he was in cover he looked at me and put three fingers up to his eyes and pointed down the trail which meant he saw three dinks on the trail.

I sneaked my head out of the bushes and looked down the trail. I saw nothing. I looked at him and shrugged my shoulders.

He leaned over and whispered to me: "Man, there are three of them up there. One is in the trees and the other two are right in the bushes waiting for us. Can't you see them?"

I looked hard at the places he was talking about. I saw nothing. Finally, he got tired of my blindness and told me to stay behind him. He stepped out on the trail, nonchalantly raised his rifle and fired three times in rapid succession. I saw a guy fall from the trees but I didn't see the other two. Leroy and I ran to where they were and sure enough there lay three dudes in black Pajamas with AK-47's, deader than a bag of hammers.

I was shocked and bewildered. I immediately reported back to Lt Waltz what had transpired. He was amazed. He told me to keep following Leroy to see if I could spot what he was doing.

I followed Leroy for a few more days and on the third day, at about three in the afternoon, he froze again on the trail. He pointed to his eyes with two fingers. He whispered to me that these dudes were real easy to see. I should be able to see them easily. I looked for five minutes but was dammed if I saw anything.

Leroy shook his head as though I was a lost cause, walked out of cover and moved ahead a bit with me right behind. He put his M-16 up to his shoulder and opened up. Two guys fell onto the trail, dead. It was uncanny. Leroy argued with me that his blind grandmother could have seen those guys in her sleep. Maybe, but I sure couldn't see them.

I went over this with David, and he told me that Leroy must have some magic, mystical power or something, but whatever, I still needed to find out what was going on because, so far, it made no sense.

That night I talked with Leroy and tried to get out of him what he was doing that was special. He tried to tell me it was just a matter walking down the trail and seeing the enemy which was as easy as if they were lit up by neon signs. He didn't comprehend why I couldn't see them.

Frustrated, I left his position and went back to David and told him this guy made no sense whatsoever.

The next morning, I got up just as the sky was getting light. I had to take a leak. I stood up just in time to see Leroy walking down the hill on the outside of the perimeter. I followed on behind him trying to find where he was going.

Leroy walked down a ways and then stepped behind a tree.

I snuck around and saw him smoking.

Vietnam – The Teenage Wasteland

He looked up at me and said, "you are about as quiet as an elephant in heat, man. Come on over here."

I went over to where he was, and to my complete amazement he was smoking a joint. I said, "Leroy, what the fuck, man? Why you getting high? You gotta walk point today, man."

Leroy took a long pull off his joint and handed it to me. "Yeah, how do you think I do it, man?" With that he laughed, coughing up his smoke.

I pushed the joint back and chided him. "This is crazy, dude. You get high every day?"

Leroy smiled. "Absolutely."

I walked back up the hill and got with Dave. I told him what I found.

David smiled. "I've never smoked dope. Could it make him have that kind of magic, walking point?"

"Absolutely. I got stoned one day and ran a snooker table from the break. So it's totally plausible. The problem is what are we going to tell the Captain and Command?"

Dave smiled. "We're not going to tell them anything. We'll just tell them that Leroy is "magic" and leave it at that.

Leroy walked point for another week, busting up ambushes and kicking ass and all was well. Then we got word to send him back to the rear, immediately. He never returned. We found out a week later that he was wanted for armed robbery in Detroit. Leroy had ducked into the Army to avoid being found and arrested.

Dave, I, and a few others sent letters to his lawyer describing how Leroy had saved a lot of lives walking point and that his brief tenure in the Army was exemplary.

We got a letter from Leroy a few months later thanking us for the letters and that our praises of him for the lives he saved resulted in him getting only two years' probation, and that he was discharged from the Army, back on the streets doing his "thang" and that he was real happy how things turned out.

Ah, ma man, Leroy! Busted up another ambush and came out smelling like a rose.

The enemy smoked a lot of dope. We found a lot of joints and opium on prisoners or dead dinks. They used to toke up quite a bit before they attacked.

I remember one particular night when Alpha Company was doing their week long security hitch on LZ Professional. I was looking at the countryside through the Starlight Scope, watching a bunch of real pretty fireflies about three hundred meters out. I was gawking at them for about five minutes when it suddenly dawned on me that the fireflies weren't moving around. They were stationary, glowed bright and then faded. Glowed bright and then faded. I finally realized I was looking at cigarettes glowing and dimming from people smoking.

I wondered why they were smoking so intently. It finally hit my dense ass that they were probably smoking dope and getting ready to attack! I had read somewhere that they toked up on dope and then attacked because the dope made them fiercer.

I put the whole perimeter on red alert. Sure enough they attacked us twenty minutes later, but we were ready for them and turned their attack back, easily.

I guess the NVA and VC used a lot of dope, but other than what I describe, there was no other dope using that I knew about.

We did a fair bit of drinking, but that was mainly on stand-down. Stand-down occurred every three months. They plucked us out of the field every three months and send us to the rear. We put our weapons away and they put us in this fenced-in area that was about 200 meters by 400 meters, gave us a container of beer and let us blow off all of the steam we wanted. Movies were on hand for entertainment. They let us do this for three days and we got good and drunk and had a good old time.

Vietnam – The Teenage Wasteland

One night we were on LZ Cork and got hold of a fifth of Seagram's Seven and got really tanked. We started throwing hand grenades over the side of the hill. We pulled the pins on them and let loose the spoon, held them for as long as we dared and threw them up in the air, trying to get an air-burst. Grenade fuses burn anywhere from three and a half to five seconds. We held them for as long as three seconds and then threw them. We were nuts.

Finally, an officer came and stopped us throwing grenades by telling us we were wasting them. I was glad he stopped us because we were getting more and more brazen with them.

Drugs and combat are a bad mix. It's not wise to use anything while you're fighting for your life. And again, I am here to tell you that I didn't see much drug use over there. I don't know what people are talking about when they talk about drug abuse in Vietnam.

10

DID YOU SEE A LOT OF ACTION?

I really had no way to judge if the amount of action I saw was a lot or a little; not until much later. I was in the field from October 1968 to October 1969 – one long year in I Corps, and saw plenty of action but having nothing to compare it to, figured it was the kind of action most everyone went through.

After returning from Vietnam I was home for a month's leave and then reported to Fort Hood, Texas for the last six months of my two year requirement.

When finally out of the Army I returned home and lived with my parents.

My father was the President of the local VFW (Veterans of Foreign Wars) chapter in Detroit and one day, invited me to debrief to him and a couple of his fellow veterans Alan and Bill. All present were from WW II and all had seen action in the Pacific. They had a tape recorder and two cases of beer. I launched into the debrief.

I started from day one and for the next three hours went over the 365 days I spent in Vietnam. They coaxed me through the rough spots and did an excellent job of getting everything. When I was done I was spent, exhausted and plain wrung out.

When it was finished they all just looked at each other.

Bill Tuttle glanced over the notes he'd taken and then announced to me and the rest: "Do you realize that of all of

Vietnam – The Teenage Wasteland

the time you were there you spent more than 260 days in combat?"

I was astonished but when I looked at it again, I realized he was right.

Bill pointed out that the WW II soldiers were in intense combat for three or four days and then spent three or four months in a safe area.

Bill pointed out that Vietnam vets never had a chance to relax in their year of duty. It was true, we were always on alert and it took its toll on us.

Bill said "No wonder your Vietnam Vets are wired so differently."

AND – DID YOU SEE A LOT OF AMERICANS DIE?

A lot of people want to know about this subject. It's touchy because it's not polite to talk about the dead. I lost a lot of friends. Before they died, I grew to love every one of them, and some I still miss them to this day.

I have seen Americans killed being heroes, and I've seen Americans killed being stupid. One fourth of all the people killed or wounded over there got that way by their own hand or friendly hands. That's an average for any combat zone. When you're in a combat zone you have to deal with a dangerous mixture of guns, grenades, ordnance of all sorts, and things that just plain explode and the most lethal weapon of all – teenagers.

The Claymore mine, for example, is a convex shaped device that stands on 3-inch legs and contains two and a half pounds of C-4 explosive (the equivalent of five pounds of dynamite) and five hundred double-ought BBs that travel faster than the speed of sound when the device is exploded with an electrical charger. Each GI carried one of them and had to be very, very careful when handling them.

When you put the mine out in front of your position at night you string the electrical wire from it to your position and then connected it to the charging device, and then it's ready to go.

It needed less than one half of a volt plus a little amperage to set it off but if you left the grounding strap on the wire nothing could set it off. So you had to use the ground strap to keep it safe. When you put it out in front of your position at night, you had to have the ground strap on it. If the ground was not on it, static electricity could set it off. If you stayed awake in Claymore class you learned all of this. However, some people must have been asleep.

One morning we woke up and were getting ready to move out. We all collected up our Claymores and trip flares.

One guy named Schmidt was notorious for never using the ground strap on his Claymore. No matter how much we badgered him, he would not use it. He was out collecting up his Claymore and was winding the wire up in a roll and was ten feet from the mine with the wire still attached to it.

I looked over at him and shook my head. But I also saw something behind him that startled me. We were on a bald hill and right behind Schmidt we all saw a Phantom jet fighter running up the valley, heading right at us. I am sure the pilot was just going to buzz and scare us for laughs. But I knew that the powerful radios of the jet produced energy: the radar on the front of it put out some major amperage, not to mention the twin jet engines that put out magnetic fields – well, my hair stood on end. Schmidt now had the Claymore in his hands.

We all yelled at Schmidt and pointed at the jet. He turned and looked and waved at it.

We yelled at him to run from the Claymore. He couldn't hear us.

The jet roared fifty feet over our heads and Schmidt vaporized. It took two hours to find all the pieces of him.

One time we were in the mountains (man, it was cold up there) and were being re-supplied with food and ammo.

Vietnam – The Teenage Wasteland

When hand grenades were given out they were in cardboard cans, like tennis ball only grenades came one to a can. You pulled a string on the top of the can, the tin top came off and you just dropped the grenade out of the can.

We built a fire to burn all the cardboard. There were about fifty grenade cans in the fire, burning nicely. I had warmed up by the fire and walked away, just in time. The fire exploded and killed one man and wounded three others.

Someone did not take a grenade out of the can and threw the whole thing away. No one ever fessed up to it. Whoever it was had to walk around (for the rest of their life) knowing they killed someone because of sloppiness.

We skirted a village one day and sent a patrol through to see what they could see. A fellow by the name of Rick was on the patrol in the village when a little kid reported to him that he'd found an RPG round.

Rick told him to go get it. The kid retrieved it and gave it to Rick. Rick took it and told the kid "this is number 10" (meaning it was bad) and slammed it into the ground for emphasis. The round, of course, exploded. It killed Rick, the kid and wounded four other kids.

A guy got a "Dear John" letter. He showed it to me one night and told me it was killing him that his wife admitted to screwing another guy. She told him that their marriage was over and that she would be sending him divorce papers.

The next day we were pinned down by a machine-gun. The guy charged it without telling anyone and got cut down half way there.

I wrote his wife a letter and told her the exact sequence of events. There was no reason for all of that.

Another incident occurred because of laziness.

At night I always had my bayonet fixed to my rifle and put my rifle with bayonet into the ground so the barrel pointed down at the ground. This was because I didn't want rain trickling down the barrel. A lot of guys just laid their rifles on the ground and let mud and water get into them and so on.

One night it rained really hard, all night long and into the morning. We got up, moved out and were ambushed immediately. The men up front went to return fire but their rifles were full of water. The dynamics of liquid hydraulics and parts of a gun that move at the speed of sound do not mix. Four rifles exploded. One man lost his face and died in the hospital next day due to the plastic embedded in his brain.

In all the time I was there, eight men shot themselves in the foot. They always did it about an hour before sun up. I guess they lay awake all night and tussled with themselves about getting out of the war. So in the morning, when they saw that it was getting close to moving-out time, they finally did the deed. Six out of the eight lost their foot by shooting themselves. The .223 bullet does not penetrate the aluminum plate in the bottom of the boot, so the foot was removed at the ankle by the three tons of energy the bullet possessed as it ricocheted off the metal plate. It's just stupid. Of course they went home and gave everyone a story about how they lost their foot in combat.

One day, we mistakenly got into a firefight with another American company. We were shooting at each other from four hundred meters away. When we called artillery on each other, the Redlegs (an artillery person is called a "Redleg") caught on and told both of us we were shooting at each other. It was embarrassing, at best. Both Captains met with each other and asked if there were any casualties. Both said there were none. It was easy to see that both were happy and disturbed at the same time about there not being any casualties.

I could go on and on, but the bottom line is that some people were careless, some stupid and others took bad risks. This was part of the 58,000 Americans killed in Vietnam. It is the same in every war.

Vietnam – The Teenage Wasteland

PERSONAL CLOSE CALLS

I had a lot of personal close calls. I've mentioned quite a few in preceding pages and there's more later in the book. I'm going to bring up some of the others here, because I want to give you an idea of how they affect a person.

I can say that I had at least a hundred bullets come within a few inches of my body during the time I was in Vietnam, especially in May 1969 when the action was the heaviest. The fact that I did not get hit by one meant I was lucky or my karma was good. Most times though, I felt like I was a magnet for bullets.

I guess the one that scared me the most was one that did not take place during an actual combat firefight. We were doing a sweep across an open area one day in the lowlands of Duc Pho in late November, 1968. We got the signal at noon to go ahead, sit down and have lunch where we were. I happened to be in the open with not so much as a bush within three hundred meters of me.

I was listening to my little transistor radio, listening to a replay of the Indy 500, eating C-rations and having a relaxing time when suddenly there was a deafening explosion in my right ear.

I went down and after a minute raised my head up to see who'd shot a rifle right next to my ear. No one was within fifty meters of me. The guys who were closest were yelling, trying to tell me to run. However, I couldn't hear them because my ears were ringing. Then it dawned on me that a sniper with a high-caliber rifle had taken careful aim and shot at me. The sonic boom from a high caliber bullet is quite loud, and I've heard them snap past me a lot – but this was deafening. The bullet missed my ear by less than an inch.

And yes, as soon as I had that realization, I took off running in a crazy zigzag motion so he could not get another clear shot at me.

I finally found a rock to hide behind and stayed there for a while. I was shaking scared as I sat there thinking that some sniper had my head in his sights, cross hairs on my ear and pulled the trigger only to miss me by a hair.

I was affected for weeks after that, by the sheer turmoil of the questions that went unanswered. What caused him to miss me by less than one inch? Why did the bullet miss me? How can anyone be that lucky?" And so on.

I guess the next scariest was Xmas Eve of 1968. We were going up to the Hill for Xmas Eve festivities, get some hot chow and do the Xmas thing. But as we were getting ready to go we got a call to go to a nearby village and check to see if any VC were there. It pissed all of us off, but we had to go check it out, and it was only five kilometers away, so off we went.

We got to the village but found it was eerily void of the usual village people. It was a rather large village with about sixty hooches. We got half way into it and all hell broke loose. There was a company of NVA in the village, and they had been waiting for us.

A machine gun opened up on me and I dove for the ground. As I was going to ground I saw bullets hitting where my head was going to land. I just told myself good-bye and hit the sand. Nothing happened. The gunner must have thought he got me and moved his sight to another target.

I just started to stir when I heard a "thump" next to my head. I turned in the direction of the noise and looked over to see a sputtering fuse on a hand grenade just a foot from my face. Once again I said goodbye as I buried my face in the sand. Nothing happened. It turned out to be a dud.

Pinned down, the enemy poured an ever increasing amount of firepower at us.

There was a strong wind blowing from behind us and towards the enemy. The Captain called "Zippo Arms" and we started burning hooches. The fire quickly spread from hooch to hooch and caused the enemy to back off. We put artillery

Vietnam – The Teenage Wasteland

on the far side of the village and marched it step by step toward the fire, catching the bad guys in between artillery and fire.

We finally made it out of that situation with no one killed and only a few with minor wounds.

The villagers had left the village before the action started and moved to a location a kilometer away. They were safe but their village was gone. We didn't like burning the village but it was the only thing we could do to survive.

Merry Christmas Vietnam.

My third (favorite?) closest call was when I was walking point. This one disturbed me.

The only person in the company that was allowed to carry his rifle with the safety in the "off" position was the point man. There was no one in front of him except maybe the enemy so he kept his rifle on automatic and the safety off.

Walking point, I was cruising along a trail with my rifle on the up and ready, safety off, when I crested a hill and saw an NVA soldier coming up the other side of the hill about thirty feet in front of me. He was more alert than I, brought his AK-47 up and beat me to the draw. I was a dead man. However, something was wrong with his rifle, it didn't fire. I saw him frantically fiddle with the side of it, but by the time he'd fixed it I had him. I fired a burst and he went down.

On looking, I found out he'd had his safety on and paid dearly for his mistake. But it took my breath away that he'd beaten me to the draw. It was just pure luck for me that he'd had his safety on.

Another time walking point I was ambushed. An NVA soldier popped out onto the trail and opened up on me with a seven round burst. I fell on my ass and shot at him but missed. The guy behind me knelt down right next to me with his rifle barrel on my shoulder and opened up on automatic, killing the NVA soldier. Well thank you for saving me, guy behind me, but the whole right side of my head was burnt from the muzzle blast of his rifle and my eardrum was severely damaged. I still have trouble hearing out of that ear to this day.

Later in August, we were walking a trail in the foothills. We moved past some bamboo trees that overhung the trail. I wasn't paying attention and I got snarled up in a bamboo shoot.

Bamboo is a very tough plant. Even the shoots are wiry and tough. Somehow a bamboo shoot became entangled with my radio chord and it stopped me in my tracks.

As I tried to untangle myself the ground right next to my right foot exploded. A shot from a sniper in a tree sounded simultaneously.

Knowing a sniper had zeroed in on me and just missed made me pull harder on the shoot to free myself.

Other guys, seeing my dilemma started to return fire in all directions but no one knew the location of the sniper.

Bang! He just missed me again.

I was yanking on the shoot with all of my strength only to get tangled more. I knew the sniper knew he might give away his position, but I also figured out he was intent on getting me because I carried a radio. I was a good target for him to shoot and there was nothing I could do about it. I had my machete out but it was not cutting through the bamboo.

The rest of the company was shooting with futility in all directions, trying to save me.

Another round from the sniper hit the ground right next to me.

Finally, Donnie Holloway rushed from his cover and came to my rescue. He pulled out his knife, quickly cut the bamboo and dragged me behind a tree.

The sniper took one last shot at me and Donnie but missed, only by inches.

Thank you, Donnie!

One more and I'll quit. This one happened when I was directing an air strike.

Vietnam – The Teenage Wasteland

As one of the Phantom Jets was making his bomb run, I saw fifty caliber tracers homing in on it. As it dropped the bomb - Bang! Its starboard engine exploded, and then a second later the port engine blew up. The jet was only two hundred feet off the ground.

Both pilots immediately ejected and there were two full parachutes in view, so we went to pick them up.

After we got the pilots to safety we were told to go and find the fifty that brought the Phantom down. We looked for three days and found nothing, so decided they must have buggered out. We called choppers to come and pick us up and take us to another part of the AO to conduct another operation.

The chopper that picked up my squad was the last one to land. We took off and joined the rest in formation when I saw green tracers reaching up for us (I always sat with my feet out the door for fast evacuation). Two rounds went through the floor boards of the chopper. Then we were knocked askew as more rounds from the fifty caliber slammed into the chopper. I saw all the other choppers in our formation ascending fast and wondered why they were doing that. But then I saw the ground coming up I realized the other choppers weren't going up – we were going down!

I looked over and saw the door gunner leaning out, looking at the back so I leaned out and looked. The tail section of the chopper had a lot of parts missing and there was sheet metal hanging off it, flapping in the wind. The craft was vibrating from a bullet hole in the driveshaft that went to the tail rotor. There were holes in the main rotor blades which were delaminating and coming apart.

We dropped like a stone and the next thing I knew we were just a few feet above rice paddies – doing eighty MPH!

I had seen choppers crash and I'd seen them explode in mid-air. What I was always feared was the ugly red-orange-black fire ball that consumes the chopper and burns everyone alive. I did not want to go out that way.

The chopper suddenly pitched upward savagely so the nose pointed straight at the sky. Ramirez, who sat opposite me was making the sign of the cross and mumbling something about "hey-zoos". That was enough for me. I jumped out.

The last thought that went through my head was: "oops, the rotor is now behind me, and I'm going to get chopped to ribbons". But what happened next was I hit a rice paddy, bounced off of it like a stone skipping on water and then landed in the next paddy doing around forty MPH. I went into it feet-first. My backpack was torn off and went straight forward, shoving my face in the water and stretching my arms in a way they should not have gone.

I pulled my head out of the muddy water and watched the chopper plowing to a stop in a rice paddy on its nose, and then looked up in time to see that aircraft come gracefully to a stop. Everyone got out and started looking for me. I was yelling but no one could find me because only my head was sticking out of the water. When they did finally find me, it took six guys to pull me out of the mud. Then we had to find my backpack and its contents because it had hit a dike on the other side and come apart.

I was out of commission for about four days because I had, well, a sprained body. That's about all I can say to describe it: a sprained body.

The chopper pilot wanted to know why I jumped. He explained to me that he put the nose up to let the rotor slow the forward motion of the chopper, and then pancaked it into the water of the paddy field. It all went according to plan. He pulled it off quite well.

I told him I just didn't know what we were doing, so I jumped.

A lot of discussion took place on how I'd made it through the rotor, and the more everyone talked about it the more scared I got.

Vietnam – The Teenage Wasteland

AMBUSHES

I hated ambushes – I thought that they were the single most dangerous activity in Vietnam and the people that sent us on them must have figured we were expendable.

Get the picture: you operate from the Hill, a firebase with several hundred other soldiers but you still feel in danger. You know you are surrounded by NVA but do not know how many there are, where they are or when they are going to attack. So whether it's the Hill or not, you still feel insecure. On top of that, your platoon leader comes up to you and tells you that you are going outside the firebase on an ambush, at night with only four other guys. You cannot say "no thanks" because you're in the Army; you've got to do what the man says.

On an ambush with four other men, one is a radio man for communication purposes. You load up with hand grenades and claymore mines, and slip out of the perimeter (and the relative safety of the hill) as soon as it gets dark, praying the NVA doesn't see you leaving, because if they spot you going out on an ambush, YOU will be ambushed.

Ever so quietly, you move to a predetermined place to pop the ambush. This is usually around seven kilometers out from the Hill. It is just nonsense to me, because if you get caught by the enemy on your way out, or on your way back, you are dead, man, dead.

When arrived at your destination, you find a point on the trail where you can see a good distance in both directions. In the dark, you set up trip flares across the trail, set the claymore mines, ready hand grenades with loosened pins and prepare everything to spring the ambush. You usually don't use rifles in an ambush because the muzzle flashes give away your location and the NVA return fire at the flashes. The whole idea is to completely surprise the enemy, disorient them and blast them with as many explosions as possible.

When the ambush is sprung you high tail it away, hide somewhere and hope to hell you didn't piss off a whole lot of people who are now hell bent on finding you. If the ambush happened to be sprung on a large, company-sized or even larger unit, then you can kiss your ass goodbye because the ones you didn't kill will come and get you. And they won't kill you right away.

I went out on about eleven ambushes. Nothing happened on five of them. The other six were pure, unadulterated pandemonium.

If nothing happened, we waited until it started to get light, policed up all of our stuff and moved back to the hill before the sun came up and anyone saw us. The chances of running into enemy at that time of the morning were pretty slim, but you never knew.

We did not sleep on an ambush. We kept our ears open and our mouths shut. No talking. We just lay still in the same spot and listened for eight hours. And the really fun thing was the fact that there was never any training for these ambushes.

One particular ambush I went on was very disturbing. Late one afternoon, during a hot game of poker, Lt Waltz came to see me and told me that NVA had been seen operating in an area a number of klicks out. He wanted me to take an ambush party out there and waste some bad guys. He volunteered to go but the CO told him to forget it.

Five of us left the LZ just after dusk and snuck away to the position, about six kilometers out.

At the ambush site we quietly set up our trip flares and Claymores on the trail and placed hand grenades in front of us, ready to go.

There was a nice little berm of land right above the trail. It was a perfect ambush site. We couldn't have asked for a better set up so settled in and waited, hoping for a quiet night.

Unfortunately, I happened to position myself in a spot right on an ant hill. They were little fire-ants, and they bit the shit out of me. They actually have a poison and it burns like crazy. I was rolling around slapping at myself while I moved to another spot, but they found me and started to bite me again.

Vietnam – The Teenage Wasteland

This went on for a couple of hours. The other guys were getting pissed at me because I was slapping myself silly and rolling around on the ground, murmuring oaths and grunting under my breath.

One of the guys came over at one point and asked me what my problem was. I told him I was covered with fire ants. He whispered to me to keep the noise down and then moved well away after he was bit crouching next to me.

I finally moved far enough away from the ant hill to stop getting bit.

As I lay there waiting for them to find me again, the night was disturbed by the sound of hushed voices and faint metallic sounds. I froze.

I looked over at Mitch, and he nodded to me that he had heard them as well. I could tell by the posture of the others that they had heard it too. This was it!

Everyone moved into position and was set. I had two claymore chargers at the ready, one in each hand, safeties off, ready to rumble. I was ready – scared shitless, but ready. And the ants had just found me again…

There was a pop and then a whole lot of light from a tripped flair. I heard yelling and I squeezed the claymore chargers.

As the ground shook from the deafening explosions of ten claymores I took the five hand grenades in front of me, pulled the pins and chucked all of them towards the mayhem.

Then I saw Mitch standing on the berm shooting downward with his M-16. I grabbed my rifle and jumped up and started shooting too.

What I saw is emblazoned on my mind forever. I saw men dancing in the strobe of the light from gunfire and grenade explosions in a macabre sort of fandango, some clutching each other and others just trying to get away from the killing zone. But they didn't know where to go. Some climbed in desperation to where we were only to be gunned down almost point-blank by rifle fire. Others were staggering off into the night. Others were already dead on the ground. It was just a meat grinder.

Finally, we all shot an M-16 magazine in the direction the NVA had come from, just in case there were more of them, and took off running for our lives. We ran about a kilometer and a half and hid in some hedges.

My radio came to life with Lt Waltz calling to find out if all of that noise was caused by us. The only thing I could do was double-click my handset in acknowledgement to his queries. I was not about to even whisper, because I knew the survivors of that ambush were probably looking for us and would definitely want to kill us.

We stayed there for the rest of the night waiting for them to come. I was scared to death. It was an agonizing wait from one in the morning until around five in the morning. The only thing that kept me from vomiting in fear was the fact that I was distracted by leftover fire ants still in residence that were biting me silly.

We moved out just before dawn and headed back to the hill and made it back in one piece. I tell you, I was never so glad to get back to the relative safety of our Hill. It took two beers to calm me down. My hands were shaking. I kept remembering the NVA in that killing caldron of hell. We killed a lot of men there, and the pictures of them scrambling to get away from the killing zone haunted me.

I went on more ambushes in the next few weeks. We popped one more and bagged about four more NVA. But an ambush was scary, and I mean scary.

I didn't care to fight like that. I like it straight up. I know the NVA and VC used ambushes on us as their main way of fighting, but I didn't like to do it myself.

11

WEAPONS

There were a lot of weapons at our disposal but the basic, standard-issue for the grunt was the highly controversial M-16 automatic rifle. The M-16 rifle struck me kind of strange when I first learned of it, in that it shot a twenty-two caliber bullet (5.56mm for you un-indoctrinated). When I found out in basic training that we were going to war with a .22 caliber rifle, I almost fainted. However, we were given a demonstration of the power of the M-16 and that calmed me down a bit.

First of all, while it is only a .22, it has a huge powder charge behind it which propels the small projectile at three times the speed of sound. That was faster than any small-arms bullet used in war to that date.

When it was demonstrated to us at the rifle range, the officer in-charge set up a shoot with a five gallon gas can filled with water. He took the venerable M-14 on which we had been trained (which shot a thirty caliber round) and fired at the can of water. The bullet rocked the can and put a four-inch hole in the back of it. We were impressed but knew what that gun could do.

Then he took another five gallon can filled with water, set it up, took the M-16 and shot it from the same short distance. To our complete surprise the can took off as if it had been hit by a speeding train. It flew through the air for twenty feet, water spattering everywhere and when it was retrieved we were astonished to see the entire back of the can ripped open. The range officer proudly announced: "Three tons of stopping power, gentlemen."

I don't need to tell you we were all sold on the round and the rifle at that point in time. However, when I got to Vietnam the rifle proved to be a piece of crap and it's a wonder we all lived through the war with the damn thing.

The first one I got looked like it had been dragged through the bush for a few years. Every part was worn completely. I was worried it would work at all but I took it to the range to "zero" the sights and found it to be a straight shooting little piece. So I felt a little better. But not much.

I am left handed. The M-16 was made for right-handers, the spent cartridge ejects from the right side and comes straight back. For a left-hander that meant red-hot cartridges came straight back and hit you in your right eye. After firefights, I always had a small burn blister above my right eye from those red-hot cartridges hitting me in the same spot, every time.

Another real sorry feature of the M-16 is that it had such close tolerances and fine machining that it needed to be cleaned every four magazines. Now, excuse me, but if you were in a hot firefight that lasted more than five minutes your rifle jammed because it needed to be cleaned. A very bad design issue if you ask me.

The opposition had the AK 47 which hardly ever required cleaning. They could blast away forever and not have to stop and spend ten minutes cleaning their rifles.

After pondering this situation, I decided to take my rifle and modify it. I sanded down the bolt and the receiver with emery cloth until the clearances were real loose and then got myself some ninety-weight motor oil and used that for lubrication. I tried it out at the range and found that it lasted nine magazines before cleaning, but cleaning was a lot harder because the carbon build up was thicker by then. But the trade-off was good because it allowed me to shoot nine

Vietnam – The Teenage Wasteland

magazines before I had to clean it – and that saved my ass more than once. The last thing I wanted was a jamming, piece-of-crap modern rifle at the start of a fire fight.

But the sorriest feature of all was that the M-16 came with twenty-round capacity magazines. We all asked for thirty-round mags, but were told they were not available, yet. So we had twenty round magazines while the enemy had thirty-round mags. We were out-magazined!

To add insult to injury; we found that you can't put twenty rounds in the twenty-round magazines. Why? Because the springs in the magazines were too weak, more than sixteen rounds caused them to jam. We were told to put no more than sixteen rounds in the mags! Absurd!

I learned all this the hard way when I insisted on putting twenty rounds in my mag. One day, we had a brisk firefight and while I was on my second magazine the rifle jammed so bad it took thirty seconds to clear it. That could have been fatal.

I used to swear up a storm to other guys about how the Army gave us a piece of shit weapon that jammed after four magazines in which you could put only sixteen rounds and which didn't work half the time. But I was preaching to the choir because everyone to whom I complained had the same stupid rifle.

That small caliber bullet, moving as fast as it did, caused serious damage to a person if it hit something solid in the body. I have seen times where the bullet entered an enemy soldier in the stomach, hit the spine and ripped the guy's back completely open. Other times it hit them in the shin and came out the top of their head. The bullet would just spin if it got deflected by anything heavier.

But the big problem with the bullet was the fact that if it did not hit bone it would go straight through the body and the person didn't know he was hit. So shooting at central mass (torso) was a crap-shoot at best; if you hit a bone, he was down. If you did not hit bone, he was, for all intents and purposes, not hit, and kept coming, unaware of the fact that he had a little hole clear through him. So it was fifty-fifty when you shot someone's "center mass" as we were taught. Sometimes you had to keep shooting until you hit bone. Then it would just mangle him.

All the mechanical problems with the M-16 were worked out and solved after I got out of Vietnam, which pisses me off. Now they have thirty round magazines, a cartridge deflector for us lefties and all sorts of other upgrades.

I carried the M-60 machine gun for a few weeks. It weighed thirty-five pounds and was too big for a little guy like me. However, it had excellent fire-power. It shot a thirty caliber bullet and had an effective range of seven hundred meters. The one I carried was made by Frigidaire, oddly enough. I knew they made refrigerators, but I didn't know about the machine guns. But it worked well and kept the enemy "chilled" – sometimes "iced".

The M-79 grenade launcher was a mediocre weapon. It shot a forty millimeter explosive round that scared the enemy more than it hurt them. But it also came with buckshot. We tore up the countryside with that. But overall, I found it to be pretty useless. I never saw an enemy killed by one, except once, by a buckshot round.

Hand grenades were okay. They came in handy when clearing tunnels and bunkers. But in the open, they didn't do anything but hurt the enemy. I rarely saw one kill someone, except in a tunnel, bunker or ambush (when we threw so many). So for those purposes it was great.

The LAW rocket (Light-Antitank-Weapon) was a forty millimeter rocket. The thing could travel as far as five hundred meters, penetrate the thick armor of a tank and destroy it. And it was very, very accurate. I used one against a machine gun emplacement and took it out; saw the machine gun flying through the air. It was disposable too. Once you fired it, you could trash the fiberglass launch tube. Kudos to the makers of that little beauty.

Vietnam – The Teenage Wasteland

The Colt .45 pistol. Been around since World War One and has been of great service to GIs through the various wars since. I carried one in a holster when I first got to Vietnam, but I never fired it once in the month I carried it. Finally got rid of it after I found out it was all rusted shut. Never carried it again.

The Claymore mine. Everyone carried one. They are concaved shaped with two and a half pounds of C-4 plastic explosive with five hundred double-ought BBs in front of the charge. They cleared a path in front of them and killed anything within fifty meters. A lot of VC and NVA died by them. It's an excellent weapon for killing, if you like that sort of thing – or if you need that sort of thing.

It took me four months though, to discover the ultimate weapon and that was the radio. I watched the Captain's radio man call in an air strike one day and realized that was the weapon of choice. I made it to the post of Captain's radio man (RTO for Radio and Telephone Operator), and used the radio for everything. I blew away my share of Vietnam real estate with the radio. I could get bombers, fighter-bombers, helicopter gunships, artillery and one day even got to use the New Jersey Battleship to silence a rocket attack on Da Nang (AND you could order food with it as an extra bonus).

We were sitting on a mountain top one night about twenty miles south of Da Nang. We watched as rockets were being fired at the Da Nang base with deadly accuracy. The rockets were being launched from behind a mountain, so Da Nang could not get to them with return fire. I called in and told them I could see where the rockets were coming from. They told me to change my frequency and tune into the New Jersey, a WW II battleship that was five miles out to sea. I called them and they asked me for coordinates. I gave them the position, and they asked if I could adjust fire for them. I assured them I would be proud to. Next thing, I saw a brilliant orange flash out to sea as The New Jersey sent a three-round volley of their sixteen-inch shells called "Volkswagens" (they were called

Volkswagens because they were roughly the same weight as a VW Beetle – sixteen hundred pounds).

The rounds from the first volley hit the top of mountain 664 (664 meters high). I adjusted fire for them and after about fifty rounds had pounded into hill 664, they had lowered that mountain to around 600 meters and silenced the rockets for good.

I was honored that I got to do FDC (Fire Direction Control) for the New Jersey because it was an awesome weapon.

I was on R&R one time with a fellow who was on the New Jersey. His job was to wind the chronometers (never called them clocks) on the ship every day. They were Swiss chronometers, the most accurate time pieces ever made. He told me he kept busy all day winding those time pieces; there were around two hundred of them all throughout the ship.

The Phantom Fighter-Bombers were very good. The napalm was very effective.

Helicopter gunships were okay. The Cobra gunships were very deadly but the Huey gunships, not.

The Spooky gunship was the best.

A description of each of these aircraft will come later.

In summary, I found the weapons we had in Vietnam very lacking. The M-16 was a piece of shit. The M-79 grenade launcher was useless. The Colt .45 was alright; I just had no use for it. The only weapons I admired were the M-60 machine gun, the LAW, the Claymore and the radio.

COMBAT ASSAULTS

I was in an airborne division called Americal. As most of Vietnam is jungle, we didn't parachute into anywhere. We used choppers to go everywhere. Sometimes we flew into a suspected enemy stronghold; we inserted the whole company or even the whole battalion right into the middle of the enemy, surprised the shit out of them and tore them up. I did thirty two of those combat assaults, but only ten of them were "hot".

Vietnam – The Teenage Wasteland

One particular "CA" happened after we received Intel of an NVA battalion operating in an area we were headed to with our whole battalion. We had been on six or seven combat assaults in a row that were not hot, so we were a bit laid back going into that one.

About thirty choppers took us to the suspected area, company by company. The space we landed in was quite big, around the size of ten football fields. Because we were Alpha Company we went in first. Bravo right behind us.

As we came in for the landing, a gunship hovered right outside my chopper door. He opened up with rockets and a mini-gun. That told me he was shooting at targets. I became concerned.

Our chopper hit the ground and came under immediate, intense fire from the perimeter of the landing zone. The incoming choppers were cut to ribbons by small arms fire from the NVA.

I got out of the chopper, hit the ground and opened fire on targets of opportunity. Bullets hit all around me. I then heard a crash and looked behind to see a chopper from Bravo Company rammed into the rear of the chopper I had just gotten off. The spinning rotor from my chopper came off and went flying straight ahead, just missing guys on the ground.

That crash triggered a series of choppers running into other choppers. People were spilt off them while the fighting grew more and more intense.

We fought for a half hour, which is a heck of a long time, finally calling air strikes in to quell the enemy.

By the time it was all over there were eight destroyed choppers on the ground. Their crews were picked up by other choppers and any wounded flown out. Now we had to do something with those damaged choppers that were sitting there with top security radios in them.

We finally got the order to burn them, in place. I took an incendiary grenade and put it on the dashboard of the chopper I had been in, and pulled the pin. It burned at twelve hundred degrees and melted right through the radios. Then the rest of the chopper caught and burned in totality.

While we were waiting for the choppers to burn, the NVA mounted another attack. We repelled them with more gunships and fighter-bombers.

The miracle of the day was that no one on our side was killed. There were about twenty wounded who were later returned to the field and another three wounded enough to go home but all in all, it was a real miracle.

But my favorite combat assault story is something that took place in Feb of 1969. We were at LZ Liz and were woken up at three-thirty in the morning and told to get ready to move out. We asked where we were going and were told that it was top-secret, we'd only be briefed when we were aboard the choppers. The platoon leaders were not even told until the choppers arrived.

We mounted the choppers at 04:45 and took off on a hundred mile journey.

At the crack of dawn, we swooped in and landed in the LZ, expecting to catch a company-sized NVA unit.

We landed and nothing happened. In front of my position I saw a white flag waiving. I called it in on my radio and yelled out to the flag waiver to surrender.

Two kids popped up fifty meters in front of me with the white flag. They had a Radio Flyer red wagon full of Coca Cola – on ice! They came to our position and started selling us chilled Coke!

I asked them where the NVA were.

They told me that they had moved out half hour before we came. "NVA find out you come, they diddy!"

I asked how the kids knew we were coming.

"Everybody know GI come now. Please buy Coke? Five dolla can."

So much for security.

Vietnam – The Teenage Wasteland

HELICOPTERS

Vietnam was the first war in which helicopters were used extensively. The use of choppers, as we called them, started a lot of controversy because when you use them in close-combat situations they get shot down so easily. However, I feel they were well used in Vietnam.

The terrain in 1-Corp was mainly mountain and jungle which prevented troopers jumping into the landscape from airplanes. Heretofore, paratroopers (parachutes) were the method for rapidly inserting troops into a hostile sector. But in 1965, the 82nd Airborne attempted a paratroop landing in Vietnam and it turned into a fiasco with a lot of troops hung up in trees and others killed while plummeting through a hundred feet of tree branches.

Shortly after, the military decided to use the chopper to insert troops into areas up to a hundred and fifty miles away. They got the troops to their destination with little or no trouble. It became a success when the 1st of the 7th Cavalry was inserted to LZ X-ray in 1965 which took the battle to the NVA for the first time, defeating them soundly.

I have seen a lot of Choppers get shot down in Vietnam, and it's not a pretty sight. But I must admit they did their job and got us transported from one place to another, but one was always wary of them.

The chopper made it easy to re-supply units in the field. Our company ran out of ammo on several different occasions, but we were always able to get a chopper out to us within 20 minutes with a fresh supply of ammunition so we could keep fighting. It was an excellent service.

And let's not forget how many lives the Medivac choppers saved by getting severely wounded men out of the field and back to the hospital within thirty minutes of being shot. The Medivac choppers probably saved twenty thousand lives during the course of the war.

My hat is off to the brave Medivac pilots and crews that landed in totally hot combat zones, unarmed without so much as a pistol on board, to carry out the wounded and get them to hospital as fast as possible. They were the bravest men I have ever seen. The enemy did not care whether or not the choppers had a red cross the size of a bill-board on them. They were still targets and a lot of them were shot down, resulting in many crew deaths.

But I cannot give kudos to Medivac crews alone. All chopper pilots and crews were heroes to me. They landed no matter the situation in order to help us out. They cared for the guy on the ground. They worked seven days a week, mostly 12 to 16 hours a day, flying for us. My hat is off to all pilots and crews; they did all they could to ferry us safely from one point to another and provide us with vital, much needed supplies.

The landscape of Vietnam is scattered with the remains of about six thousand choppers, evidence of the sheer number of missions flown to ferry troops or supplies to and fro and testament to the bravery of the men who flew them, many of whom made the ultimate sacrifice to help us out.

To me, the venerable helicopter made our job a lot easier. We would have lost many more men, and left behind a great number of wounded without them.

Helicopter gunships became of ever increasing help to the troops in the field. The mini-gun really proved the value of the helicopter gunship. The mini-gun is a six-barreled Gatling gun with an electric motor that churns out six thousand rounds per minute. That's unprecedented fire-power.

The introduction of the Cobra Helicopter Gunship put the effectiveness of gunships over the top: the Cobra could make a pass on a football field and put lethal ordnance in every square inch of it, in just one pass! The Cobra had one mini-gun, one automatic 40mm cannon and could carry as many as 72 lethal rockets, real firepower from the sky. I can safely say

Vietnam – The Teenage Wasteland

that I am here because of Cobra Gunships. They were the greatest support.

Overall, helicopters and their crews were a great asset to the troops on the ground. I am happy they were there. I am here today because they were.

PART TWO

THE TOUR

Vietnam – The Teenage Wasteland

12

THE BUSH

"Nothing is as exhilarating in life as to be shot at with no results."
– Winston Churchill.

I arrived in Vietnam on October 15th, 1968. I flew in on a TWA Boeing 707, landed in Saigon and was there a week waiting out a typhoon that arrived in the area right after I did. After the storm passed, I was sent to my company at a place called LZ Baldy in Duc Pho province and spent a week on the beach going to different training schools.

I met a guy on the long plane flight over, a fellow draftee. We joked around so much that by the first day of that week long indoctrination we started a comedy routine. I played the perfect straight-man. Most of the material we came up with was spontaneous. After a few days we had huge crowds of soldiers coming to watch us.

By the end of the sixth of the day an Air Force sergeant came to see us and explained that he had heard of us and wanted to know if we would like to be on the Armed Forces Radio Network.

"Hell yes!" we both said – anything to get out of going to the killing fields. He told us to do our routine and we did five minutes or so for him and he said "Fabulous".

He replied that he was going to check with his Commanding Officer and let us know if it was okay for us to arrive, tape recorded our routine and took off, promising to return the next day.

He did return the next day and announced upon meeting with us that he had good news and bad news and said he would give it to us at the same time. He said, "I can only take one of you."

We decided to draw cards. The one that drew the high card would be the lucky one that went to work with the Armed Forces Radio Network studios.

My friend pulled a card first, a three of clubs. I was elated. I drew mine, but to my horror I pulled the two of hearts. I didn't believe in bad luck but I did believe in Karma, and at that moment understood that I was going to war whether I liked it or not and nothing was going to change that.

For the rest of the year I listened to that asshole do fifteen minutes of comedy each day on the radio. Fifteen minutes! What a job! He wasn't very good, either. I could have done better.

DAY ONE

My first day in the field was an utter nightmare. I was choppered out to my company about thirty miles inland from the rear. It was just about forty minute to sundown as we circled above a clearing with heavy jungle all around. It looked very green and very foreboding. As we circled above the jungle I suddenly saw a wisp of red smoke coming up from a clearing and the chopper spiraled down to it, flared and then quickly landed.

I jumped off the chopper and someone came from out of nowhere and ordered me to sit next to a hedgerow. I sat down and watched shirtless men scurrying back and forth unloading the chopper. They were in an awful hurry and I thought that maybe it was because they were hungry. Suddenly the engine of the chopper raised its RPMs and the craft left scattering debris all around as the GIs hunkered down low to keep from getting hit with stuff from the chopper wash.

Then the guys with no shirts were running to and fro carrying things and quietly giving out orders. It all looked hopelessly confusing to me. I sat there waiting for someone to come and tell me what to do or where to go.

I sat in front of the hedge for around ten minutes and then everyone disappeared and everything got deafeningly quiet. I wondered if someone had forgotten about me, but I sat there not moving, determined to make sure I did nothing wrong.

After a few more minutes of silence I heard someone running behind me. Suddenly a man jumped over the hedge and landed in front of me with his Colt .45 pistol pointed at me and declared, "You're dead."

I looked at him and tried to figure out who he was but he had no insignia on his fatigues.

"Do you have a round chambered in that rifle?" he demanded.

"N...no," I stammered. We weren't allowed to have rounds chambered in the helicopter, so I didn't do it yet, or at least not until someone told me to.

"Well, where in the fuck do you think you are right now, downtown Dayton, Ohio? You better get your shit together FNG (Fucking New Guy) or you aren't going to last a week."

I chambered a round.

He yelled at me to put the safety on. Then he asked me, "What platoon are you in?"

I told him I didn't know.

He looked at me in disgust. "Didn't you ask?"

"No," I replied weakly.

"I have two weeks left in this god-forsaken place and I'm not going to let idiots like you take me out before I get home, so you better get your shit together because if you endanger my rotating back, I'll shoot you myself. Got it?"

I nodded.

"Okay. Come with me, shit-bird." And he took off.

I followed him for about twenty feet when I realized I had been sitting outside the perimeter. Guys were snickering at me as we passed the perimeter guards. I realized that the Captain probably wanted to know where the "FNG" was and sent someone to look for me at the spot where the chopper had landed and found me there, outside the perimeter.

The man wearing no insignia walked over to another man and told him to take me to the 2nd platoon. The other man introduced himself as Sammy. Said he was the Captain's Radio Man. He told me that the man who handed me over was the Captain. I swallowed hard.

On the way over to 2nd platoon, Sammy told me not to worry about the Captain being so gruff, he was a little testy and "short" these days, but was a great Captain.

Sammy the radio man, took me over and introduced me to a Lieutenant and left. I can't remember the Lieutenant's name for the life of me, but he seemed like a nice guy. Daylight was waning when the Lieutenant took me over to a spot, introduced me to a guy named Mark and asked him to take me under his wing. Mark smiled at me and said, "Sure, no problem."

Mark was a grizzled sort of guy with a shank of hay colored blond hair, weathered face and dark brown eyes. Think Robert Redford. I noticed he had an easy grin and he seemed laid back. But there was an aura of confidence and certainty about him that made me feel at ease.

Mark simply said to me "You're going to be under my wing, I'm going to show you the ropes here. Keep your mouth shut and your eyes and ears open, because you've got a lot to learn. They don't teach you shit in The States about this place." He put me more at ease by asking where I was from and all that. He told me he wasn't going to start teaching me anything right away, he just wanted me to chill for the night but I would be with him until he left. In three weeks his tour was finished and he asked me to help keep him alive until then.

I assured him I would do my best.

That night, I fell into a troubled sleep only to be rudely awoken by an explosion followed by a second, bigger explosion. Everyone was awake and on alert. I was scared shitless. After a while, things calmed down.

The next morning I was told that someone had thrown a grenade at us in the night and the second explosion was a Claymore mine triggered by one of our guys. No casualties on either side. Mark said it was no big thing, but I wasn't so sure. I hadn't slept the rest of the night I was so frazzled by it. I lay awake thinking about what a fool I was not going to Canada when I had my chance. It knew I was going to die in this place. It was looking to be an impossible gen-in for me. I'm not a fast learner and I'm not known for my intelligence. I was screwed, that's all there is to it.

DAY TWO

The next day we broke camp and got ready to move out. I was told by Mark that we were going to hump about eight klicks and find a new place to stay for that night. I wondered how he knew that.

We set out and walked for a few hours. Then we stopped. I asked Mark what was up, and he shrugged his shoulders. "You never find out what's going on until you see it."

We moved forward slowly from that point, but no one showed the slightest indication there was any trouble. Then I heard the sound of rushing water – a waterfall.

Mark turned to me and said, "Oh, we're crossing a waterfall. This is going to be fun."

It wasn't long before Mark and I stood at the edge of the top of a waterfall and I saw guys walking across it right where the water went over. I couldn't see how high it was, but it sounded huge.

I pulled on Mark's shirt and said, "Uh, I was never trained on how to cross a waterfall. How do you do it?"

"Watch those guys cross. Notice they quickly step on rocks right where the water goes over the fall, they don't stop. Watch me as I go across. The main thing is not to stop – you just keep moving until you reach the other side. Where the water goes over is the shallowest part, but it has a lot of force so you've got to keep moving. That's the most important thing." And with that he was off. It was like watching a ballet dancer with a rucksack. He tip-toed from rock to rock, gingerly moving and dancing from one rock to the next near the edge of the falls.

Mark made it across and then waved for me to cross.

It looked easy so without thinking I just took off. I was amazed at how easy it was. I did the same dance, just tip-toed from rock to rock. But I got about half way across when I made a huge blunder – I looked down while I was dancing across the crest of that falls; a fatal mistake. I saw it was about sixty feet high and froze in horror.

The force of the flowing water hit, swept my feet out from under me and over I went, so fast I didn't even have a chance to call out.

I was certain I was going to die. I can remember falling, knowing I was going to die. I landed on my back with a remarkable thud, and that was all I remembered for about a minute. Then I remembered being washed up against rocks and just kind of bobbing around, floating aimlessly, looking up at the sky wondering if I was dead.

I saw a GI looking down at me and heard him announce, "He's dead."

"No, I'm not!" I shouted as I panicked and forced my body to move.

Then some guys pulled me out of the river and lay me on the bank shouting at me, asking if I was hurt anywhere. I kept shaking my head but they looked all over my body for broken bones while others gathered up my equipment or fished it out of the river.

The medic came over and asked me if I was okay. He had me move my arms and legs.

I said, "I think I'm okay. My back hurts a bit."

"I'm not surprised," the medic cooed, "that was a long fall."

I heard the Captains voice, heard him shouting "Where is he?"

"Over here, Captain," someone said.

He came over and looked at me, instantly pissed. "You again. That's two," and he held up two fingers. He started barking out orders to get my pack put back together and then asked where my rifle was and I said I didn't know. This really set him off. It really enraged him not knowing where my weapon was. Finally, someone fished it out of the broiling water and he told him to give it to me and then came back over and looked at me angrily. "You're a first class fuck-up, you know that?"

I just looked down.

He yelled at me again. "You ain't gonna last at all. I might as well shoot your ass right now and save us all a lot of trouble." He looked at me for a while longer and walked off in disgust.

The Captain truly hated me. It was not just a matter of busting my chops anymore; he really did not like me.

Later that day when we were setting up for lunch, Mark looked at me and saw that I was really down. He told me that the CO was just busting my chops, trying to get me "grooved in". I wasn't so sure, never seen training like that and thought about it for the rest of the day as we walked. I would have quit right there and then, if I could have. But you can't quit the Army, so I decided by the time we entered night-camp to brace up and make it through the first couple of weeks and then re-evaluate my situation. I became a little calmer and restored my resolve to make it through Vietnam. I was a little more confident. Go figure.

DAY THREE

That night went without trouble and the next morning, as we were getting ready to move out, Mark announced that we were to move four klicks south, fast, because choppers were going to pick us up at an LZ, and we were going to do a "combat assault". Once again, I wondered how Mark knew. I started to worry because I never saw him being briefed. I wondered if he had a hidden antenna that picked up briefings. How was I going to know what things were going to happen like he did?

A combat assault is an operation where choppers pick you up, take you to a hot location and dump you right in the middle of it. The concept scared me though I was up for it, but maybe only because I felt safer in a chopper.

We walked quickly to the helicopter pick up spot. Mark told me to stick with him no matter what. The choppers came and we boarded. This part we did in training so I was a little more familiar with the action.

I ended up being the last one on our chopper so sat right next to the door, near the starboard door gunner.

We took off and had been flying for about fifteen minutes when I spotted jet fighters on the scene and grew a little more concerned. I heard the pitch of the rotors change and saw we were losing altitude. Everyone was loading their rifles and adjusting their gear. I did the same.

Finally, the chopper slowed its descent and hovered over some elephant grass. I bent over, looked out the door and down at the elephant grass to see how tall it was. It looked to be about ten feet high. While I looked down at the grass, the chopper hovering there, ten feet above it, the door gunner reached over, grabbed me by my rucksack and threw me out the door.

Vietnam – The Teenage Wasteland

I landed on my back with a thud, the wind got knocked out of me and my rifle discharged as I hit the ground.

The discharge of my rifle caused everyone else to start shooting, helicopter gunships opened up with rockets and even the jet fighters rolled in and started strafing the area with their automatic cannon.

I lay there, still trying to get my wind back when I heard the Captain shout, "Cease fire! Cease fire, god dam it!! "Who the fuck are you all shooting at?""

Everyone stopped shooting. There was no enemy fire or any other fire coming back at us. The Captain announced, "This is a cold LZ, no bad guys here. I don't know what you idiots are shooting at.

By this time I was on my feet, the Captain was asking everyone who fired the first shot. Three guys pointed at me.

The Captain walked over to me and said "Did you shoot first?"

"Not on purpose, Sir. I was thrown out of the chopper, hit the ground and my rifle went off by accident."

That was the worst thing I could have said to him. He was enraged. "By accident? By fucking *accident*?" he demanded and then stomped off, swearing at nobody in particular. And just when I was thinking he had forgotten about the third strike he stomped back to me and held up three fingers and then walked off, yelling, "I'm rid of this bastard. He is a complete fucking idiot. Somebody please shoot him for me."

I sat down wondering what was going to happen to me. I was really down, worried I was going to get a lot of people killed. I just didn't know what to do.

Mark came over and sat down, asked me how I was doing, and I told him I was worried – not about me getting killed but getting others killed. Mark smiled his easy smile, took his helmet off and then spent thirty minutes giving me a "no shitter" talking to.

"Okay Tom, I don't know what is really going on, but you are fucking up. Don't believe you're doing any of it on purpose, but you're causing these things to happen, and you really do have the Captain pissed off at you. I want to help, because I think you're a good guy – you don't complain, and you aren't a pain in the ass, but there is something going on. Do you agree?"

I nodded yes, because I knew what he was saying was the brutal truth, and I really did appreciate it.

Mark pressed on, "Look, you need to change something here. Maybe you disagree with being here, or you're still against all authority or something like that. But what I want you to do is decide that you are here in Vietnam and decide you're going to contribute here and make the best of it. Know what I mean? Okay? All you need to do is start soldiering and you will be okay."

It made perfect sense to me and was the talk I needed. It was weird, but I agreed with Mark that I was not there on the same terms as most everyone else. My plan was to try to skate through the mess and get out of it without soldiering. I made up my mind, right there and then, to soldier. I didn't like it, but I was in a combat zone, so I needed to soldier.

Mark was a good guy. He had great insight and I really appreciated him. I think he saved my life that day.

We continued on for a few weeks and nothing much happened. We walked and walked, checked out villages and engaged in do-little motions. I started to get into the groove. No more major screw-ups from me.

Then one day on my second week in country, our Captain left. He said goodbye to everyone. He even shook my hand and gave me a nod and a wink which said a lot to me. It said, "Glad to see you making it."

That day I felt like an old-timer. I no longer felt like a trainee or an FNG, I felt like a part of the group.

Mark left too. I really hated to see him go. He gave me another talking to, told me I looked like a natural and he was proud to see me take to the bush like I did. He had a tear in his eye, but it was not for me, it was for all the guys. He hated to

Vietnam – The Teenage Wasteland

leave his friends, but he was also glad he'd finally made it through his time in Vietnam.

Our replacement Captain came on the chopper the CO left on. He looked like a dork, and it turned out he was. His very first action was to announce to us that he wanted us to give correct data only and ordered us to report things exactly as we saw them and not to "cook any data". He had coke-bottle-bottom glasses and buck teeth – I kid you not. He had no business being a Captain in my estimation. He looked like a little boy that peed in his pants. I wondered where in the world the army had gotten him.

We took off into the bush with him in command and started to travel all through Duc Pho Province.

One day, about two weeks after the new captain arrived, we marched into a valley somewhere. That night we parked on level ground right beside a river. The river was a hundred meters wide, shallow water about half of that and the rest a beach of brilliantly white sand, studded with thick bushes. The beach was on our side of the water. On the other side of the river we were overlooked by a large hill.

To me, camping in that location looked stupid as we set up a large perimeter and more than a hundred men bedded down for the night.

I drew the second shift for guard duty so a few hours later I rose from my "bed" and guarded my section of the perimeter, staring out at sand, shallow water and the local water buffalo as they wandered aimlessly up and down the riverbed.

After a while, I noticed something wrong with the picture I was staring at and thought I was tripping under a partial moon. One of the water buffalo seemed to have six legs, not the usual four. And as I continued to watch it, I saw the six-legged water buffalo lazily pass a thick bush in the sandy riverbed and noted that after it was beyond the bush it seemed to have only four legs. Somehow it had lost two legs. Then I saw another six legged water buffalo and the same thing happened, it lost two legs as it passed a bush.

I ran around and quietly alerted my whole section of the perimeter, then grabbed a radio and called it into the captain stationed in the center of the camp, and reported that the NVA were using water buffalo as cover to move into position to attack us. He refused to accept or believe my report and brushed it off.

So I returned to my position and told everyone within earshot to shoot at the bushes in the riverbed as well as the other side of the river and to start when the machine gun in our position opened fire. This was going to be my first good fire-fight, and I was happy that we had the element of surprise, rather than breaking my cherry on an ambush rigged by the bad guys.

The machine gun opened up. I shot straight into the first bush that I'd seen someone hide in.

We received a horrendous return of gunfire from the other side of the river. So we sent back even heavier fire as everyone on our side joined the action.

I heard the Captain yelling for us to cease fire and report in, but we all ignored him and put it to the enemy.

When we finally called artillery to put ordnance on the other side of the river, the fight ended.

The firefight only lasted ten minutes and after that, and only after that, did the Captain come over. He asked us what we were shooting at. We told him but he denied hearing any enemy fire. We told him he was crazy, that we received a horrendous return of fire. He accused us of being stoned and said he was going to report us. He was in a serious case of denial because enemy tracer fire was seen all over the perimeter; he had to have seen it. Their tracers were green, ours red. You had to have your face in the sand not to see the green ones.

Vietnam – The Teenage Wasteland

The next day we wrote it up and sent it into command. They replaced him a few days later, never to be seen again, thank God.

That firefight was a good one to introduce me to real action. No one got hurt and I know we killed several NVA. So I got my cherry popped with us coming out on top. That was good.

A few weeks later was the first time my life was in jeopardy. We stopped for the night on an "island" of slightly high ground in a valley surrounded by rice paddies. We all placed our trip flares and Claymores on the interconnecting, surrounding rice paddy dikes.

The next morning I went out to bring in my flares and Claymores from the point on the dike where I had set them up, walking out onto the dike with another guy. I only had my M-16 with me and the single magazine that was in it.

I had just gathered in one flare when I saw a splash in the rice paddy water right next to me and was still wondering what it was when I heard the shot, but it still didn't register until a bullet hit the top of the dike directly in front of me. Then I knew what it was.

I turned around and capped off a few rounds in the direction the shots had come from. Then a whole bunch of water erupted in front me, spraying me all over including my face. I opened up on automatic and then jumped into the rice paddy, sheltering behind the dike.

Bullets hit all around me. I fired off two more rounds in response but then my magazine was empty. I reached for more magazines but didn't have any with me. Panicking, I jumped up and ran back towards the perimeter as fast as I could while bullets landed all around me.

As we had camped on a small hill I had to climb a slope to get back into the perimeter but dare not. Instead, I hid behind an outcropping of dirt, bullets hitting right at my feet while I was screamed for help.

The perimeter finally opened up with return fire, and I made it back inside our lines.

I was shaking for an hour after that. It was the first time I personally had been shot at and yes, it was scary.

It was a few weeks later when I shot and killed my first man. I thought it would be a big deal and I would feel bad and all that, but it was not what I expected, probably because of the way it went down.

I was walking slack. An infantry unit in a jungle area has to move single file through the terrain. There is a point man (the first man) and then all the way back in the rear is the last man, called the "slack". It is not as harrowing as point, but it has its moments.

It was my first time on slack. I didn't know what to do and spent a lot of time looking behind me. After an hour or so of walking I looked behind once more and, not seeing anything for the umpteenth time, began to feel more relaxed. Just as I thought everything was cool, someone took a shot at me. The bullet hit a tree just a foot away.

I grabbed a little earth and the guy in front of me came to see what was going on. I told him someone shot at me. He told me to get the bastard and then hurried off to catch up with the rest of the patrol.

I lay there for a few minutes and then had an idea. I pulled out my Vietnamese/English book and waited for him.

All of a sudden, I saw him stick his head out. He was an NVA regular: classic pith helmet, backpack, AK-47 and so forth.

I looked in my book real quickly and told him to surrender, in my best Vietnamese. "Chu hoi!" I shouted.

His answer was a short automatic burst from his AK-47. I replied with a short burst in his direction from my M-16.

I got up and ran back to my position at the back of the line and resumed walking slack.

Vietnam – The Teenage Wasteland

The person in front of me asked if I got him. I told him I thought I had but that was just wishful thinking.

Thirty minutes later my NVA friend shot at me again. The guy in front of me told me to get him and not to fail this time.

I hunkered down in a bush where I had a good view of the trail, and waited for him to show and while I waited, I pulled out my little book and learned a phrase in it: "Let's be friends."

The little guy came around the corner. I could have nailed his ass right there, but hey – I was a hippy, I believed in love and peace.

I called to him and he froze like a deer in headlights. I told him in Vietnamese that I wanted to be his friend. He walked backwards ever so slowly and disappeared behind a tree. I called to him again and told him I wanted to be friends. He fired off a burst in my direction. The bullets snapped branches right above me.

I held off firing back at him and called to him again. He fired another burst at me. This time closer. Wise guy, hey?

The man in front of me came back and had clearly heard me call to the NVA soldier in Vietnamese because he yelled, "Hey Tom, quit fucking around and kill him, god dam it!" and took off to resume his place in the line.

I fired a burst at the little guy and then took off too.

Twenty minutes later I was at the rear of the line, walking backwards, when I saw him again, he was running up the trail toward me.

This time I hid behind a tree. I figured he didn't know where I was, but when I looked around the tree, he shot at me and missed only by inches. That kind of pissed me off so I pulled out my book and looked for another phrase, but then I realized something big. I was in a war and the guy chasing me wanted to kill me, for real, truly and actually. Somehow, realizing the facts of it made me feel affronted. I needed to put an end to him before he put an end to me.

I took off in the open, so he could see me running. I ran twenty meters and hid behind another tree. Sure enough, here he came. I drew a bead on his forehead and squeezed the trigger. He rag dolled, slumping to the ground. I waited a few seconds and then ran up to him, grabbed his AK and kicked him. "You should have listened to me, asshole," I yelled.

I ran back to the line to resume my position.

The man in front of me turned around when he heard me coming. "Get him?" he asked.

I held up the AK 47.

"Good man!" he beamed

That night I was the talk of the company. Having nailed the NVA stalking me made me a celebrity of sorts.

I thought about it before I went to sleep and worried that I might feel bad at ending someone's life. I waited for the depression to hit, but the next thing I knew it was morning, and I woke feeling very refreshed.

We went the next month with very little enemy contact. To me, it was like a big camping trip. The only problem was the rain. We were now into the monsoon season and it was getting wetter and wetter.

We were in a pretty thick jungle area, in a ravine with a river running through, when we bumped into an enemy underground field hospital complex. It was one of the most amazing places I have ever seen. It was like a gopher complex. Tunnels were everywhere. We actually found rice still cooking on fires when we arrived and found a lot of medical supplies, food, tons of rice and operating rooms.

The thing I admired most about it was that it had running water. They used bamboo to pull water from the river and route it all through the hospital. It was ingenious.

We took everything we could find and then pulled out. We called a B-52 strike on the complex later that day and erased it from the face of the earth.

We actually got pretty slack as time went on. We let our hair grow and accumulated love bead necklaces, peace rings

Vietnam – The Teenage Wasteland

on our wrists and long mustaches. We were Army hippies and loving it.

Around the middle of December, we were told that Command was going to send some of us up north to fill in for a battalion there that had been decimated. I was one of the guys picked to go. We were put on a transport plane and flown a hundred miles north to Chu Lai. I had no idea how we looked when we arrived, that is until we were put before our new First Sergeant of the battalion.

First Sergeant Thomas Alt looked us over and was furious. "What in the blue fuck are you people?" He roared.

It was then that I realized I had all the love beads going, with five peace bracelets, mustache long, hair long and so on. He asked another sergeant to take us for haircuts and get us cleaned up. We lost our hair and beads and bracelets and were made to "look like real soldiers".

I was sent to Alpha Company, 1st of the 46th Infantry, sans bracelets, beads and hair. I was back in the Army.

13

DAVID

There is no great genius without a tincture of madness.
Seneca – 3 B.C.

One of the first people I met in the new battalion was Lt. David Waltz. I was introduced to him by the Captain's Radio & Telephone Operator (RTO). Dave Waltz was around five foot-ten, of average build, with a semi-dark complexion and bright, happy blue eyes with wrinkles on the sides from lots of smiling. I could tell David was a happy person with lot of friends. He seemed easy to be around.

Lt. Waltz greeted me with warmth and welcomed me to his platoon.

I thanked him with a "thank you, Sir."

He shook his head and leaned into me with a conspiratorial whisper: "Don't call me Sir; the bad guys might hear you. Just call me Dave." He smiled at me again.

I liked Dave instantly and we eventually became good friends. I could tell he was looking for a playmate, someone like me who was willing to do fun and wild things.

David told me he was from a small town in Maine and asked me if I'd seen the movie "The Graduate" with Dustin Hoffman.

"Sure," I said, nodding.

Vietnam – The Teenage Wasteland

"Picture me driving an old two-seater Jaguar with the top down, wearing a cap and sipping a martini as I cruise the back roads on my way to one of my girlfriends' houses. That was me."

David was drafted into the Army in August, 1967. After boot camp, he decided to become an officer and enrolled in OCS (Officer Candidate School). He graduated a year later and was immediately sent to Vietnam where he planned to stake a claim for fame and leave the Army, after his obligatory four-year stint, as either a Captain or a Major. David was smart; he decided to turn being drafted to his advantage and eventually leave the Army with lots of kudos to further his career after the military.

He took me into his platoon with such grace and made me feel so at home; I couldn't help but admire the man. The rest of my new platoon seemed to feel the same way about him which made me feel more confident and safer, knowing we did not have a looser for a platoon leader.

Our whole Company was taken to Landing Zone (LZ) Baldy, named after the treeless, five-thousand foot Mountain in Southern California. The LZ was huge and housed our battalion, the 1st of the 52nd battalion, some Marine regiments and some Navy. I had no idea what the Navy was doing there, but then again, they support the Marines.

David, it turned out, was a rascal and was not afraid of anything. At the same time, he was not suicidal, but his balls were definitely bigger than his common sense.

It was around two weeks after I joined his platoon that he made me into his RTO. My duties were to carry the radio for him, answer calls from the Captain and generally make sure our platoon had all the supplies it needed.

One day we were slacking at LZ Baldy when Dave came up to me and said: "Get your radio; we're going for a walk to have a look-see."

The area we were in had been quiet since our arrival. I was now in the eighth week of my tour and was starting to think that duty in Vietnam was a cake-walk. So I liked the idea of going for an excursion in the countryside, jumped up and got my gear on.

We packed light and moved through the wire, heading for a point five kilometers out to investigate reports of VC action in that area. There were seven of us all told.

We had gone around four klicks and were walking along a berm, a raised piece of ground, when all of a sudden David looked off to his left. I was right behind him and looked at what was grabbing his interest. I saw a clump of trees and that was about it.

Dave motioned for me to follow him, and then he motioned for the rest of the patrol to circle around the far end of the clump of trees.

I followed but moved fifteen feet to the left of David to watch his back.

David headed right toward that clump of trees. He was right on top of it when he opened up at the trees, on full automatic.

It shocked me at first and I wondered what he was up to, but the next thing I saw was a man fly out of the foliage with blood and brains blowing out the top of his head. I saw another one running away with an M-1 Carbine, I popped a few caps in him and he went down.

Dave screamed at me. I turned around just in time to see an NVA soldier running behind me in black pajamas trying to bring an M-1 carbine around on me. I blasted him on automatic and he went down. Then Dave nailed another one who was pretending to be dead until he tried to shoot me when my back was to him.

It was all over in less than thirty seconds.

Slamming a new magazine in my rifle, I surveyed the scene. Looked over at Dave and his eyes were as wide as saucers and his face taut with the effects of adrenalin. I started to walk toward him when the first guy I shot got up and started running for the wood line to the west. I took careful aim and shot him in the back. He went down again but then got up and started running again.

Dave said, "Let me have him" and shot the man twice, dropping him for the last time. Then he looked over and lectured me: "You have to shoot them in the heart or the head in order to get a kill. You were sloppy, Tom."

Just as he said that, the same man got up yet again and staggered toward the west. David looked at him in horror, looked at me and took off running towards the escaping NVA soldier who was now fifty meters away from us and around a hundred meters from the wood line.

I had just yelled at Dave to stop chasing him when the entire wood line erupted with gunfire. Dave went down in a hail of bullets.

I jumped behind an old headstone sitting out there in the middle of nowhere as bullets hit the spot I had just vacated. I knew Dave was dead, and I was crushed. I sat there for a full minute (that's a lot of time when people are trying to kill you) listening to bullets hit the headstone I was hiding behind. I decided I better see if they were charging me from the wood line. I looked over at the rest of the patrol, and they were pinned down by gunfire, but were returning fire. I figured I was alone, so I'd better start putting out fire to defend myself. I took a deep breath, checked my rifle and swung around the headstone, ready to shoot when I saw Dave running right at me. He saw me and made a bee-line for where I was. I pulled back and Dave did a home-plate slide, head first and rolled behind the headstone. He looked at me, his big blue eyes were as large as the moon. It cracked me up and I started laughing, half at the sight of him and half from nervous relief that he was alive.

Dave looked at me and said, "It's not funny," as he nervously tried to change magazines.

At that, both of us rolled around the rock and started putting out a lot of gunfire, just enough to give the rest of the patrol relief to maneuver out of their wide open position.

Dave grabbed the radio and called for gunship support.

A helicopter gunship came a few minutes later and chased the rest of the bad guys away.

Later that night, back at LZ Baldy, Dave came by my position to see me. I went outside with him and lit a smoke.

"What was so funny, today?" he asked, looking a bit embarrassed.

"Aw shit Dave, you should have seen your face. I thought you were a goner and when you came sliding in there like that I thought I was going to pee my pants."

We both laughed and then recounted the story.

It turned out that we killed five bad guys between the two of us. Dave said that we were a good team, and that he liked working with me. He went back to the CP (Command Post), leaving me with a good feeling. For the first time, I was actually happy in Vietnam.

Our Captain (I will omit his name here) was a murderer. He was always pushing us for body count and didn't care who was killed as a result. He pushed us to kill prisoners, farmers and other innocent people. Most of the guys told him to go fuck himself and ignored his tirades. Others were afraid of him and complied.

The funny thing about this guy is that he never carried a weapon of any kind. To me that was the flakiest thing I'd ever seen. I asked him about it one day and he told me that it would be a distraction because he should be running the company rather than shooting. It was a good reason, but I knew the real reason was that he didn't want to be accused of or held responsible for shooting anyone. Having no weapon was his insurance. In the final analysis, he was just a coward.

Finally, a lot of the guys got tired of his shit and wrote him up. He was replaced by Kern Dunagan, a big, green-eyed Irishman who was everything you ever thought a combat Captain should be. He had the rare ability to be tough, demanding and at the same time caring and friendly. It was

Vietnam – The Teenage Wasteland

astounding how he carried out his captainship while being all that. He was quite a man.

Captain Dunagan had been with the company about two weeks when we were sent to LZ Cork, way out in the middle of nowhere. It was a frightening place that gave you the idea there were a whole lot of NVA in the area.

It was shortly after we arrived at LZ Cork that I realized David had become a little cracked in the head.

It was March '69 and our company was searching for a battalion of NVA suspected of operating in our zone. Dave worked with the Captain to figure out where we should go to find them.

I overheard Captain Dunagan tell Dave: "Don't go out any further than four klicks.

Dave assured him we would not.

We put together a patrol of Dave, me and five other guys, including a machine gunner and a grenadier.

As we set out, Dave launched himself into the patrol with a new kind of intensity but after a while he was unusually quiet as we walked along and I wondered what was up, until I realized we had gone more than five kilometers.

I didn't want to get on the bad side of the new Captain, so I said, "Uh, Dave, we are a lot further out than four clicks, you know."

Dave snapped at me. "I know, but I'm onto this battalion and I think we can find them."

"Dave, listen, we are out too far. If we get cut off we're going to be in the shits with the Captain, not to mention getting our asses blown off."

Dave then used the co-conspirator approach on me: "Think about it, Tom. If we find them we'll get feathers in our caps. I know they're just a little further; we can find them and save a whole lot of lives by catching them out here. Just a little further. Okay?" And with that, he proceeded down the trail.

I stood there for a few seconds, looked at the other men in the patrol who looked back at me noncommittally. Then I turned and followed after Dave.

We were making our way down the center of a valley. Running right down the middle was a series of small islands, a chain of islands, areas of high ground thick with tall trees and bushes amid the expanse of lowland rice paddies.

The trail between the islands ran along top of some of the dikes, the narrow ridges of land slightly raised above the dry rice paddies which served to separate them when in use and full of water.

After moving from island to island along the dike paths, we finally got to a rather large island at the end of the chain. It was about three acres in size. On the other side of the island the trail went out forty meters and then hung a right and went another three hundred meters or so to a cut in the foothills that led around mountains and into the next valley.

David stopped and looked at that trail. He looked hard and thought.

At that point we were seven kilometers from the base, beyond radio range and so out of contact with the rest of the company.

Dave rubbed the stubble on his chin and finally looked at me. "They'll be coming up this trail from the cut in the foothills over there. I can feel them. Let's set up here."

I told him we were out of radio range and needed to report in, in another twenty minutes.

He brushed off my complaint, assuring me we'd be out of there in twenty minutes or less.

Five minutes later Dave turned to me. He had that look in his eye; that twinkle – the one that scared me, the one he had just before we got into trouble. "I got an idea Tom. Look, they will be coming along the trail over there. They'll be in the open for three hundred meters or so. They'll be walking the standard thirty-five meters apart, arriving here twenty seconds apart. We can capture them, one by one. There're two large bunkers on this island. I can set up over there in those bushes, you can stop them over there, and I can bop them over the head, tie them up and throw them in the bunkers. We can capture the whole battalion."

Holy shit! I knew Dave had cracked. I tried to handle him the best I could, but his energy and charisma were too hard to deny. I was just no match for him. But I tried. "Dave look," I said, "we have to get back to the company. If you're so sure the NVA battalion is going to come by here, we can call spotter planes to find them. There are only seven of us and…"

He cut me off. "That's the beauty of it. They will hide if they see planes. With us hiding here we can catch them off guard. They won't expect it, Tom. It's a perfect plan. Go in the bunkers and see what you can find."

I stood my ground. "Dave, I think you've blown a head gasket or something. It's crazy, you're going to get us all killed out here, man."

Dave just smiled at me and put his hand on my shoulder. "I know you're scared. I understand, but we can do this. All we have to do is decide to do it and it is done. Picture it done in your mind, Tom."

I just stood there looking at him as though he were diseased.

He saw my support slipping away so pulled rank on me. "Go find some rope. Move it."

So there it was. That was an order and I knew it was the end of conversation. I got up and looked at the other guys.

The machine gunner put a finger to the side of his head as if it were a gun and pulled an imaginary trigger, blowing his brains out.

"No shit, man," I murmured

I looked in the bunkers and to my chagrin there was about two hundred feet of twine in there. I came out with it.

"Good man, Tom!" Dave said, seeing the twine, ecstatic.

As I sat there cutting the twine, I finally thought "What's the worry, there is no battalion out here anyhow, he'll get tired of dicking around after an hour and we'll go back." I cut the twine into useable two-foot pieces and laid them next to me.

Dave had stripped off his gear and was down to his pants, T-shirt, M-16 and a couple of magazines of ammo he stashed in his pants pocket. He had his bayonet in his hand.

I shook my head at his foolishness. He was delusional. I was afraid that he had gone crazy from the heat and the war. Maybe he needed salt. Maybe he spent too many nights tripping under the full moon. Whatever, I now had a madman for a leader and some day he was going to get us all killed. Most likely today. Still, I loved him dearly.

The other guys had set up their positions as ordered by David. The machine gunner guarded the foothills in case we ran into the battalion, or something went wrong and the NVA tried to out-flank us. The rest covered the trail and were assigned fire zones.

We hunkered in the noon heat and waited; only Dave expected something to happen.

Fifteen minutes later we saw motion at the entrance to the trail, near the foothills. A person dressed in black pajamas and a straw hat stepped out on the trail and walked along.

I watched from behind my tree as the figure drew nearer. Then we saw it was a woman – nothing unusual about that. She reached the half-way point along the trail and stopped, turned around and motioned behind her for someone to follow.

To all of our amazement a man in a pith helmet with tan fatigues and an AK-47 stepped out onto the trail and followed the woman.

Dave turned to me and mouthed, "bingo".

My heart sank.

It was not uncommon for a woman to walk point for a battalion of NVA. In fact, it was routine. The women knew the neighborhood well and knew the safe routes. It was also common to see a woman walking by herself in the open so no one would suspect she was leading a battalion of NVA.

Vietnam – The Teenage Wasteland

Thirty five meters behind the first man, to my horror, another man appeared on the trail with an AK-47, backpack and pith helmet.

"Son of a bitch", I thought, David did figure them out. But I felt dizzy with the mere thought of what we were doing. It was pure insanity. We were going to try to capture three or four hundred enemy soldiers, an entire battalion. We were mental cases! It would have been surreal but for the fact that it was actually happening. The show was on. There was nothing I could do about it. I straightened up and got ready, stuffing a few lengths of twine in my belt.

The woman walked right up the trail toward us, walked right past Dave and up to my position.

I was scared to death but finally threw all caution aside and forced my body into the open, stepped out in front of her with my rifle on her and quietly said, "Chu Hoi" (put your hands over your head and surrender).

She turned around to scream but Dave was on her and bopped her on the forehead with the heavy hilt of his bayonet.

She collapsed into my arms. I tied her hands behind her, rodeo style, and threw her unconscious body into the bunker.

I got back to my position just in time for the next guy to make the turn and come up the trail past Dave.

The girl was easy, she was unarmed. The guy approaching had an AK -47, and if he saw me first, we were dead meat. For either of us to shoot would be certain disaster.

He came on up the path. I stepped out and did my "Chu Hoi" routine. He was stunned. Before he had a chance to raise his rifle Dave was on him from behind, slapped his helmet forward and whacked him hard on the back of his head with the hilt of his bayonet.

The NVA soldier went down like a sack of hammers. I tied his hands behind him and threw him into the bunker.

"Two down." I said to myself as I slipped back into position.

Dave turned and looked at me, nodding with a, "hey, this is working." He had his bayonet in his teeth and looked like a swashbuckling pirate from the Caribbean.

We put our attention on the next victim.

I actually started to believe that the plan might work, started to marvel at it and began to think just how smart Dave was and how brilliant his idea. We had two so far and it was easy. I got a little light headed and giddy and stifled a laugh. I felt like capering and leaping around yelling, "We're so cool, we're so cool."

The next guy arrived but stopped just short of Dave.

Oh, oh - I stopped capering in my mind.

The NVA looked into the island and called to his friends.

Dave looked at me and I looked at him, and then I looked at the soldier.

The NVA called out again.

I called out with my best Vietnamese accent; "Lai Dai" (come here).

He frowned. Then he called again while bringing his rifle up to ready, sensing something was amiss.

I'll say something was amiss. Dave and his merry band of idiots were about four cans short of a six-pack. That's what was amiss. I had to do something or we were going to be in deep trouble. So I jumped out onto the trail and pointed my rifle right at his chest. I tersely called to him to move forward.

He shook his head "no" as he took a few steps backwards. He moved his hand to flip his AK onto automatic.

Aw shit, here we go. I fired a burst of three rounds into the NVA soldier's chest and quickly ran down to where he was, at the same time noting out of the corner of my eye that Dave was rapidly getting his gear on.

I saw the next NVA in the open and blew him up as he tried to unstrap his rifle from his shoulder.

The other guys from our patrol selected targets out in the open and started methodically shooting them down. The rest of the NVA in the open ran for cover.

We downed about seven of them in the initial volley, but now it was time to go. The whole thing was blown and we were now a force of seven against a pissed off force of three hundred or more. This was not good at all, damn you Dave!

Dave was dressed, ready to go and told everyone to get down the trail. He ordered the machine gunner to stay behind to cover us.

The gunner started working the wood line because, sure enough, the NVA were trying to flank us. The rest of us took off running. We crossed an open area by way of a dike path and ran to the next island.

Enemy gunfire was coming from the wood line with increasing intensity.

We set up at the island and covered the gunner as he crossed to us. When he arrived, Dave told him to set up at the entrance of that island. We peeled off, returning fire as we ran to the next island.

The battalion of NVA was on our heels. They were flat out running at us, bent on catching us. We were doing the stop, shoot, and peel. It did not slow them down, though, and the bullets were whizzing past us as we ran. We all ran to the next island and Dave shouted to set up. We set up and waited rifles at the ready.

Five seconds later a group of NVA came charging across the open area. As soon as there were thirty or so we opened up and mowed them down. They got all bunched up trying to get back onto the island they'd just come from, trying to reach cover while we poured fire into them. They backed the hell off and we took off, leaving the gunner behind again to keep them at bay.

We ran to the next island and set up at the entrance again. This time the NVA were coming around the sides, running through the dry rice paddies and not on the trail. Too bad, we expected that and we nailed them. They turned tail and ran.

We broke off and peeled out of there running our asses of.

By now the NVA had taken serious losses and were more cautious, but they did not stop their pursuit. They still came, not as hot as before, but just as pissed. This bought us precious time, and we ran like never before.

We ran two more kilometers before we set up again. We checked our ammo and were down to half. Not good with just a little less than four kilometers to go.

We waited and they came. When they were just about on top of us, we opened up on them, almost point-blank, downing ten more. They turned tail and took off, back to where they had come from.

Dave held up his hand to stop us from peeling, and we waited. Sure enough, they thought we had left that spot and came straight down the trail at us. We mauled them again. Once more they took off running in the opposite direction and so did we.

We got about two kilometers from the rest of Alpha Company when I heard my radio. It was the Captain and he was shouting at us to report in. I heard him ask about gunfire, and I knew I had to answer him. I picked up the headset while I was running and keyed it.

"Hercules five-zero, puff, puff, this is… puff, five-two Juliet… puff, puff, takin' heavy fire…. Over."

He was fast to respond.

"Where are you? Report in. What is the situation, over?!"

I didn't answer him because the bad guys were catching up to us, we were running out of gas and they were shooting again. I wanted to give him some sort of answer, but I just couldn't breathe! I keyed the hand set just as gunfire came across to us. I let go of the hand set and ran harder. I knew that would worry him even more, but I physically could not talk. I was running for my life and there was not enough available oxygen on the planet at that point in time to help me.

We had just enough ammo for one last stand. We set up at the entrance of another island. I figured we were just a little

Vietnam – The Teenage Wasteland

more than a click out from Alpha Company but it now took forever for me to catch my breath.

The bad guys came at us once again. I knew the Captain was listening in. He would hear the action loud and clear. We opened up on them as soon as they came across and downed another ten of them. We broke and took off again.

My radio was just churning with the Captain screaming at us for information.

I finally called him. "Hercules, we are a klick….puff, puff … out. Need cover, puff … soon…puff, over."

He shot back, "get five-two on the radio now, over."

But at that moment the gunfire intensified from the bad guys, and we ran even harder. There was no chance to stop and call.

Running like never before, I finally saw the perimeter and raised the hand set. "Coming in NOW!" I signaled as we ran the last stretch to the perimeter.

We got there just in time. The bad guys caught up to us as we dived through our defense perimeter.

The lead portion of the NVA battalion ran into a hailstorm of bullets from thirty GIs and got knocked down, hard.

A few seconds later everything went quiet. I lay on the ground next to Dave fighting for breath. I didn't think I would ever catch it.

The Captain's RTO, Brian Shaw, came up to me and Dave and addressed us. "Captain wants to see both of you right now. On your feet, let's go!"

We got up and staggered over to the Captain.

He looked pissed. He looked at both of us threateningly. "What the fuck is going on. What's the situation?" he hissed.

Dave was almost white from lack of oxygen and was soaking wet with sweat. So was I. Dave got that silly look on his face while he was panting and announced, "We found the battalion Captain."

Dunagan looked at him and narrowed those bright green eyes and focused on Dave. "You watch your tone with me

Lieutenant. I want a straight answer on what happened. Report!"

Dave sobered and took a deep breath. He looked at me as if to say, "don't say anything about the thing, you know…" as he started to explain his way out of it.

The Captain caught the look and cut him off. "Don't say anything, not one more fucking word," he said as he wagged his finger at Dave.

Dave looked silly because he knew he'd been caught in a lie before he'd even told it.

The Captain broke his intense glare off David and put it on me. Those green eyes were like laser beams boring into my head. "Report, Tom," he ordered.

"We, uh, went out and ran into the battalion. We almost got cut off and we, uh, fought our way back here."

He didn't buy it. He looked at us one after the other, suspiciously. He looked at me menacingly. "How far out did you go?"

I looked at Dave.

"Don't look at him for the answer, answer to me, now!"

"Uh, five clicks or so." I said with my eyes downcast so he couldn't see them.

He still knew I was lying. He looked back at Dave and got into his face. "How far out?"

Dave looked defeated. "Around seven klicks."

The Captain was not satisfied as he asked Dave, "Now, be careful here – who shot first?"

Dave threw caution to the wind. He looked directly at Captain Dunagan. "We set up an ambush and tripped it when they came in." Dunagan was stunned and Dave got braver. "But we killed around forty of them and…."

Dunagan cut him off with the wave of an admonishing finger and walked around in a circle. He was deeply disturbed and was making a decision. He made another two circuits becoming more and more disturbed. Finally, he stopped in front of us. "You know, I let you take a patrol out to see if

Vietnam – The Teenage Wasteland

you could see signs of a battalion of NVA. I figured you would see something and report in so we could handle it intelligently. Even if you did run across them, I would have figured you would call an air strike, you know, in a coordinated fashion. But no: I had John Wayne and Audie-fucking-Murphy on patrol and you two and five other idiots decided to ambush them and then, and then, AND THEN you bring them right to my doorstep! You actually invited them over for dinner. Now tell me, what the fuck am I supposed to do with a battalion of NVA that is a hundred meters from me? Call an air strike on them? No, they are too close. Call artillery on them? Nope, too close. How about we just go charge them?"

The logic from the Captain hit me like a hammer. He was right. God, were we stupid.

Dave weakly tried to calm the Captain down. "Sir, I take full responsibility…"

The Captain cut him off by charging at him and sticking his finger in his face. "You shut up, right now. Not one more word." Then he addressed both of us, sternly. "I am going to try to figure out what to do with this mess and how we are going to get out of it. By now they have figured out we are a company sized unit and they have us outgunned. If they attack us they will hurt us, bad. If we do get out of this, I will have both of you court-martialed. Now the two of you get out of my face."

We both walked away. Dave tried to say something, but I cut him off. "Dave, you need to get your shit together, man. That was way over the top today. You are going to get a lot of us killed if you don't knock it off, not to mention my going to jail if I do live. So I don't want to talk to you right now."

Dave looked at me and smiled his smile and put a placating hand on my shoulder. "Look Tom, we're not going to get into trouble and besides, look how many bad guys we bagged today. We kicked ass. So chill out, man. We had a good day."

And with that, he went to check out the rest of the platoon and carried on as if nothing happened.

As it turned out the NVA battalion was badly hurt and they snuck off in the middle of the night.

We moved out the next day and never heard about the incident again, that is until six weeks later when I was Dunagan's Radio Man. We were camped for the night, and I was talking with the Captain about it and he asked me: "You remember that incident with you and Dave and the Battalion of NVA?"

I nodded.

The Captain looked a little amused. "How many do you figure you guys killed that day? No bullshit, now." He was smiling.

I dropped my guard a bit. "I figure we killed a minimum of forty, possibly as many as sixty and severely wounded another thirty or forty."

Dunagan was taken aback. "Really? That's the truth?"

"No shit, Sir." I told him we did it by setting up and letting them come to us and so on.

Dunagan smiled as he doodled in the dirt with a stick in deep thought and then asked, "What were you guys really doing that day?"

I looked at him shocked that he pulled the trigger so fast and his smiled grew broader and totally disarmed me.

"You want the real truth, Sir?"

"Yes. Give me the real skinny. I know David and I know you, and you guys were doing something off-the-wall."

"We, ah.., well we, um, well, we tried to capture that entire battalion."

Dunagan looked at me to see if I was telling the truth. He could tell by my embarrassment that I was. He laughed. "Capture the whole battalion?"

"Yep."

He was astonished. "Tell me about it. I gotta hear this."

I told him the whole story.

After I was done, he sat there and thought for a moment as he doodled in the sand. Then he shook his head and laughed. "You two really are cowboys," he said. Then he patted me on the back and walked off smiling and shaking his head.

Down deep he loved it, because he loved soldiers that showed initiative and guts. But he was wary of men who had more guts than brains, and I think that is why he got rid of David, sending him to Echo Company's Recon Platoon.

And it turned out Recon was the perfect place for David. He had done so well finding that battalion and now he got to run Recon which is what they do, sneak around all day and locate the enemy. It was perfect for him.

I loved David. He had a contagious personality and took on the war with aplomb and flippancy and you know what? That was the only way to fight that war. I adopted Dave's philosophy for myself, and it definitely made things go better.

I thank God for introducing me to David, and feel a better person for having met him. I do love him dearly.

14

LZ PROFESSIONAL

We were briefed one day in early March that the 1st of the 52nd battalion had been wiped out and we were to replace them on an LZ called Professional.

We flew out there on big Chinook helicopters. Our company (Alpha) was to go in first and secure the Hill. As we came in on our final approach, fire from an enemy .51 caliber machine gun ripped several holes in our chopper.

The Chinook behind us was shot down. It managed to land without casualties, but still, it was sort of an omen for us. Chinooks just don't get shot down at altitude except by anti-aircraft artillery so that's what it must have been.

We landed on LZ Professional. As we climbed off the chopper we saw thirty or so grunts waiting to board. They looked scraggly, dirty and beat up. I asked one of them if they were part of the 1st of the 52nd. He nodded he was. I asked him where the rest of his battalion was. He pointed out toward the valley below and said, "out there" and with that they all boarded the chopper.

I was shocked because I knew what that meant. They really had been wiped out. We were later briefed that they had several MIA, and we were going to go out and find them.

My company secured the Hill while the rest of the choppers unloaded Bravo, Charlie, Delta and Echo companies who then walked down the hill and melted into the bush.

Vietnam – The Teenage Wasteland

I was glad we were to secure the hill and weren't going out in the bush because the area looked like a foreboding place. Everywhere was jungle. The hills all around LZ Pro looked dangerous. The place just gave me the creeps.

LZ Pro was a hill about seven hundred feet high at the east end of a long valley called the "Valley of Death" or as the chopper and fighter pilots called it: "fifty caliber alley". The real name of the valley was the Song Thien, the valley in which the Song Thien River flowed.

The valley had high mountains to the south and smaller mountains to the north. About twelve klicks in was another large mountain that seemed to block the end of the valley. The mountains were all covered in triple-canopy jungle. The valley floor was sparsely populated with old, dried up rice paddies, abandoned long ago – probably because of the fierce fighting that occurred frequently in the area.

LZ Pro was put there some two years previously for the purpose of guarding the infamous "Burlington Trail" which was a branch of the Ho Chi Min trail that came in from Laos. It was actually a paved road and before the LZ was put there, it carried a lot of supplies by truck into Quang Tin Province to supply the NVA. LZ Professional was strategically situated right next to the Burlington Trail.

Since its establishment, LZ Pro had been a major target for the NVA. They wanted to get rid of it so they could resume supply traffic into the south.

LZ Pro was a heavily fortified installation. It had large, heavily sand bagged bunkers along the perimeter with inside bunkers all over the place. It was entrenched all around the perimeter with covered firing positions every twenty feet or so. The bunkers all had rocket fences in front of them to keep the rockets from hitting them directly.

The hill was guarded with seven rows of concertina razor wire. In between the wire rows were various mines, trip flares, fifty-five gallon drums filled with napalm and so on. It was a fortress.

My squad (five men) went to our assigned bunker and the moment we arrived, mortars started falling all around the perimeter. They fell one per second and the bombardment lasted for three days without let-up.

It was a message from the NVA to let us know that they still owned the valley, and that we were in for more than we had bargained for.

Three days of mortar fire killed us, quite literally. During the bombardment, GIs ran from bunker to bunker trying to avoid the bombs. On the 2nd day one guy ran from one bunker to the next but was killed by a mortar.

Going out to take a dump was a crap shoot (pun intended). You waited until you really had to go, ran to the latrine and took the fastest dump in history.

The mortar fire subsided on the fourth day and we went about repairing the massive amounts of damage but every now and then, they fired mortars just to keep us on our toes.

It was five days after that I had the incident with the rockets and my .50 caliber machine gun.

By the time it was our turn to go out into bush I was only too glad to go.

Our mission was to find MIAs from the 1st of the 52nd and to mop up any other organized NVA elements. We followed a shallow river down the valley to a place where none of the other companies of our battalion had gone.

On the third day, we found the remains of a GI from the 1st of the 52nd. He was in a tunnel off of the river bed. We found a note on him that read:

Dear Mom & Dad,
We have been in heavy combat for several days now. My company got overrun yesterday and we all scattered. I am hiding in a hole in the ground, hoping I get rescued. If you get this letter, it means I didn't make it. I just want to tell you that I am sorry I left you and sorry I did not come back home to you. I love you both. I need to go now, I hear voices...

Vietnam – The Teenage Wasteland

The letter was never finished. He was stripped of his weapon, his clothes, and any valuables and was left lying there with the letter clutched in his hand.

I cried like a baby. It was the saddest thing I'd ever seen.

My new Lieutenant, Lt. Edwards, was pissed, and I mean really pissed. He quietly avowed revenge.

We called a chopper and evacuated the body and then continued with the rest of our patrol. Later that day we came across a lone hooch in the middle of nowhere, and found the GI's wallet hidden in a bucket of rice. We took everything out of the wallet but left it hidden in the rice. Then we took off.

Around twilight we made camp some four klicks away from the place we'd found the wallet. Lt. Edwards asked for volunteers to go back to the hooch with him. I raised my hand and he nodded.

We took off down the river with Lt. Edwards, a machine gunner and one other grenadier. I carried the radio.

Arriving at the site of the hooch, we saw there were three AK-47s leaning against the outside. We heard talking inside. Lt. Edwards told me to give him the rocket launcher. I handed it over to him, and he got it ready. He told the rest of us to open up on the structure as soon as he fired the launcher.

Edwards was from New Jersey. You could tell he'd been around the block. Even though OTC had shined him up really well, it is a fact that you can never take the street out of someone from the streets. He raised the rocket launcher as the NVA in the hooch talked and laughed, slipped the safety off, aimed and shouted out: "This is for the boy in the tunnel, you fucks!" and with that he mashed the trigger.

We opened up with our small arms but shot into nothing but an empty space because the exploding rocket left nothing standing.

We took off running and made it back to our camp. Edwards was in high spirits, laughing that the hooch had blown up like it did.

I pointed out to him that straw or bamboo would not set off the rocket and we all looked at each other knowing that the rocket hit one of those cats and blew up the rest of them.

For the next few weeks we patrolled, killed quite a few NVA that we caught in various places and found two more dead GIs.

We kicked pretty good ass and chased the bad guys out of the AO (Area of Operation) and things settled down to a good routine. There was just enough action to keep us on our toes. We basically got into some sort of firefight just about every day.

From the start to the end of March 1969 we lost five guys with another twelve or so wounded badly enough to go home. But we killed a hundred or so NVA in the process.

We walked into village in the middle of the day and saw that it was empty. The Captain slowed down and looked around. The quiet was deafening. The Captain said "Easy, there's something…" His sentence was cut short as a machine gun opened up on us from the center of the village from a well that had a brass bell over the top of it. Off to the right, AK 47's ripped into our flank. We were trapped and under heavy fire.

Sometimes you get a break, and sometimes you don't. Our company must've had good karma because we always got the breaks when we needed them.

This one particular day the wind was blowing at a steady twenty knots with gusts up to forty. The Captain surveyed the situation and knew we were completely screwed, but you could see the wheels turning and all of a sudden his face lit up and he called out to put one of our pigs (machine gun) on the bell.

He gave the order and a GI named Kirby brought his pig from the second platoon and opened up on the bell, ringing it like an old telephone. You could see Kirby's red tracers

Vietnam – The Teenage Wasteland

ricocheting down the well and in a short time the NVA machine gun was silenced.

Captain Dunagan then made a very peculiar call. "Zippo Arms" he shouted above the din of AK and M-16 fire.

A few guys got it, pulled out their Zippos and started burning hooches.

Burning fronds were carried by the wind as sparks flew from hooch to hooch, in all creating one of the biggest blazes I've ever seen. We followed the burn with our backs to the wind and blasted our way out of that village. Oddly enough, even though we were completely suckered into the trap and the trap was sprung well, no one was killed or seriously wounded.

15

CAPTAIN KERN DUNAGAN

The world knows nothing of its greatest men.
– Sir Henry Taylor

Shortly after the bell ringing and hooch burning incident, I was promoted to Captain's RTO, which surprised me. I thought I was in trouble with Captain Dunagan, but just the opposite; I was invited into the "command circle". It was a great honor.

Brian Shaw had been the Captain's RTO up to that time but he was graduating up to be the Battalion Radio Operator on the hill, So Brian grooved me in as his replacement.

I ran the Company radios. My job was to relay orders to platoon leaders from Captain Dunagan, keep the platoon RTOs briefed and basically run them or replace them.

Captain Dunagan was his own man. There was no one quite like him. He was smart as a whip and confident.

He started training me immediately, wanted to make sure I was HIS radio man; that I did things his way, not the Army way or any other way. It was his way and that was it.

Like I said, Dunagan was a sweet man, but he was also tough as nails. If I was doing the right thing I was his best

Vietnam – The Teenage Wasteland

friend. If I screwed up, I got his wrath and he withdrew, distancing himself which hurt more that the wrath. It made you want to do better because the great reward was being allowed back into his warmth.

I remember the day I first met him. We were walking to a rendezvous point where a chopper was to land and pick us up. We were running late. We saw the chopper fly over us and land a kilometer or so beyond. Dave Waltz was in charge of the company at that point and said we should "double-time it" to the rendezvous point. We high tailed it and arrived within minutes and there, in the middle of an open field, all by himself was Captain Kern Dunagan, a bear of a man standing with his M-16 looking at us in amusement.

"I thought you guys were going to leave me here by myself, all day. You're going to have to learn how to be on time from now on," he said, with a mischievous twinkle in his eye.

He took over the company at that point and whipped us into shape.

The only thing about him I didn't like was that he had a really bad habit of walking point. No other officer in the Army walked point. But he did, and no amount of cajoling or pleading or lecturing on my or Brians part changed his mind on the matter. He always answered me or anyone else that complained with, "Whatsamatter, you afraid?" "Can't you keep up with me?" or "Am I scaring you? Well, take it up with the Chaplain."

Yes, Captain Dunagan had a horrible habit of walking point and I never really understood why he did it. I asked him why but he never told me. In retrospect I imagine he walked point for the most unselfish reason of all – he didn't want anyone to get hurt or killed walking point for him so he did it himself.

He was an excellent executive and officer – the kind you rarely find, anywhere. But if he had a flaw, walking point was it. He thought he was doing the point men a favor by taking their position but it made them feel uneasy, they wondered why the Captain felt he had to do their job for them. They figured they were failing him in some way. In short, it affected morale.

It was my only beef with Captain Dunagan and I objected often because, in addition to all the other reasons, when he walked point I had to walk with him.

One particular day, I was angry with the Captain for walking point, as usual. That time we were doing it while hacking our way through very thick jungle.

All of a sudden, we cut through the jungle grass and broke out into a clearing. In the middle of the clearing was something no one could have predicted.

The clearing was isolated, out in the middle of nowhere, far, far from civilization yet in the center of it stood a solitary, smiling NVA soldier with a North Vietnamese flag draped over his outstretched arms. An apparition worthy of any Frances Ford Coppola movie because he was also immaculately groomed with clean, newly pressed and starched fatigues and was an unusually healthy specimen.

It just didn't fit. "Where the hell did he come from?" was all I could think. It looked like he had beamed down from the Starship Enterprise after eating a good meal, taking a shower, a massage and manicure. It was just too weird. And how the HELL did he know we were going to be there? I just couldn't handle the number of questions multiplying in my head. It was just too much for me to process.

The Captain moved around the outside perimeter of the clearing to the right.

I moved around to the left so that we were not quite one hundred-eighty degrees apart. "Careful, Sir, he looks crazy," I warned.

Dunagan nodded.

I motioned to the others to stay back, out of the clearing.

Vietnam – The Teenage Wasteland

The NVA soldier looked straight at me with a grin, and then stepped toward me one pace, offering me the Flag in supplication. "This is for you," he said, in perfect English.

The way he spoke sent chills down my spine, my shields came up, a flashing red light and blaring klaxon did double time in my head. I flipped my rifle on automatic and said to him in plain Vietnamese; "Chu Hoi" (put your hands over your head and surrender).

He brushed me off with a quick shake of his head and, still smiling, repeated, "This is for you", placing real emphasis on the "you".

I looked at his smiling face and looked into his eyes. His eyes were death. That was all I needed to see. I did something I had never done before. I shot a man who was apparently unarmed. I hit him with a three-round burst right in the chest.

A minute later I sat up and looked around, my head ringing like a church bell on Sunday, my mind spinning. I was dazed and couldn't understand why I was I sitting down and why I had been flat on my back.

There was a smell of cordite in the air and I saw smoke wafting through the clearing, carried on the breeze.

GIs rushed to me and Captain Dunagan who was also sitting on his ass the other side of the clearing. The men made sure we were okay.

Besides not being able to hear anything, I felt like I was alright. I stood up and looked at where the NVA soldier had been. There was a small crater there and one sandal. Then I saw pieces of meat everywhere and realized he had blown up.

I collapsed again and just sat on the ground. The medic gave me some water and a candy bar and I started to feel better.

Captain Dunagan appeared. "I think you blew him up, Tom. I really wanted him prisoner," he said, with that little gleam in his eye that meant he was kidding.

I smiled and said, "Sorry Captain, I'll get you another one."

We sat and chatted for a while and the medic finally asked me if I was okay and I assured him I was. I stood up, adjusted my rucksack and looked at the Captain.

The Captain nodded at me and I back at him. He turned around, moved off in the direction we were originally going and resumed walking frigging point.

For the rest of the day, as we humped though the jungle, the Q&A in my head drove me nuts. "If the First Platoon had been walking point would they have handled the NVA dude correctly? Would they have botched it? Was it a good thing the Captain and I found him first? Was it right we were walking point?"

I brought up the matter to the Captain that night and his answer was, "who the hell knows, Tom? Did you dig our foxhole yet?"

End of discussion.

In our CP (Command Post) we had the Captain and the Battalion Radio Man – which was Brian Shaw whose job it was to maintain contact with Battalion on our situation, position and all that. He also got to call air strikes, gunship strikes, artillery strikes and all communication between our company and battalion command. Then there was the Company Net Radio Man. That was me.

My job was to communicate with the Platoon Leaders of the company, relay information to the Captain and orders from him to the Platoon leaders.

When the Captain figured that I had learned how to displace troops he let me call the shots. During fire-fights he would look in my eyes as I gathered data from the platoons and then I'd give orders. If I was doing the right thing he would just nod his head.

If I gave the wrong order, he would tighten his face or shake his head or narrow his eyes depending on the severity of the screw up. I would correct myself and if I didn't get it right, he would tell me what to do or grab the handset from me and give the correct order himself. After a bit he just let me go because he knew he had trained me well.

I would yell to Lieutenants over the radio during a fire-fight something on the order of: "Five-two, get your god dammed machine guns up on that high ground now with the rest of your troops and pour fire down on that clump of trees. Get them up there now! Move it!!" Then I would ride them for compliance: "Five-two, I don't hear the guns yet, what's the hold up, over?" And then: "Where the hell is the fire power you were supposed to have five minutes ago? Do we need to come up there and do it ourselves?" and so on.

I loved my job. The radio was a powerful tool. It all worked fine. It always worked. You just pictured the situation in your head and then moved the troops around and made them do what you needed them to do. It always worked!

The next part of our CP was the "Mule", the biggest guy in our company. He carried the scrambler which was a forty pound radio of sorts that hooked up to the Battalion radio (Brian's). Through this set up, you could talk to Battalion and tell them anything you liked because the communications were scrambled into 36 different frequencies and unscrambled on the other end. The Mule's sole job was to carry that device.

Then we had the medic, Doc Johnson, but he left in May. He was replaced by another fellow (Richard Belanger) who was not as fun as Doc Johnson but a nice guy all the same.

The Executive Officer, or the XO, operated in the rear. He ran all of the logistics for our company. We rarely saw him.

The first Sergeant was also in the rear. He recruited for us and also took care of logistics.

Last, but not least was the Supply Sergeant. His name was "Epstein". It was not his real name – we gave it to him because he was as good a Jew as any when it came to bartering. He was also in the rear and he took good care of all of our gear and got us the impossible when it was needed.

We got a new Supply Sergeant when "Epstein" was promoted to battalion. The new guy was a slacker. We called him "Ghost" because he was invisible most of the time and hard to contact. He was a camouflaged hole and we realized how good Epstein had truly been. Now, equipment was not being cared for and what had been possible was now the impossible.

One day one of our machine gunners, Gerald Porter reported that he had a broken M-60. We sent it back to Ghost to get fixed. It came back three days later (after a lot of calling to find out what the holdup was).

It finally came back with a note saying that it was fixed and worked fine.

The following day, the first platoon was ambushed. Porter set up his "repaired" pig and opened up with twenty rounds, announcing to the NVA that he had an M-60. Then it jammed.

The NVA responded, pouring fire into his position, and Porter was killed.

Captain Dunagan was really pissed. He ordered the Ghost out to where we were. When the Ghost arrived, the Captain asked him point blank if he worked on that gun.

The Ghost told the Captain that he had, in fact, worked on the gun, and that it worked fine when he tested it.

It was more than obvious to those present (including me) that the lazy-assed bastard was lying.

Ghost started to blame Porter for not taking care of the gun and said that was why it failed.

Captain Dunagan became even more infuriated at that and screamed at him, called him a lying son of a bitch.

Ghost said that he did not find anything at all wrong with it other than it was dirty, and that he cleaned it and there was nothing wrong with it.

"Good," Captain Dunagan said, "then pick it up and walk point with it."

Ghost was stunned and told the Captain that it was not his job. Clearly, he had no idea where he was and got a rifle butt upside the head from yours truly to re-enforce the Captain's order. Ghost had the nads to tell me to go fuck myself. I gave

Vietnam – The Teenage Wasteland

him another shot to his solar plexus to remind him where he was.

Again, the Captain told him to pick up the gun and when he didn't pick it up fast enough, Brian moved him a little faster with a swift kick in the ass.

Ghost reluctantly picked up the machine gun and started walking. He finally realized where he was. He also learned to keep his mouth shut.

We put him on watch at night in case he tried something foolish.

At the end of the third day, Ghost shot himself in the foot and was sent back to the rear and then on to LBJ (Lon Bien Jail).

We got Epstein back and all went well again.

Our CP was a formidable group, we kept things running smoothly and we always kicked ass. Whenever we got into a firefight I maneuvered the platoons according to the Captain's orders and our troops always decimated whatever we came across and with minimal casualties on our side. Under Dunagan's leadership, we were a smooth, well-oiled fighting machine that never lost a fight, big or small. We always maintained the upper hand.

However, all good things come to an end, eventually.

16

MAY 1969

"... from this day until the ending of the world but we in it shall be remembered. We few, we happy few, we band of brothers. For he today who sheds his blood with me shall be my brother."

Shakespeare

By now we were all seasoned combat vets. We had seen a lot of action and were used to being shot at or ambushed and we always came out smelling like roses. We had an excellent team that just seemed to work well under any circumstance. We were fearless and competent. We were a formidable fighting unit, and as if to prove our sand the enemy put up "wanted posters" for Alpha company even placed bounties on us. They didn't scare us. Far from it; we felt like celebrities because it meant we were the bad asses of the neighborhood.

On May 2nd, our company was travelling to the Hill for our week of security duty. We were two klicks from the Hill, walking through a small basin with hills on all sides, excited to get up to the hill for a much deserved rest.

Our CP group (The Captain, myself and the rest of the Command Post) were right in the middle of the basin when two machine guns and a whole bunch of AK-47's opened up on us from the surrounding hills. We all went down in a hail

Vietnam – The Teenage Wasteland

of bullets. The NVA had waited until they saw two radios together (which signified a CP) and opened up with everything they had, bullets flying everywhere.

Once we'd gone to ground, they zeroed in on me and the other RTO to shut down the radios. I was in grass two feet high trying desperately to hide from the raking gunfire.

"Do I move or do I stay? Should I move to where they've already shot or will they keep shooting at that spot? Are they about to fire at my current position or not? Is their fire accurate? These questions and others like them rolled through my mind faster than the fastest computer ever made, but I was alive right now and that was because I hadn't moved, so I decided to stay put. Don't ask me how I came to that decision, because I don't know.

The NVA gunners were still raking my position and bullets hit all around me. I played dead and it seemed to work.

They went after Captain Dunagan and raked his ass but good. He was writhing around yelling at me to get helicopter gunships in to silence the "god dammed machine guns". So I dropped my act of being dead and got on the radio.

Brian was on R&R, so I was carrying the Battalion radio. I got my handset out and started calling the rear for the gun ships. No dice, my antenna was parallel to the ground, and we were in a basin surrounded by hills. The only solution was to raise my radio antenna. But that meant signaling the NVA gunners that I was alive and calling for help, and they weren't going to be too excited about that. But you gotta do what you gotta do. So, I raised my antenna and put out a call.

The NVA machine gunners saw my antenna sticking out of the grass and came after me again. I actually ate dirt from the bullets hitting right in front of my face.

I rolled five meters to my right and ran into the Captain. He told me to get the fuck away from him because I was drawing fire. He took off, crawling toward the wood line at the end of the basin, and I was left out there alone.

I got a hold of artillery and gave them coordinates for some rounds to hush the machine guns. They served up a salvo but the arty was off target.

Battalion got a hold of the Firebirds – the chopper gun-ship people. They called me and said they were on their way – ETA ten minutes. Ten minutes is an eternity in a fire fight.

I was rolling all over the place to get away from the raking machine gun fire and finally rolled behind a dry paddy dike where one of our machine guns was set up and was returning fire. I saw more rounds hitting around us and then the assistant gunner landed on top of me. I pushed him off me.

His mouth and his eyes were wide open. I could see he was trying to scream at the top of his lungs, but nothing was coming out. I saw blood on his arm and investigated. His elbow had been blown out by a bullet. It made me wince because I imagined it hurt more than anything in the world. The poor guy was just trying to scream, and he couldn't. I figured his arm was a loss, so I put a tourniquet on it and then gave him a shot of morphine (I always carried 2 shots of morphine on me, just in case I needed it). I watched him after I gave the shot but nothing happened. He was shaking as waves of pain racked him, and he was still trying to scream, so I gave him another shot. The second shot took, and he let out a long, loud howling scream. Then he lay down and stared at the sky. I asked him if he was okay, and he nodded at me. I asked him if the pain was gone, and he shook his head, no. I asked him if he gave a shit if it hurt, and he said, "No". At least he was in a good place.

I left him and tried to cross the open area again, but again, the machine gun opened up on me.

The gunships finally came on station. I vectored them onto the enemy machine guns. They rolled in and opened up.

At first I was a little relieved, but when I saw Firebird One open up on our guys, I was horrified. I called up to him right away and told him to cease fire.

Vietnam – The Teenage Wasteland

They backed off and went back up to orbit, and I could hear screams for "Medic!" from the men that had fallen.

I called Firebird One and asked him why he opened up on an American platoon. The idiot pilot radioed back to me that he saw soldiers in the open and figured them for NVA. I told them to break off and go home. Last thing I needed right then was a bunch of idiots working against us.

It turned out Firebird One wounded five men from the 1st platoon. None were hurt badly enough to be critical, but they were out of action. The fact that the gunships showed up chased the bad guys away. So I didn't need them anyway.

I called in the Medivac chopper. We had four seriously wounded and five others wounded less seriously but they needed to go to the hospital for treatment before being returned to us. The NVA had wounded four while the Firebirds got five.

When the wounded were evacuated we continued on our way up to the Hill.

The incident set us up for a bad next month because it left us nine men short, and they were all good men. Two were platoon sergeants and one was the RTO for the 3rd platoon. The ambush should have been a lot worse than it turned out. In one way we were very lucky to have only a few wounded. But it left us handicapped with the loss of the two sergeants and the RTO which set us up for a real situation later on.

That was the time we got the new medic. A nice boy from Massachusetts named Richard Ballenger. He was a little overwhelmed by the antics of the guys and how wild we were. We also got five new greenies but that was it. We lost another five to R&R and another five to various medical situations. It seemed four of the five suddenly had hemorrhoids. That was a good one; once you had your hemorrhoids taken out it took four to six weeks to heal. That meant six weeks in the rear, away from the action (no pun intended). I guess the pain was worth it to some. Anyway, those particular four were a pain in my ass anyhow.

After our week on the Hill we were ready to go back out into the field. But we had to leave three more of our best warriors on the hill to pull some sort of PR duty. So with the wounded from the previous week, the R&R people, the medical and hemorrhoid people as well as the warriors off on PR duty, we were severely shorthanded when we left LZ Professional for out next duty assignment.

Just before we left we received a briefing that we were going to go where none of our battalion had gone before, some fourteen miles away to the south-west.

After being choppered east, down to the end of Death Valley, we humped south, crossed a thirty-five hundred foot high mountain range and strode down into the valley on the other side.

We arrived in the valley with the Captain walking point, me and Brian (just back from R&R) behind him. Scouting here and there we began to see signs of large amounts of NVA in the area. The signs were trodden paths, trash, old camps where they stayed for the night and so forth.

Having crossed a valley that was four kilometers wide we were just about on the other side when suddenly we ran into someone wearing white PJs and sporting an AK-47. Brian nailed his ass and he went down, but then got up and ran to the wood line at the base of another five thousand foot mountain.

We chased him but held up a hundred meters short of the wood line. You never fall for stuff like that twice. We fired a few rounds of machine gun into the woods and the whole wood line opened up on us so we retreated and reported in.

Intelligence came on the radio and told us they were sure this was the 3rd NVA Regiment and wanted us to pull back and put an "Arc-light" air strike on the mountain (in other words a B-52 strike). We were to move four kilometers back from the strike, but our position should be on high ground where we could observe it.

Vietnam – The Teenage Wasteland

We went back up to the top of the mountain we had earlier crossed and set up a beam above the target with a special radio apparatus that was brought out to us.

We waited to see the strike but waited for nothing. We waited and waited. It became dark. At around 10:00 at night, we heard what sounded like a woman screaming. Then we heard several women screaming and saw flashes in the area where the targeted mountain was.

The "women screaming" were thousand pound bombs falling from B-52's from 35,000 ft. The bombs fell and fell, and I am here to tell you that the ground shook from the pounding of 200 seven-hundred and fifty-pound bombs with delayed fuses. The shaking went on for ten minutes before it finally stopped. It was most impressive and I started feeling sorry for the bad guys who were on the receiving end of unleashed hell.

The next morning we walked, ever so cautiously, back to the target area to investigate the Air Forces' crime scene.

I call it a crime scene because the air strike missed the mountain entirely. The bombs landed in the valley two kilometers east, and took out a small village of about fifty men, women and children. The only thing left in the churned up ground was a human arm sticking out.

We were all grossed out. Brian called in the crime to battalion and he was not kind in his estimation of the incompetence and carelessness of the air crews and their mission. There was absolutely no need for this "collateral damage".

Calling another Arc-light was out of the question, so we were ordered to go in and investigate. We were wary of the NVA on the mountain and its surrounding hills. They knew we were onto them. We were outnumbered by more than ten to one and did not want to walk into a meat-grinder. We called a regular, controlled air strike on the mountain and called in a battalion of South Vietnamese Rangers to go up there in front of us.

The ARVN Rangers were flown in and went up the mountain. They made it half way up when they were caught in hellish crossfire. They came running down at half strength screaming and yelling. They also left their weapons up top. We shot at their feet and forced them back up to collect their weapons, dead and wounded. They went back up but came back down without any weapons, radios or anything, and they were now at one quarter strength. For all intents and purposes they were wiped out. Think of three hundred of them lying up there dead and/or wounded and a battalion of weapons lying up there as well. It was a big flap.

We got the remaining ARVN rangers out of there on choppers and sent Bravo Company up there to scout it out. They too ran into heavy, heavy gun fire, including several .50 caliber machine guns with two killed right away. They came back down.

We sat and considered how to crack the egg.

The Regiment of NVA was probably fifteen hundred or so. That sized group was easy to decimate for us because all we had to do was find them, stay at arm's length, put artillery on their location and then mop them up with air strikes. But no one had come close enough to the main body of NVA to get accurate ranges on them.

Captain Dunagan went into a twenty minute meditation with his map and then called Battalion. He talked to Colonel Uphill and they hatched a plan. The Colonel ordered Bravo Company back to the Valley of Death to act as a screen along with the other companies there in case we were unable to contain the NVA Regiment.

Meanwhile, my company moved to a hill directly across from the mountain the 3rd NVA Regiment was on and Captain Dunagan told Brian he wanted air strikes on that mountain for the rest of the day and to pound it into dust.

Brian and I both got on our radios, starting around ten thirty in the morning.

Vietnam – The Teenage Wasteland

We got our first sortie fifteen minutes later. (A sortie is a flight of 4 jet fighter-bombers). We vectored them onto the top of the mountain and to work their way down, pounding it area by area. They slammed the mountain with five hundred pound bombs with delayed fuses but nothing happened. The bombs exploded but there were no secondary explosions or other evidence of any damage inflicted on the enemy. The air strike departed.

Brian called in another but the BDA (Bomb Damage Assessment) was the same. Nothing.

This went on for the next three hours. Ten sorties were flown using bunker-busting five hundred pounders but all we got on the mountain was churned up earth.

Right around 1:30 PM, I had an idea. I remembered seeing huge rockets on twin launchers back in Chu Lai. I knew they were for tactical purposes and were most likely ready to launch with small nukes on them, but I also knew they could carry 3,000 pound explosive warheads that made a very big bang. They belonged to the Air Force, so it would not be an easy sell.

I jumped on the radio a little after 13:30 hours and started hammering the Air Force for a few of them. I worked for two hours and was told they were being saved for emergencies, they cost too much, they were not meant for the use I intended and other excuses, but I finally got them thinking when I said the rockets had probably been sitting there forever and needed to be changed out, anyway. I was told I had a point there; they would get back to me.

Around five o'clock in the afternoon we got a call from battalion that the Air Force was going to give us some of their rockets. We were thrilled. Brian cancelled any aircraft flying within ten miles of the area and told battalion to keep everyone away because major fireworks were about to commence. Ten minutes later we got a "heads up" from the USAF for "incoming missiles."

We all got up and watched but saw nothing but four streaks, smoke trails that suddenly appeared and heard four loud cracks (sonic booms). But a few seconds later there was a thundering explosion on the side of the hill. It was spectacular. The rockets came in at Mach 3 and just plowed into the side of that mountain with 3,000 pounds of explosives each, almost simultaneously.

After the dust and smoke cleared, we saw four sizable craters in the side of the mountain. But there was nothing else to report. Another disappointment.

We called the Marines and had them send more sorties of bombers out to continue the onslaught. The South Vietnamese Army even flew a sortie of old Navy propeller "Hell Divers" that dropped thousand-pound block-busters, but to no effect.

It was starting to get late, the sun was moving below the mountains. We got a call from Battalion that told us we had used up almost twenty sorties, an ungodly amount of bombs and had nothing to show for it.

Captain Dunagan was not pleased. He gave us both a talking to. "Alright guys, we have to come up with something, or we are going up that mountain to do the job ourselves. So figure something out. Top brass is pissed at us for spending so much money for nothing. Get on it and get bright."

I got up and put my binoculars on the site. A sortie was heading in and we needed to use them to make something happen. I looked over the mountain and saw a large outcropping of rock. I pointed it out to Brian, and he thought it might work so called the bombers as they were rolling in and had them target the rock. They delivered the goods right on it but after 24 bombs they were "Winchester" (out of bombs and down to their pistols only) and went away.

It was now twilight and we were told we had one more sortie for the day and that was it.

All of a sudden the rock outcropping gave way and the whole side of the mountain started sliding; a massive landslide that shook the earth.

Vietnam – The Teenage Wasteland

We yelled to the Captain and he looked through his binoculars. The whole side of the mountain was in avalanche leaving dozens of exposed tunnels behind. It was overwhelming to see the length and intricacy of the tunnels complete with strung lighting. The amount of work and trouble they must have gone to build … the next thought was "There must be a shit-load of NVA in there!"

Brian quickly called the next sortie and told them to bring napalm only.

They came supersonic and when they arrived they too were astonished at the sight they saw and dropped napalm on the tunnels with deadly accuracy. We actually saw people running out of the tunnels, on fire. It was a ghastly sight.

It finally got dark, the jets had long since left and things settled down. After we set up camp some of us sat around talking and figured we hurt that Regiment of NVA bad, real bad. We were giving out a lot of congrats to one another.

We then got a radio message from our intelligence officer at LZ Professional that none of us will ever forget. "Do not, repeat do not transmit by radio from this point on. Your air strikes knocked out the NVA upper echelon of radio communication, enabling us to find out that this is not the 3rd NVA Regiment, but the 2nd NVA Division. They are actively looking for you, have triangulated you and are moving in on your position now – do not, repeat do not communicate by radio. Use only clicks from here on out. Evacuation Plan Four. Repeat – Evacuation Plan Four NOW! God speed. Out."

There are four evacuation plans for infantry in the field:

EP 1: Orderly, pre-planned evacuation.
EP 2: Immediate evacuation. Fast planning, fast evac.
EP 3: Immediate Retreat
EP 4: Run for your lives in any direction.

We just got an EP 4! My hair was standing on end. Thousands of NVA were looking for us and wanted to get a little more than even for the air strikes.

Captain Dunagan was visibly shaken as he got out his map and ordered me to get the platoon leaders together ASAP. I went to get them, and as I rounded them up, I told the other RTOs not to use their radios – only reply to mine with clicks (one click means "okay" or "yes" two clicks means "no" or "not okay").

When I returned with the platoon leaders, Dunagan showed them the map. He didn't mince his words but told them the superior force of NVA were going to try to prevent us getting back to LZ Professional, cut off our retreat and wipe us out. He said there were two ways out of our current location, one was back across the mountain trails we came along, and the other was down along a river that would take us back to our valley.

Lt Edwards pointed out that the river had straight cliffs in places along its sides and there was nowhere to hide along the river. He said that if we got caught there it would be like shooting fish in a barrel.

Dunagan agreed and pointed out that it would be pretty stupid for anyone to try it, that's why we were going to go that way. He said we would never make it back across the mountain anyway, the NVA were likely already up there in force, waiting for us. He ordered the platoon leaders to get everyone to camouflage their faces and hands with dark camo paint and to tape up anything that rattled. We were moving out in ten minutes and had to move with stealth.

We all taped up our sling hinges and anything else that could make noise and moved out.

There was a half moon and partly cloudy skies. A half-moon was still a lot of light as we tip-toed the five miles through that river canyon. We moved about ten feet every minute and made sure we made not one sound because one click of a rifle butt or one jingle of a sling swivel would cause

Vietnam – The Teenage Wasteland

the death of a hundred dead men. Luckily, it was mostly cloudy that night. But whenever the clouds broke and the moon shone through, we hunkered down and pretended to be rocks, not moving an inch, and we stayed that way until the moon went back into the clouds. We moved that way for the rest of the night: one step, stop and freeze. Take another step, stop and freeze. Moon out, hunker down and freeze – look like a rock. All the way like that, all the way down that canyon. It was stressful, physically and mentally.

12 MAY

Dawn came just as the company point element (Captain Dunagan, Brian and then me) broke into the Valley of Death. We were now twelve clicks from LZ Professional.

We walked out of the mouth of the river canyon and into a field, careful to hang close to foliage and not out in the open. The Captain walked around the side of the clearing. Brian followed him. I took the cue and went in the opposite direction. The rest of the company split up and followed both ranks, skirting the clearing on opposite sides. As we got to the end of the clearing, the Captain motioned for everyone to get down and get out of sight. With intensity, he scanned the valley that lay ahead of us. As he did, I heard some choppers above. I turned to their frequency, and immediately heard chatter between them.

"Look – there's a bunch on the right side over there. See them Red Knight?"

"Roger 69 and they're headed for LZ Pro. I've never seen anything like it before. They just look up at us and wave, over."

"Red Knight, let's RTB and regroup there, over."

"Copy 69, out."

Alarmed, I decided to use the radio and cut in: "Ah, Red Knight, this is Ashcan five-zero Juliet, ah where did you see the bad guys, over?"

"Ashcan, uh, hah – they are – uh, everywhere, they're headed towards LZ Pro by the thousands. Looks like it's going to be a busy night for the boys at Pro, over."

I thought maybe I misheard him when he said *by the thousands*. "Ah, got it Red Knight, can you give me an estimate of how many on the ground? Over."

"Uh, Ashcan, I have seen at least two thousand. They were just walking in the open. Back a ways; we saw another thousand or so. They normally hide whenever we come around but this morning they are just waving at us. Some of them actually flipped us the bird. Ah, overall I would guestimate five or six thousand down there, over."

I was stunned. Brian and I looked at each other. The Captain shook his head. My skin crawled at the thought of us, less than a hundred Americans, sitting out in the open with five or six thousand NVA all around.

Red Knight brought me back, "Copy, Ashcan?"

"Ah, roger Red Knight, that's a lot, over."

"Roger Ashcan, are you ground pounders, over?"

"Roger."

"Copy that. If I were you guys, I would find a hole and hide in it. Copy?"

"Roger, Red Knight. Thanks. Over."

"Good luck, men. And God Bless. Out."

I wished with all my heart I was on that chopper at two thousand feet, away from harm.

Captain Dunagan was studying his map, working it out. I knew he was up for whatever the day had in store for us. I knew what he was thinking: we have to make it to the LZ Pro, no matter what. The LZ was our island of safety, where we could make a stand. Out here in the open, we were alone. Sanctity was on the Hill with friendly forces. The higher our number, the better the chances.

Dunagan looked at me and Brian and spoke, evenly. "I know this looks bad guys, but we are going to make it to the Hill. I need you guys to perform like never before. Speak

Vietnam – The Teenage Wasteland

clearly and give succinct orders and get them carried out no matter what. We need the rest of the men in the Company performing flawlessly, and it is up to us to get them to do that. Rog?"

"Rog, Sir," we answered, in unison.

"Alright." He pointed at the map. "We're going to cross the valley to the northern side, move through the wood line at the base of the mountains and work our way to the Hill. We need to avoid contact. It seems the NVA are moving down the Burlington trail on the south side of the valley. So we'll tool on the north side. The going will be a lot tougher, but we need to avoid contact. In all likelihood, we'll not be able to avoid all contact, but it will be less over there. Now, the NVA have radios, and if we get into contact, they'll try to surround us. If they do that will be our end. The secret is to avoid contact, and if we can't, fight only long enough to get the upper hand, then break off and move as fast as we can to the east, toward the Hill. Copy?"

We both nodded.

"Good. We'll stay in single-file and move across the valley one at a time, but we move fast. Tom, brief the platoon leaders and then get them going. Brian, find out about air support but use the radios as little as possible. Let's get busy living guys. Let's go!"

The Valley of Death was long but thin, no more than a hundred meters across in some places, north to south, with LZ Pro at the far eastern end. We were coming from the west.

I found the first platoon leader, briefed him and sent him and his men on their way, moving single file. I briefed the rest of the platoon leaders on the plan. They all got it and started out.

Catching up with the Captain, I stepped in alongside. Dunagan was moving ahead cautiously but as fast as he could. We were all alert.

About an hour later, we were across the valley and moving along its northern side when we came across a knoll. We crept up it and saw around twenty five NVA ahead of us, all talking together with their weapons slung over their shoulders as if they were in downtown Hanoi.

We might have made it past them, but if we didn't, if only part of us made it past, they'd be in amongst us and carve us up. The only option was to cut them up now. We wanted to avoid contact but they were right across our path and that many NVA in the open was impossible to get around with any chance of success.

Dunagan had me bring up Sgt. Kirby with his machine gunner and the rest of us got ready with our '16's. We aimed up the knoll and fired on them.

As I was shooting I saw the rounds plucking at them, they were trying to get away from the swarm of bullets buzzing around them and chopping them down and were running into each other.

We dropped them all, and then we took off running east.

We hit them but good and sent twenty or more off to Nirvana. It was a good first jab to the ribs of the NVA. That was the good thing. The bad thing was that they now knew we were there in the valley.

Brian was still trying to get an answer from Battalion about air support. So far, the answer was that there was nothing available. Both the Marine fighter-bombers and the Army helicopter gunships were claiming "maintenance problems" or that they were "assessing the situation" and would "get back to us" when they had "taken stock of the situation."

To me it was nuts because why the hell did they think they were in Vietnam, to be safe? They needed to get jets and choppers out now to attack and decimate the bad guys before they organized and got into position to do some real damage. So what if they lost a couple of jets or choppers? No "assessing the situation" was needed. There were thousands of targets of opportunity. If they flew over the area at twenty thousand feet and blindly dropped bombs, they would get plenty of bodies bagged for their statistics. Plus, our company was about to go down and probably the whole battalion – no way could our battalion hold off six thousand enemy troops without air support. No way. It really jerked my ass that they lagged like this. What the hell?

But the real problem that nagged us all was how the hell were we going to move a hundred men all the way along the valley to LZ Pro without being seen? It was impossible. We knew it was going to be a daunting task – especially now we had loudly announced our presence in the valley.

The Captain finally decided to move out, and we took off ever so cautiously. It was around nine thirty in the morning and we made just a hundred meters before we were found out.

A large contingent of NVA hit us on our flanks with small arms fire. The Captain was ready for it and gave the orders. I maneuvered the first platoon and third platoon in a pincer on the ambush. It worked and we rebuffed them. I immediately pulled them off, and we boogied to the east again, on the run. We were lucky because we only got a few minor wounds in that skirmish.

We moved another couple hundred meters east when the valley narrowed, so we stopped. The Captain decided to move us all across to the south side of the valley where the majority of the NVA had been spotted. He knew they'd now be looking for us on the north side.

We crossed the valley without incident and holed up while we watched the valley floor.

It turned out the Captain made a good call because the NVA were now moving on the north side of the valley, the side we just came from. They were in large numbers, looking for us. We called artillery on them and made them pay.

Since the north to south maneuver worked, the Captain figured it would work again, that the NVA would now move south to search for us so we should move to the north side again.

Lt Edwards and the 2nd platoon were the point platoon, strung out, single file, heading north across an open area of the valley when they got into trouble. They were rumbling with a company sized unit of NVA. It was not good. The rest of us moved across, got behind the NVA and poured a ton of small arms fire on them. It worked. They broke off and moved north, out of the valley and into the hills.

We moved east.

Once again, The Captain had us hole up and wait. It wasn't but fifteen minutes later when Lt Waltz (Recon platoon, Echo Company) called us and told us he was ordered by Command to hook up with us. He was on the south side of the valley with his platoon of eighteen men.

We told him to come across, and they got half way across when they got ambushed by a contingent of NVA hiding in spider holes. We tried to help them, but the NVA were between us, and we ended up in a vicious cross-fire. So we had to use hand grenades. We threw them in the spider holes and took out the NVA that way.

Dave came over to meet with us. We were in the open, greeting each other when I looked behind Dave and saw a bunch of bushes I didn't remember seeing before. They were around seventy five meters to the south.

I raised my rifle and shot a bush, and it fell over. I shot another one and it fell over. Then Captain Dunagan and Lt Waltz joined me and started shooting the bushes and toppled a bunch of them. It was a turkey shoot.

I stepped aside from the others a short distance to get a better angle. I aimed at a bush, but before I could get off a shot it exploded and I saw that friggin black dot with that friggin' orange halo around it coming right at me. I swear that RPG roared over my helmet by a few inches because I could feel the heat from the rocket as it went over.

It hit a tree twenty feet behind me. The explosion knocked me flat on my face. It knocked me silly. Dave shot the perpetrator and then picked me up. I was shaken up but I was okay.

Vietnam – The Teenage Wasteland

I picked up my helmet and saw that it had a big crease down the middle of it from a piece of shrapnel. I was real lucky. Two days later I felt the back of my head itching and when I scratched it, my hand came back with blood all over it. Turns out I had a shit load of pepper shrapnel in the back of my head from that rocket. Some infection set in and the medic treated me in the field, hence my purple heart.

We left the moving bushes and took off east. Dave and the rest of Recon went up ahead of Alpha to scout the terrain.

It was getting on to five o'clock, and it was time to find a place to hole up for the night. We walked to the north looking for a hill to settle in when the NVA hit us hard on our west flank. Then more NVA moved in on us and hit us from the east as well.

The firefight was severe and we started taking casualties. This time they threw a lot of rockets and machine gun fire right into our perimeter.

Billy Lutz was killed by an RPG and we had several more severely wounded. We finally disengaged and moved further north and then went straight south into the valley, carrying our dead and wounded with us.

Things were getting serious and our men were starting to get scared. They knew we were being chased by a superior force but we hadn't told the platoon leaders about it being seven thousand NVA; we didn't want to give out that much bad news. But by now, the men were starting to understand the gravity of the situation and were freaking out.

We got a chopper in quickly and got poor Billy Lutz and the wounded out of there. James Sowers died that night in the hospital.

We took off again, looking for a place to spend the night. We decided against going into the hills because the NVA would be waiting for us there. They knew that American doctrine was to find high ground for the night so all they had to do was wait for us in the hills.

We walked on for another hundred meters and found ourselves in five foot high elephant grass. Captain Dunagan decided it was a good place to hide for the night. No one in their right mind would attack or try to maneuver in grass that high, so it seemed like a good plan.

I spread the word for everyone not to dig but to just keep quiet for the night, no smoking, no eating, no nothing, just lie down and be quiet.

It was a great call because we were quite safe in the tall grass and for the first time in what seemed like weeks (but I knew was forty-eight hours), we were at peace. I sat down to enjoy the quiet.

LZ Professional – 21:00 Hrs.

Echo Company is the weapons company of the 1st of the 46th otherwise known as the Battalion Combat Support Company and was permanently assigned to LZ Professional. Echo maintained the 80mm mortars, the 4.2 (Four-Duce) mortars, Ground Surveillance Radar Section, the 106mm Recoilless Rifle as well as rifle defense of the LZ. Recon was also a platoon of Echo Company.

The following occurred on LZ Professional the night of 12 May 1969 while we were hiding out in the elephant grass. This account was told to me by survivor, Norm Ellis.

Just after 21:00 hours, Specialist Fourth Class Norm Ellis was awake and ready to pull his shift on the bunker line security. He headed for bunker seven on the south side of the hill to relieve Specialist 4th Class, Jackie Owens. When Norm got to the bunker he found Jackie peering intently into the Starlight Scope that was mounted on a tripod...

Norm climbed up on the bunker and lay next to Jackie. "What's up man?"

"We got Dinks in the wire, man," Jackie announced, not taking his attention off of the scope.

Vietnam – The Teenage Wasteland

"How many?"

An illumination round lit up above them and blinded Jackie. He pulled back from the scope: "Can't tell, I can see a few of them humped down in the grass between the concertina wire, but every time we pop an illumination round out of the mortar tube, they duck down before it ignites. It washes out the scope too."

Norm peered through the scope as soon as the illumination round burned out before another one popped out of the mortar tube. He could see several "humped" shapes in the green lit landscape.

The next illumination round lit under its parachute, lighting up the hillside and washing out the scope screen, again.

After the round burned out it took up to two minutes for the Starlight scope to come back on line from the washout. Just as it came back on line another illumination round would flare and the scope would wash out again.

Jackie made the call and put the whole of the hill on red alert. Everyone was up and ready for action.

Norm sat there watching. He and Jackie figured out that the NVA were following the rhythm of the illumination rounds fired from the tube. As soon as the NVA sappers heard a round shoot out of the tube, they moved up the hill and hid just before the round lit in the air.

Norm had an idea. He called the Fire Direction Control officer and asked him to fire two rounds exactly at the same time. The first illumination round to go up on its usual shallow arc, ignite and then flare for a minute. The second round fired to go a lot higher so it began to illuminate just as the first one died out. That way they would use the rhythm against the sappers and the second round would ignite just as the sappers made their move.

The FDC officer said they would try it.

The two rounds went at the same time and sounded like one tube firing. The first round went up a hundred feet, ignited and lit up the landscape.

Norm and Jackie had a case of hand grenades in front of them ready to toss, pins pulled on the ones in their hands.

The first round burned out just as the second round fell from a thousand feet and ignited right on time, washing the hillside in brilliant light.

Standing right in front of Norm and Jackie's position were dozens of NVA, frozen like deer in the headlights. Busted! Behind the now exposed NVA were dozens more enemy that had been working their way through the wire and were now scrambling for cover.

The men on the bunker line started chucking their grenades while the mortars pumped out more and more illumination rounds to keep the fire zone lit up like Hollywood Boulevard on a Friday night.

The NVA were trapped between rows of razor-sharp concertina wire and were dancing in the wire as the grenades exploded all around them and rifle fire cut them down.

The bunker line had a field day. The NVA were either dead or hanging on the wire, their bodies jolting from the concussion every time a grenade went off near them.

The first wave of the attack was thwarted due to the ingenuity of Norm and Jackie. But there were more NVA further down the hill, bent on following through with the attack, and they started working their way through the eight rows of wire.

An air strike was called and while the jets were on their way, the troops on the hill threw flares down the slope from the bunker line, in a straight line. It was like a neon sign pointing to where the NVA were, enabling the Phantom pilots to see the location of the enemy with ease.

The jets, guided by the flares, dropped deadly napalm at the base of the hill so it washed upwards toward the bunker line.

Vietnam – The Teenage Wasteland

A tidal wave of liquid fire engulfed the remaining enemy before they had a chance to get through the wire.

As Norm put it: "It was beautiful! The napalm rolled up the hill like a wave. I marveled at the beauty of it. For the rest of the night, we were gazing at imaginary shadows because we had killed everything in sight."

The Hill was quiet, for now, but the men of Echo Company remained on red alert. They knew more was to come.

<u>Alpha Company in the grass – 0200 Hrs 13 May</u>

About two o'clock in the morning I was monitoring the radio from the other companies. Everything seemed quiet. I listened to Echo Company on the hill and watched the air strike and figured they had thwarted the sappers and probably discouraged the massive attack they had planned.

The NVA were probably regrouping and figuring out what to do. Their attack was obviously in stages: first sappers with satchel charges to blow up key defenses on the hill's perimeter and then mount a major attack and take the hill. With the sappers eliminated, they would have to change their plans.

I was musing on this with Captain Dunagan when static suddenly took the place of a report coming in from Bravo Company. They were just to the south of us up in the mountains. The static went on for a minute and then it was replaced by music – the organ solo from *In A Gadda Da Vida* by Iron Butterfly. I automatically changed the radio to the alternate frequency but the alternate frequency was playing the same thing. In fact, as I spun the frequency wheel, I found that every channel on my radio had the same thing. The hair on the nape of my neck went up as I realized we were being jammed.

There were few times I have been as scared as that. You have to play the organ solo of *In A Gadda Da Vida* in pitch-black dark to understand. It will scare the shit out of you in the dark of your own bedroom. Find it and listen to it.

The solo was looped and went on for five minutes, and then it stopped. It was replaced with another twenty seconds of an organ death dirge and then a voice screamed out "YANKEE – YOU DIIIIEEEE!"

I saw flashes way off in the south-west as several NVA rockets were launched toward LZ Professional, landing right in the middle of the Hill exploding with magnificent force. More rockets rained down. You could see RPG rounds going up the hill as well as B-40 rockets rain down on LZ Pro. The bombardment lasted for more than twenty minutes.

LZ Professional – 02:13

Dick Pils, Commanding Officer of Echo Company, suspected the Hill was going to be hit that night. He had his riflemen up and trained on the perimeter. His four-duce mortars were pumping out round after round of high-explosive mortar shells, landing them in the rows of concertina wire further down, near the base of the Hill.

The men manning the eighty millimeter mortars were busy providing illumination.

Reports were coming from all sides of the Hill and they were all the same, "dinks in the wire."

The FDCs of the eighty millimeter and four-duce mortars were trying to keep up with the demand for fire.

Enemy rockets were pouring in and the hill started to sustain casualties and severe damage from incoming shells and recoilless fire.

All four B Battery 155mm cannons were immediately manned and started to return fire at hill 899, the source of the enemy recoilless and rocket fire. They lost two of their 155mm cannons in the very next volley from the enemy recoilless rifle. They lost two of their 105mm cannons shortly afterwards. By the end of the night they had no cannons left operational.

Vietnam – The Teenage Wasteland

The same held true for the Echo Company gunners. They lost all of their four-duce mortars, their 106 recoilless sustained severe damage, and the quad-fifty was also knocked out.

By the end of the night the accuracy of the NVA gunners took out every weapon on LZ Professional that could be a threat to them. Afterwards, the NVA recoilless gunner shot at targets all over the Hill at will because there was nothing on the Hill to stop him – plus the cloud cover was right down on top of the LZ which made air support impossible.

The NVA recoilless gunner had a free pass and had what seemed like an unending supply of ammo, as he took his time aiming, firing and finally neutralizing the defensive and offensive capabilities of LZ Pro.

An hour later, the rockets and recoilless let up and the ground attack started. And no, back in those days, air strikes were not done in the dark unless the night was clear and the moon was out.

Back in the grass we watched the battle rage. We could see RPG rounds going up the Hill, green tracers going up the Hill on the West Side, and red tracers going down the Hill. It was a ghastly, nauseating sight. LZ Pro was taking a pounding. Delta Company was on the Hill for guard duty. I listened in on their radio as they were screaming for medics and calling for more support on the west side of the Hill. We witnessed large earth shattering explosions on the bunker line as sappers tossed twenty-five pound satchel charges into bunkers, blowing them to smithereens. Then we heard that the NVA had breached the west side of the bunker line and were in the perimeter.

It was unthinkable that the defense on LZ Pro was collapsing. Without LZ Professional we were orphans in the middle of no-where, and we would not last another day. In short, not only LZ Pro, but Alpha, Bravo and Charlie companies were just hours away from being annihilated.

The battle for LZ Pro raged on for the next two hours. The NVA, at one point, took over half the Hill. Echo, Delta and B Battery made a good goal-line stand with their small arms as the NVA threw everything they could at them. The infantry units on the hill were joined by the cooks, the clerks and everyone else who worked on that hill and those brave souls not only held LZ Pro, but pushed the NVA attack back down the hill. By dawn, it was announced that the Hill still held, while the jet fighters streaked in, in the early morning light and napalmed the west side of the hill, pushing the remaining bad guys all the way down to the valley floor. Those that didn't get fried by the jet fighters limped back to their staging area with their tails between their legs.

Colonel Uphill called out to the rest of the companies in the bush and announced to us that LZ Pro had stood up to the attack in grand style and that the American flag was still waving proudly. Even though it was a corny speech, my heart swelled with pride.

We knew the attack was designed to take the hill in one night, and they almost did, but our guys fought valiantly and held. I felt better about facing the next day because we still had our Hill. Crippled though it was, it was still the place we could go to and have some sort of unity for a coordinated defense.

Four of our guys had gone to LZ Pro two days prior. They were supposed to go from there to Chu Lai the next morning for some sort of ceremony but were caught up in the attack. One of them was killed by a rocket during the siege, Sgt. Michael Raymond Tucker. His was a real loss because he was our best platoon sergeant, a very brave individual who already had two purple hearts and a Bronze Star for gallantry. My friend, John Miner was with Tucker and was also hit during that attack. He spent the next eight months in hospitals being operated on and put back together. Their loss to us was critical. Both were excellent warriors and not having them over next few days was crippling.

Vietnam – The Teenage Wasteland

<u>Alpha Company – 13 May 1969, Saturday Morning.</u>

Captain Dunagan spent quite some time that morning checking with the rest of the companies who were also winding their way back to LZ Pro. They were in the mountains and pretty much out of harm's way. We asked them what they saw in the valley. They could not give us much data, but promised to keep their eyes open for us. Captain Dunagan wanted to be able to move on with as much Intel as he could gather.

We got a call from S-2 (intelligence) on the Hill. They wanted us to get to some specific coordinates a few klicks west of the Hill, and wanted us there by mid-afternoon.

It was an eight klick hump and in normal circumstances would have been a snap, but we knew we were going to have to fight our way there.

We set out again to the north side of the valley, skirting thin jungle, cutting some of the way. We only made three hundred meters when we walked right into a company of NVA.

We had a brisk and fierce firefight but broke contact as fast as we could and went around them, leaving Echo Company's Recon platoon behind to make the NVA think we stayed for the fight.

As soon as we were in the clear, the Recon platoon broke off and joined back up with us.

Brian was still trying to get air strikes and was told nothing was available to us and that resources were working with the 101st Airborne just to the north of us.

Why in the hell was our air support working with another Division? We found out later that Hamburger Hill was happening at the same time and because most of the reporters in our sector hung with the famous 101st, the show was sent there.

We asked for gun ship support, and we were told that they had already lost three gunships yesterday and were "re-evaluating the situation". We were also told that there were no cannons on LZ Pro that worked. So we were definitely on our own. This was significant because there was never a time, in the history of Vietnam warfare that an infantry company was out in the open without the support of artillery, bombers or helicopter gunships. We were going to engage heavy numbers of enemy without support, and would be doing so for the next few days. The thought of no support was not welcome and things were going to be tense if we got into more heavy contact.

We shook off the bad news and kept moving east. Brian was getting calls every fifteen minutes by S-2 wondering what our progress was on arriving at the coordinates we were given.

The Captain told S-2 we were moving but the going was tough, so they should just hang in there. The Captain wondered aloud why S-2 was busting our balls to get us to the coordinates.

Around noon we were in another firefight. We tried to disengage and run, but the NVA guessed our tactics and surrounded us. We got trapped, and were fighting our way out of it slowly but surely, but we were running low on ammo.

We called for an air strike, no go. Called for gunships; no go. Artillery was still no go.

We finally pretended we broke contact, and hid behind trees. The NVA came to investigate and we charged right through them and back out to the east.

This time though we had major casualties. We had seven or eight that were severely wounded. One fellow, who was lying next to me, got up to take a shot and took a round in the belly. He was a big boy from Nebraska, and he stood there in shock before I tackled him to the ground. I noticed the hole in his shirt, ripped it open and saw a perfect .30 caliber hole there in his belly. There was no blood and there was no exit wound.

I looked at him and said: "Good going Jones, you're going home."

I put a bandage on him and when the chopper came with more ammo, I put him on it myself, and made sure he made it out of there. He was still in shock and hadn't really come to grips with the fact that he had been shot. He would later.

When the re-supply chopper lands, it marks your position for everyone to see for miles around.

After we received ammo, we set out to put as much distance as possible between us and where the chopper landed.

We made it another kilometer east when we got into another firefight with heavy automatic and intense RPG fire hammering us. It was a company of NVA and from the intensity of the firepower coming at us we knew they had orders to finish us off and, as they had us pinned down, they called for their buddies to come help. And their buddies did come. They surrounded us and we were trapped again.

We fought on for the next hour and it was lucky we'd just gotten a fresh supply of ammo. But we were taking more casualties, and we needed to break contact fast. We were running out of ideas. The NVA was really on us and they were pouring it on.

The Captain was studying the map. It was around five o'clock in the afternoon, and it would be getting dark in an hour and a half.

Captain Dunagan decided to do what the NVA now wouldn't expect. He wanted to run right through them, to the north, run up into the hills and secure Hill 62 for the night's defense. He decided we should head for high ground that night to better defend ourselves.

We briefed all the platoons and jumped up and ran right through the enemy lines. The plan worked and we were in the hills and worked our way toward Hill 62.

We finally made it to the base of Hill 62. Echo Company's Recon platoon went up the hill with Alpha Company's first and second Platoons on their flanks. The third Platoon would guard an exit while the fourth Platoon would follow up the hill. It looked like we were going to have a place to stay for the night and it looked very defendable.

As Recon crested the hill, the NVA opened up on them from the front and from both sides. The NVA pulled the perfect "horseshoe" ambush on Recon and dropped them in their tracks.

The other two platoons fought to relieve Recon, but they also got trapped and started getting chopped up. Automatic gunfire was raining down on the platoons. RPG Rockets were exploding in and around them.

Dunagan was listening in as the platoons reported they were stalled on the side of the hill taking heavy casualties. He commanded me to get them to take the hill NOW.

I yelled at them to move up and take that hill. I pushed them hard, but the return fire from the top was too intense, and they remained stalled.

Recon platoon was taking cover behind trees as the NVA opened up on them with machine-gun, AK-47 and RPG fire. The enemy fire was intense. Recon was getting chopped to ribbons, so were the first and second platoons. They tried to disengage, but the fire from the enemy was so severe they had no chance.

As the NVA held the three platoons in check, another NVA unit moved in and closed the door behind us, attacking from the south. The fourth platoon got busy fending off that attack. Another good friend of mine, James Dye was killed there. At the same time Michael Blea was dragged down Hill 62 by the medic. He was also dead.

Recon platoon, or what was left of it, pulled their dead and wounded out and came back down the hill. The other two platoons followed them. Because we were trapped, we were burning ammo like never before. The NVA were coming right at us in suicide charges to use up our ammo. They were determined to finish us off right then and there. No artillery,

Vietnam – The Teenage Wasteland

no air support, no chopper gunships. Our asses were out on the line and no support whatsoever.

We got everyone in a tight perimeter at the base of the hill 62 and defended ourselves. Everyone was shooting their M-16's on automatic, downing dozens of NVA, but they kept coming and we were almost out of ammo again.

I saw Brian and he had no backpack. I asked him where his radio was but he couldn't answer me. He was dazed. Now we'd lost our Battalion command radio.

Dunagan told me to get ammo out to us now.

I rapidly switched frequencies and called Battalion at LZ Pro and told them to load a chopper up with ammo only, and drop it on us from five hundred feet – any chopper that landed here was going to be destroyed. I told them we needed ammo NOW! I also told them that they had to communicate to us through the company frequency because we'd lost our battalion radio.

Captain Paul Lukins was on the pad on LZ Pro with his Huey 1-HD chopper's engine running, waiting for the call. Battalion had been listening in and knew we were going to need ammo soon, so had the chopper loaded and waiting.

He took off right away and flew the seven kilometers to where we were in just minutes. He called in and asked what our situation was.

I told him we were heavily engaged, that the LZ was closed and to hover above us at 500 feet and drop the ammo.

He asked if we had any "criticals" (badly wounded troops).

I told him yes, but once again reminded him the LZ was closed. I put out an orange panel for him, so he could drop the ammo, but to my horror. he came right in on the panel. I yelled at him on the radio to break off his approach, but he wasn't listening.

I saw him flare for the landing, and I stood right in the middle of where he was going to land and I yelled at him to break off and get up to altitude.

He landed right on top of me, hitting me over the head with his chopper, knocking me flat on my ass. He yelled at me to get the wounded onto the chopper.

Dunagan had guys emptying the chopper and putting the wounded on it in record time. They could only get half our wounded on it – the rest and the dead had to stay behind.

I ran over to Captain Lukins' window and yelled at him over the radio to get the chopper out of there. I was screaming at him as bullets plucked at the chopper. I was being cut by tiny metal fragments hitting me in the face.

Captain Lukins was looking straight forward, ignoring me when suddenly his head snapped backward, and then he slumped forward, blood pouring out of his facemask.

I ordered the co-pilot to get the chopper out of there because bullets were just cutting it apart.

He told me he couldn't because Lukins was lying on the controls.

I opened the pilot's door, unhooked Lukins' harness so I could pull him out of the chopper. Big mistake. Captain Lukins had died instantly and his hands were frozen on the controls. When I pulled him out of the chopper his hands still held the controls in a death grip, so I inadvertently yanked on the pitch and collective.

The chopper started bouncing all over the LZ. The rotor came perilously close to some of our guys as the chopper lurched and tilted. I ran alongside, moving with the craft trying to push the Captain's dead body back into the door. The skid of the chopper landed on my foot and it hurt so badly, I saw stars.

I pushed harder to get the Captain back into his seat. It took tremendous effort and finally the port door gunner got out and assisted me and we finally got Lukins back in his seat. Then I pried his stiff fingers off of the controls one finger at a time. After which we pulled him out of the seat and both of us levered him into back with the rest of the wounded and yelled to the co-pilot to get that chopper out of there.

Vietnam – The Teenage Wasteland

The co-pilot pulled the chopper up as his windscreen disintegrated. He started backing up, screaming for us to cover him. Smoke poured out of the exhaust. I saw that the door gunner on our side was dead as the bird backed on out of there.

It was twenty feet off of the ground when I saw Captain Dunagan jump out of the chopper and land with a thud on the ground. I wondered what the hell he was doing in there.

Then the co-pilot turned the bird around and flew it downhill, smoke pouring out of it.

I yelled at him over the radio to turn left, as a stream of green tracers followed it down the hill. He gave me a "roger" but I could hear him crying. He then asked me if his pilot was dead, and I told him I thought so.

He followed my direction and turned left. I told him he had seven klicks to go to the hill and to keep the chopper alive for five more minutes. He gave me a weak "roger" as he sobbed.

The chopper made it to LZ Pro with the co-pilot barely able to control it, shot up like it was. He landed on the executive pad with a thud. He planted it down so hard the spinning rotors bent down and cut off the tail. People rushed to the chopper to get the dead and wounded out of it and put out the fire.

No sooner had the chopper left we started getting mortared. The NVA had four mortar tubes on us and were sending over 81 millimeter mortar rounds as fast as they could. They were landing all around us and we all lay on the ground as flat as possible to avoid the deadly shrapnel that was flying in all directions.

I found myself laying on my back looking up at the sky to see if I could see them coming down at me. I was in terror at the thought of one landing right on top of me. I did see one at the last second, but it was too late for me to do anything about it.

The mortar landed right between me and the Captain, who was sitting up. I saw him get knocked flat on his back and it looked like he had bought it.

Brian jumped up and ran over to him and pounded him on the chest, screaming "No!"

Dunagan sat right up with blood spurting out of his face, pointed across at a point on the perimeter and asked if the man over there was dead.

He was asking about Ronald Marrs, whom we'd put on an outgoing chopper the day before because he only had a week left in Vietnam. However, he was sent back out to us on Lukins' chopper and was killed a few minutes later by a mortar round.

Brian pushed the Captain back down, and waited for the mortar rounds to subside.

After another fifty rounds or more landed, the mortar attack subsided. The small arms fire finally stopped, and it began to get dark. There was a chance we could slip away under the cover of darkness.

Despite his facial injuries, Captain Dunagan got the men together and led them out of the area.

As everyone was moving out, I looked over at the LZ where the chopper had landed and saw cases of food, the mail bag, of all things, five new M-16's and three new M-60 Machine Guns and a bunch of machine gun ammo. Why in the hell they sent food and mail when we were getting slaughtered is beyond me.

I couldn't leave food behind and especially the mail, and I was not going to give the bad guys good machine guns and ammo to use on us. I needed to destroy it all. I put an incendiary grenade on the food and lit it. It would destroy most of the food; there's no sense in feeding the enemy our wholesome C-Rations. I grabbed the mail bag, ripped it open and dropped an incendiary grenade into the bag.

The NVA likes to find our mail and write nasty things to our loved ones, so the mail had to burn.

Vietnam – The Teenage Wasteland

I then gathered up the machine guns, the M-16's and around 1,100 rounds of machine gun ammo but it was too heavy for me to carry. I looked around for help and realized I was by myself. This was not a good feeling to be alone just after a fight like that with NVA all around.

It was totally dark and I knew the NVA would arrive on top of me any second as I hauled my own hundred pounds worth of backpack, plus two hundred pounds of guns and ammo.

I didn't know how long I would last carrying all that stuff, but I didn't want to leave it behind for the bad guys to use on us. So I walked like a duck, grunting and sweating like a pig in the direction I saw the last of our guys heading.

After 150 meters I ran into the company. They were holed up on a little patch of high ground, but were well hidden.

I found the Captain and he was surprised to see me with so much stuff. With his teeth clenched from the pain in his cheek he asked me where I had been so I told him what I was doing. He asked me why I hauled it by myself and I told him in between gasping breath that no one was there to help me. He shook his head.

I was pretty spent from carrying all that crap and rested for about ten minutes still gasping for breath. Then the Captain asked me to make sure we were deployed to defend ourselves and to do a head count and let him know what the situation was. He was straining to talk and I know his wound was killing him. It even hurt to look at it.

Following the captain's orders, I went around and made sure we were set up to repel any attack, counted the living, the wounded, the severely wounded and the dead.

I returned fifteen minutes later and reported in. "We are down to 59 in good shape and able to fight, around twenty of them are wounded but are okay to fight. We have ten severely wounded, not able to fight and one dead. Three of the severely wounded may not make it through the night unless we get them to a hospital."

Dunagan swore and shook his head. I checked with Brian only to find him completely caved. He could hardly talk. I asked him if he could shoot his weapon, and he nodded.

I sat back and rested. Oh crap. The Captain was out of commission, Brian was a mess and the only officer left, Dave Waltz, was tending to his own men. I was on my own. I didn't want to be in charge of anything but I knew I had to do something. So I did the only thing I could think to do - I called into Battalion and asked to talk to Colonel Uphill.

He got on the radio and asked how we were. With the captain sitting next to me I gave him a cryptic report on where things stood and told him we were going to need a miracle to get through the night.

He said he was working on something and for us to hang in there. LZ Pro was under a fierce attack again. The Colonel really had his hands full.

I noticed the captain was sitting there shivering in pain. I asked him if I could do anything for him, and he grimaced "no". He sat up and was holding his face. He looked tired, too. None of us had slept for the last forty eight hours. I felt vey alone and scared that he was out if commission. He was in pain and I thought to myself that if he could sleep for a while he would feel better and run the company. I knew he would not do anything for himself, and he would not sleep but sit there shuddering in pain, so I decided to pop him with some morphine so he could get some rest. I pulled out the syringe and got ready to nail him. He saw me with the syringe and asked me "What's that for?"

"You. You got too much pain." He didn't say anything to me; he just slapped the syringe out of my hand. "Don't come near me with that stuff. What's your problem?"

"Captain, you are in severe pain. Brian and I can handle things tonight; you should sleep, because if we make it through the night we're going to need you to be lucid tomorrow."

Vietnam – The Teenage Wasteland

He shook his head: "I need to stay alert right now. Stay away from me with that shit."

I went back to my radio and called around to the rest of the platoons. No one answered up.

I crawled out to the platoons and found out that everyone had dropped their backpacks and no one had a radio except for James Sargent in 2nd platoon. But his radio caught a bullet and could only receive, not transmit. In fact, Captain Dunagan, Jim and I were the only ones in Alpha Company who still had a back pack, I was pretty dismayed. That, to me, was the pits. We had to have radios, but the one thing worse than not having our radios was the fact that the NVA now had them and were listening in on our traffic. But recon did still have one of their radios, so that was something.

I went over to Doc Ballenger who was treating the wounded. He told me William Robert Hale had just died. He begged me to get the two other critical ones to the hospital. I told him I would do what I could.

I went over to see the 4th platoon leader, Sergeant Kirby, and asked how things were. He told me he and his guys would stand guard and fend off any attacks. Kirby was a good sergeant and a good platoon leader. He was a sandy haired fellow from Massachusetts with a friendly face and an easy smile that was always present. He could be counted on for anything.

I went back to where the Captain was. He was holding his face. I knew he was in a lot of pain; he had a hole in his cheek with cheekbone fragments sticking out. I heard later, that the mortar shrapnel that hit Captain Dunagan in the face also took out three molars, so imagine the pain he was in. He looked up at me and motioned me away from him. I sat down next to him anyhow and chilled. I had a chance to reflect on what had just happened and the fact that we had just gotten our asses kicked, severely. That did not happen to Alpha Company. We never lost a rumble, but now we were hiding and scared shitless. We had never been in this situation before. We had never been sent back to mama with our tails between our legs. I thought about all the radios and backpacks out there. It outraged me. Sure it was easier to run for your life without ninety-five pounds on your back, but you just don't leave your gear out there.

The more I reflected on the events of the day the more frightened I became. I had the urge to just get up and run, run and run, and then some more, all the way back to Detroit.

At that moment my radio crackled to life and snapped me out of my reverie. Colonel Uphill was calling. I answered. "This is Ashcan five-zero Juliet, go ahead."

"This is Eagle five zero, how is Ashcan, over?"

"Ashcan is in pain."

"Sorry to hear it, Juliet, but I called because I have good news for you, over."

I moved the handset to the captain and he brushed it back to me and motioned for me to talk. I put it back to my face

"Can't wait, Eagle, do tell, over."

"Roger, we have a Spooky gunship headed out to your local, ETA ten minutes. Can you hold on that long, over?"

A Spooky gunship? Holy shit, that was great! A Spooky was just about the only thing that could save us. I knew the NVA were planning the finish of us, and would probably pop it on us in the next hour or so. But with a Spooky, we had a chance. The Captain actually gleamed and said something unintelligible.

"Roger Eagle, we will hang in here for Spooky".

"Roger, he will contact you in a few. Out."

A Spooky is an old WW II vintage twin engine Dakota or C-47. It is equipped with three mini-guns and state-of-the-art computers with side-looking radar, infra-red sensors and metal detectors all hooked into one computer that tells the operator that the infra-red blobs moving on the ground with metal on them are in fact not cows, but soldiers. They can then put the cursor of the computer on the infra-red signature, push a

Vietnam – The Teenage Wasteland

button, rain bullets on the target and watch the little green glows diminish as heat leaves the dead body.

I waited and finally heard the drone of the twin-engine plane as it flew overhead at three thousand feet.

The Gunner of the Spooky called down to me and what follows is the transmission, remembered to the best of my ability, with Spooky Four-zero, the operator of the weapons on the Spooky gunship.

"Ashcan Five Zero, this is Spooky Four-Zero, over."

"Spooky, this is Ashcan Five-zero Juliet, go ahead."

"Ashcan, we are on station here and have enough fuel to loiter on your position for eight hours. We will guard you the rest of the night and try to take out as many of the bad guys as possible. Copy Ashcan?

A big grin came on my face. "Copy, Spooky, over." Captain Dunagan gave me a thumbs up.

"Roger, Ashcan. What I need is for you to make sure your guys are in a tight bunch and that everyone lies down so as not to get hit by ricochets. Copy?"

"Roger Spooky, over."

"Okay, Ashcan, now I need you to take your Zippo lighter, put your helmet upside down and light it in the bowl so I can see it on my screen. Flick it when I tell you, copy?"

I took my helmet off and turned it upside down, held the Zippo that my dad gave me that he carried in the Pacific during WW II. The lighter had now been through two wars, but still lit first time, every time! I held it in the helmet, ready to go and called back up to Spooky "Okay Spooky, I am ready, over."

"Roger Ashcan, light it… … … … now!"

I flicked the Zippo and she lit first try – I could feel the heat from it. Spooky called down immediately: "That's good Ashcan, close it. I got a fix on you, and you seem to be in a nice tight group. Get your heads down because some bad guys are coming to you from the south, and I need to handle them right now. Get everyone down."

"Roger, Spooky."

I went around to the perimeter and gave everyone a briefing and told them to lay flat down.

I went back to the Captain and helped him lay on his back. He nodded. I brought up the morphine again and got bitched out with a long sentence that I didn't understand, but I did get the meaning. I then lay down on my back and I watched the lights on the Spooky as he orbited our position. All of a sudden, a red line came out the side of it just for a second–like a laser beam. Then I heard a sound like a chain saw. Then I heard a scream as an NVA soldier was cut to ribbons by the mini gun. Then another red laser came out of the sky and another, and another. The Spooky gunner was laying his cursor on green spots on his screen outside of our perimeter and mowing them down. I never felt so safe in my life.

He circled around for the next hour and a half and then went back to LZ Pro where I could hear the tearing sound of his mini-guns as he knocked down insurgents over there.

About 2 a.m. Spooky came back to our position only to learn that the NVA was mounting a full-out attack on our position with a full company sized unit. Spooky took them all down spending the next half hour mopping up stubborn infra-red signatures.

Spooky stayed on station for the rest of the night, alternating between our position and then LZ Pro to give them much needed cover.

He came back from LZ Pro one time, announced we were being rushed by NVA, opened up on them and then went quiet for a spell.

At one point he said we were being rushed by a company sized unit. He destroyed that unit in five minutes. It was a spectacular sight. The NVA were screaming as the vintage warplane with modern weapons cut them to ribbons. He spent another half hour rubbing out those stubborn infra-red signatures that lay still on the ground.

Vietnam – The Teenage Wasteland

Spooky saved our asses that night of 13 May 1969. What a piece of machinery!

17

———————————

14 MAY 1969

It was just about dawn when Spooky told us he had chased everyone at least a kilometer away from our position and as soon as we were ready, he would plow a path for us so we could get a chopper in and get our wounded out. We gathered all our wounded and dead together at the crack of dawn and Spooky gave us cover until a chopper delivered fresh ammo and took our wounded out. Our numbers were now down to about half. We were a unit of around fifty-five men, trying to get back to the Hill.

The Hill was attacked the night before, but Spooky took turns defending us and then defending LZ Pro. The hill still got hammered with recoilless and rocket fire, but the ground attack was thwarted.

Captain Dunagan catnapped all night long, so he was feeling a little better and was a little more refreshed.

After our wounded were placed on the chopper, we moved swiftly off down toward the river that would take us straight to LZ Pro. The Captain did catch some sleep when Spooky was with us and he was definitely looking and acting better. He told me that he didn't have the energy to talk on the radio, and that I was doing fine, so carry on and he would let me know if

Vietnam – The Teenage Wasteland

and when I screw up. But he did tell me that I better not cause him to talk on the radio.

The river wound its way through the Valley of Death in an east-west direction but in places it meandered back on itself in a series of "U" shaped bends. On both banks it had abandoned rice paddies dotted with trees and brush which became denser close to the river. To the north, dry rice paddies gave way to a dense tree line and then foot hills.

The remnants of Recon platoon went ahead on point while we unloaded the chopper. They wanted to scope out the river banks, see what was ahead and pave a path for us to get out of there.

Recon was about three hundred meters ahead of us when we heard AK-47s mixed with a little M-16 fire. Then I heard frantic calls on the radio from the Recon point man reporting another KIA and that he was shot in both legs and pinned down. He was screaming.

Dunagan told me to tell him to shut up and use clicks on the handset only. He was giving his position away by yelling into the radio. He was in an absolute panic but I got him to shut up and to use clicks while we rushed to the scene.

As we closed in on Recon's position we saw a GI floating face down in the shallow river and moved more cautiously on both sides of the stream.

The river at that point had steep, five-foot high walls on both sides that afforded us cover while we approached.

We were thirty feet from the dead GI when the dinks opened up on us from ahead. I ordered some guys up on the banks. They climbed up and immediately started shooting at dinks moving towards us through the trees on both sides of the river.

We sounded ahead of us by shooting sporadically as we moved up.

Dunagan, Brian and I got as far as twenty meters short of the dead GI floating in the river. He was now reduced to bait.

That was what he was. The NVA had guns trained on him waiting for one of us idiots to go to him.

The point man was in a clump of bamboo and trees another twenty meters up the river on the north bank. We could see his boots from where we were. The Captain wanted to know if he could walk. U asked him but he said both his legs were broken so didn't think so. Guns were trained on him as well. His life was also reduced to being bait.

We tried to move up to him but the return fire was way too heavy. The NVA were keeping him alive as long as we were trying to rescue him. A few guys tried to get to him again but were driven back; We stalled trying to rescue him.

Captain Dunagan stripped off his gear, put a new magazine in his rifle, charged a fresh round in it and looked at us kind of crazily. "Cover me," he said, and to our complete astonishment he took off running towards the trapped GI.

What the ….? Both Brian and I automatically brought our rifles up and opened fire down river, shooting right past Dunagan, on either side of him. We poured as much fire as we could into the trees on both sides of the river. I was changing magazines as fast as possible.

While I was shooting I was amazed to see Captain Dunagan run to where the GI was holed up, bend over, grab the wounded man, radio and all, throw him over his shoulder and run back to us.

Making his way back he ran as fast as he could, so fast he found it difficult to stop upon arrival and skidded as he crashed down at our feet in the shallow river water, with the recon man and everything in a big splash. I was on my fifth magazine by the time he arrived.

NVA Automatic gunfire followed the Captain back and we all dove for cover as bullets homed in on all of us.

As the gunfire died down, the Captain stood up.

I stood up and faced him. "What on earth is your problem, Captain?" I asked, wondering why our leader had put himself at such risk.

Vietnam – The Teenage Wasteland

He looked at me sheepishly. I could see he was holding his left arm, which was covered in blood.

He looked at his arm and then looked back at me as if to say, "I fucked up."

At that point I realized he'd been shot. I looked over his left arm. A bullet had gone through his forearm and another through his upper arm. Both bones were broken. I called for the medic.

As the Doc patched him up I wondered if I might have shot my own captain. Brian and I were both shooting to the side of him as he charged down the riverbed, either of us could have hit him, but after examination we saw the rounds were thirty calibers, so they were from an AK.

I am sure the Captain was in excruciating pain. He had a smashed cheek-bone with broken bone fragments protruding through his face and three molars knocked out. He had two broken bones in his left arm from gunshots and I found out much later he also had a broken foot! I think he broke it when he jumped out of the chopper the day before.

The Captain was a complete mess. The medic told him he should take some pain pills but the captain refused and told the medic he needed to keep alert and on the ball. Then he looked at me as if to punctuate that he needed to be alert.

How he was up to walking around at all, let alone dealing with the stress of running a company surrounded by thousands of NVA and fighting for its life was a mystery, but miraculously he was still Captain Dunagan, still in control and you knew it.

Where do men like this come from? Where can you find them? That day, I witnessed something you don't see often, a real man. Not a John Wayne in the movies, but the real thing, real heroism, action above and beyond the call of duty, conduct above that of mortal men. Despite being in more pain than anyone could endure and while refusing drugs because they might affect his ability to function, Captain Dunagan held his command and would not relinquish it, not by order or wish or by lack of action or competence. He kept a steady hand on the situation and a firm grip on what was happening around us.

I have not met anyone since that came even close to the caliber of that man. I have always been in awe of Kern Dunagan. He will always be my hero.

After he was patched up, the Captain came to me and Brian and ordered an update on the current situation. He looked horrible with his left arm in a sling and a big patch on his swollen face but in his right arm he held his M-16 and a map, which he was back studying, looking for a way out of our situation. He ordered a patrol to go back down the river where we came from, but they only made it thirty meters before they came under heavy small arms fire. We were now officially surrounded now that the back door was closed.

By now the NVA knew they had us where they wanted us. We were trapped in and around a river bed and they had us surrounded. It was too late to go anywhere; we were cornered. However, the NVA knew that they still had to be careful. They couldn't just waltz in on us. They knew we were a pissed off wounded bear, in a corner, fighting for its life. I am sure they were studying maps too, only they were figuring out how to finish us off.

We were still without Artillery and air support. To make things worse Spooky had been sent somewhere else. We were on our own again and we knew it.

The Captain asked me where we stood on ammo. I went around and did a count and reported back to him that we were about sixty-five percent.

"Not good enough. Get us up to two hundred percent. I want everyone doubled up on ammo. We're going to have to make our stand in this river. I don't want to run out again and have to have a chopper come in during a fire fight and lose another crew. Have the chopper drop it in the river this time, don't let him land. That's an order, Tom."

"What about food, Captain? The guys haven't eaten in three days."

"No food. They can eat next week. Right now we need ammo only. Get on it."

I jumped on the radio and did a silent figure-out in my head on ammo. Then I called the hill. "Alright, send Charley-Charley out with twenty-four thousand rounds of .223, four thousand rounds of M-60, two crates of grenades and two hundred rounds of M-79 (grenade launcher ammo). And this time no chopper lands here. They drop it from five hundred feet into the river. No landings. Copy?"

They assured me that the chopper would be right out and it wouldn't try to land.

I put together my panel and put it downriver, away from us by fifty feet, so no one would get hit over the head by a fifty-pound crate of .223 ammo going fifty miles per hour.

We were going to be loaded up with enough to defend the Alamo. We would have enough to stand for the rest of the day, no matter what.

The chopper came fifteen minutes later, hovered and dropped the ammo. He almost didn't make it because he got hit thirty times by machine-gun fire as he dropped his load. But because he was at an altitude of five hundred feet, none of the hits were fatal to the chopper. And it's a good thing we re-supplied because we laid down one hell of a covering fire for the chopper while he was there, burning a lot of ammo.

Per the Captains orders I made sure everyone was fat on ammo and had the men take turns cleaning their weapons for the first time in three days. The Captain wanted them ready for action with clean, good-working weapons. We were going to make our last stand at the river, and we were not going to succumb to the NVA, no matter what. The last thing anyone needed at a crucial moment was a jammed rifle. So, we cleaned our weapons, cleaned them good and made sure we were battle-ready.

I had some guys put out a bunch of Claymores that I'd had delivered along with the ammo. We set up fortifications in our river shelter. We got ready. They could send thousands at us but our group, though now less than fifty-five would be able to defend itself.

We settled into a quiet mode, everyone still, trying to keep from sweating too much while we waited.

The good news was we were in a river and had unlimited water. That wasn't going to be a problem. But we were trapped and now we had to wait to see what the enemy was going to do. We had no offensive plans because we had no offensive posture. The Captain was trying to figure it out.

It was eight in the morning, and it was already too hot for any activity at all. It was going to be a real hot day, one of those days where it goes up to one hundred twenty degrees with a hundred percent humidity.

I was tired. Dog tired. I realized I hadn't slept in three days, and it was taking its toll on me. I hunkered down in the shade and fell asleep.

My radio crackled to life. It was Colonel Uphill. He told me that some Helicopter Gunships from somewhere I'd never heard of before might be joining us soon. He also wanted to know about the Captain. I told him about the Captain's newest wounds and the Colonel wanted to know if we should get him out of there.

Captain Dunagan was about to rip the handset from me when I answered: "You should get us ALL out of here, over".

Dunagan smiled, he was real happy with that reply.

Uphill answered with a mumble about how he was working on it or something.

The Colonel and I went over the casualties and he was astonishingly apologetic about what happened to us. He actually grieved a lot about the dead on the radio, actually started crying. I had heard him do that a couple times before. It was totally unnecessary and annoying. I mean I don't need to hear a superior officer crying over the radio. I would expect

Vietnam – The Teenage Wasteland

to hear something more like, "You're taking too many casualties – you need to tighten it up out there or I'm gonna come out and kick the living shit out of you and if I hear of one more killed you're all going to get Court-Marshaled." That would have felt better and would have been more effective. Every time someone dies in your company, you take it personally and feel somewhat responsible: Maybe the day before you saw it in his eyes, or you should have talked to him that morning, or something. Or maybe it was your fault for not maneuvering his platoon properly or whatever. You just take it personally. Every death is your fault, somehow. To get chewed out for a death would have been welcome. A senior officer crying just made it worse.

It had been an hour since the supply chopper came in. I got up and walked around again and made sure everyone was up and awake on the perimeter. None of the guys had gotten much sleep in three days so they were tired. I talked with just about everyone, checking their health and mental state. Seemed like everyone had some sort of wound, but most not too serious and our new medic, Ballenger, had done a good job of caring for everyone that needed medical attention. In this climate it was easy to get infections. Everyone got a tetanus shot and the Doc cleaned everyone's scratches, holes, gashes and any open wounds and we all were sporting red splotches on our arms and legs from mercurochrome. He did a great job, considering he'd only been in country two weeks.

The men were in good shape and they were all scared. That was good - anyone who was not scared right now would be in la-la land.

I was talking with Jessie when Sergeant Kirby yelled: "Heads up, incoming dinks on north side. A lot of them."

I got up on the river bank and looked north. There were around sixty or seventy NVA charging at us from around five hundred meters out, just running flat out at us. It was a really odd sight. It took a little bit for it to sink in that these people were running at us to kill us. I raised the barrel of my rifle at them. Apparently they had gotten orders to finish us at all costs. So be it. It was going to cost them big.

Dunagan came up on the bank and yelled to me to tell everyone to wait until they were on us and then shoot single-shot only. I repeated his command so to make sure he was heard. He added that no one shoots until he does. I relayed that order.

We watched them charge at us across the five-hundred meter open space of dried up rice paddies, yelling and screaming. They knew we had no air support, choppers or artillery. We were going to be fighting them on even terms, so they threw all they had at us to finish us off, and then get back to finishing off the LZ.

I sat there watching the craziness of these men running at a meat grinder knowing they were going to die. I realized they intended to take as many of us with them as possible. I was certain that was their strategy.

I looked away from them for a split second and looked at the beautiful blue sky with fluffy clouds. I wondered if I were going to see the sky again in two minutes from now. I looked back at the charging men and drew a bead on one of them. I had a giddy thought about all of our men aiming at the same guy I was aiming at but it was too late to do anything about that. When they got close in, the captain opened up and then other guys started shooting, and when I shot, my man dropped. I found another target, shot, and he dropped, then another.

They all went down. The closest one to get to us was twenty five meters from our line. The rest lay dead or wounded in front of us.

We put two more bullets into the bodies lying out there to make sure no one was playing dead, surveyed the scene and then went into the routine of checking our ammo and gear.

I picked up my radio and reported to Battalion on the quick battle and gave them their ever-precious "body count" of 66 NVA K.I.A.

Vietnam – The Teenage Wasteland

I sat down next to the Captain. I remember looking over at him during the rush. He was up on the line with his M-16 blazing from his right arm with his left arm in a sling. He was in there with the rest of us slamming away.

We sat there for ten minutes or so and he called to me with a silly smile on his face: "Hey Tom, did you call your mother today?"

What the hell kind of question was that, I thought. Had he become delirious?

He looked at me drunkenly, "It's Mother's Day."

"Holy shit, you're right."

He said, "We should call them. Is there a phone booth around here?"

We both laughed. I thought about it for a minute and then I realized it was Wednesday. The Captain was out of it. Mothers day was going to be next Sunday.

I sat back and chilled while my mind went back to Detroit. I started thinking about home and wondered what my mother was doing right then. When I realized she was probably sleeping because it was around two in the morning there – Mothers Day morning, I started to wonder what she would do later in the day. I pictured my brother and his fiancé taking mom and dad to breakfast. I wondered if they would talk about me at all. I wondered if they remembered me at all, if they even brought up my name. Then I thought: if they knew the situation I was in right now, they would vomit and my mother would have to be taken to the hospital due to the chest pains she often suffered during times of stress. They could not even handle knowing about us being surrounded by hundreds of NVA who had one intention -- to kill us. And since they had no idea of my predicament, I was probably not in their thoughts at all.

It hit me that everyone in my family back in the states was sleeping like a baby and tomorrow would be a la-di-da day of taking mom to breakfast and all of the niceties that went with it. They would talk about mundane stuff and mom would open her Mother's Day gift and give a gleeful look of thanks and they would all talk about the weather and all of that kind of thing, but they would not talk about me.

I felt sorry for myself. I wanted to be home so badly. I wanted to be going to Mother's Day breakfast with my family. I did not want to be here, waiting to die. I wanted to live. I almost started to cry from self-pity so I shook my head to rid myself of all negative thoughts but one managed to linger. The one lingering thought was how ironic it would be for all of us mother's sons to die here on Mother's Day.

Ten minutes later I was still thinking about mothers and sons and all of that when my radio came to life. "Ashcan five-zero this is Blue Ghost One, over."

I'd never heard that call-sign before. I picked up the handset and called back, "Blue Ghost One, this is Ashcan five-zero Juliet, go ahead, over.'

"Roger Ashcan, we are en route to your position, ETA seven minutes. We are flying Cobra gunships and are going to be dedicated to you for the rest of the day, copy?"

Cobras! I'd never seen a Cobra gunship in action before. They were real kick-ass gunships, brand new and powerful. I had heard they were in Vietnam, but I had never seen one. They were tremendous weapons and I felt honored to be getting that day. Our priority must have gone up. A Cobra was the first real gunship helicopter. It had a mini-gun, automatic forty millimeter cannon and a pile of missiles. It could make one pass on a football field and put lethal ordnance in every square inch of it. That was the kind of fire-power we needed.

"Roger Blue Ghost, our coordinates are one-four-six, four-four-eight. Look for an orange panel in the river."

Captain Dunagan nodded at me. "This will help. Thank God." I nodded to him.

I used an orange panel that folded into sections one foot by one foot, so you could place it in the shape of an "L" or a "T" or an "E" or an "F" and it could be seen from the air only. It was used instead of a smoke grenade because smoke gave away your position to the NVA mortar guys.

Those beautiful Cobras have rotor blades that are three feet wide so you can hear them coming from miles away. They finally came on top of us and the ground shuddered as they flew over with power and authority.

"Ashcan, Blue Ghost One, I copy letter "Echo", over."

"Roger Blue Ghost One, "Echo". They had us!

"Roger Ashcan, give us your layout so we don't impact any of your guys."

I didn't want to give our exact situation because the NVA had our radios and were tuned in, I was sure. "Uh, Blue Ghost, just figure we are around the panel and that's all you need to know. Bad guys have some of our radios. Copy?"

"Roger Ashcan, I copy that. Thanks for the warning. We're going to scout around for a bit to look over the terrain, and then we'll go into orbit waiting for your call. Over."

They flew around, looking things over, looking for runs in and out, escape routes and so forth. After ten minutes he called to me.

"Alright Ashcan, tell me your current situation. Copy?"

"Roger One, the last re-supply chopper that was in here kicked up dinks all around us, and a rather large amount of dinks, seventy or so, charged us from the north, so there is a large staging area in the wood line to the north, over."

"Thank you Ashcan, yes, we can see the bodies lying there in front of you. They'll probably rush you repeatedly to try to run you out of ammo. We'll help from up here the next time they do. Also, watch your south side, we saw some movement there."

"Copy One, thanks. We will watch for them."

This was good. We had an eye in the sky.

I told the Captain we should put more guys and a pig to the south of us, per Blue Ghosts report.

He nodded okay.

I went over to Kirby and told him to set up on the south side and put his men on high alert because the NVA were going to attack us from that direction. He put three men over there and gave me the sign he was ready. We hunkered down again in the stifling heat and waited.

Twenty minutes later my radio crackled to life and Blue Ghost called to me, the pitch in his voice relayed urgency: "Ashcan, heads up - you have a hundred or so coming at you from the north – we're rolling in."

I alerted the north side of the perimeter and we all got ready for the NVA onslaught.

But this time Cobras rolled over our heads just a few hundred feet up and came in side-by-side, letting loose with their mini-guns, cannon and rockets as the ground churned up all around the charging enemy.

Only half of the NVA came running out of the smoke and dust, and we easily chopped them down.

Meantime thirty or so NVA attacked from the south. Kirby and his boys easily shot them down.

Blue Ghost was rolling back in again when he called down urgently. "Ashcan, you guys okay? Did any get through? Over!"

I called back to him calmly because he seemed real shaken. I got the idea that this was the first time he'd seen real combat like this. "Uh, Blue Ghost One, this is Ashcan, all enemy are down and none got through. You guys did a spectacular job and took down half of them. That was real impressive, over."

Blue Ghost was still on adrenalin. "Okay, okay uh, you guys take care down there now. That was close. Copy?"

I smiled. Nice guy. "Copy Blue Ghost. You guys did really good on that. Appreciate you being there, over."

He calmed down a little. "Copy Ashcan. I am glad to be here for you guys. We were fully briefed on your situation before we came out. You all are in a bad situation there. You realize you are surrounded, copy?"

Vietnam – The Teenage Wasteland

"Copy Blue Ghost, we fought all the way here and finally got bogged down, and now they have us by the nads, copy?"

"Copy that Ashcan. Know that we will do everything we can to help you guys out. I know they want us to come after them so we run out of ammo, but we are not going to do that, we will just wait until they play their hand. We got plenty of ammo. Copy?"

"Roger Ghost. Keep your eyes peeled for us. Copy?"

We chatted a little more and then I told him I needed to conserve my battery. He apologized for chatting me up and wasting my battery. He really made us all feel at ease.

The Captain was still reading the map, but was dozing off. That was fine with me. He needed the sleep.

It was only eleven thirty in the morning but felt like it should be around five in the afternoon.

Dunagan dozed for twenty minutes and woke up with a start. Then he bitched me out for letting him sleep. He looked better though, but still in pain.

I said to him, "Might as well catch some more shut-eye, we're not going anywhere fast."

He grunted at me as he looked at his watch. "It's been a while since they charged us, they might be coming soon. Check out the guys and make sure we're ready."

I went around and checked the guys, they were all okay. Some were sleeping, most were on the alert. The unbearable heat plus lack of food and sleep was taking its toll.

The only good news was that we were by the river, water was plentiful. Drinking water with a friend of yours floating in it was not very welcome, though. But you gotta do what you gotta do.

It was noon and Jessie yelled out: "Incoming Dinks from the north side, everyone up".

I called to Blue Ghost: "Heads up Blue Ghost, dinks charging us from the north. Over."

"This is Blue Ghost, we are on it."

We all got up and looked out over the shimmering heat coming off of the field. There seemed to be only twenty-five or so coming this time. Were they running out of people?

Blue Ghost One and Two were on them. They nuked the dinks right out of the dust with rockets, and mini-guns.

We only got a few shots off. Blue Ghost One and Two made their pass and were coming back around when out of the dust came another seventy or so NVA at a dead run at us. I looked at the choppers and they were half way through their turn – the NVA had sent the first twenty-five as a decoy for the Cobras and then sent another seventy at us while the choppers were turning. Smart!

We were on our own. They came hard and fast. We opened up on them but they kept coming. We blew all the Claymores when the NVA were on us, but they still came through. We were in a fire fight right at our doorstep.

A lot of the NVA died right at our line, but three of them made it through, jumped over our heads and into the river where they opened up on is. Before we got them, they shot four of our guys, wounding them badly.

I could hear Blue Ghost calling me all through the battle but we were all too busy shooting and then mopping up the wounded NVA that were still trying to shoot at us. There were at least twenty five of them right in front of us, and five or so were still alive. We had to methodically shoot each body to locate the ones who were still alive.

Finally, I answered Blue Ghost because he sounded so frantic. "Okay Blue Ghost One, a few of them got through and caused a little damage. Nothing bad. We're okay, over."

"Thank God, Ashcan. Can you believe that? They outsmarted us."

"Roger, Ghost, we're fine. We'll just get them the next time, over."

"Roger Ashcan." He was feeling bad he got out-maneuvered, and I had to chill him out.

Vietnam – The Teenage Wasteland

"Listen, Ghost. You guys are saving us. We are wasting the bad guys. I think we have eliminated two hundred and fifty so far, so we are doing alright. The strategy is still working, and we are pulling through this. We still have plenty of ammo down here. Copy?"

"Roger that Ashcan. Listen, ah, we are bingo (out of gas) and Winchester (down to just the pistols in their shoulder harnesses). Blue Ghost Three and Four are almost here to cover, we're going back to re-fuel and re-arm. Be back in an hour or so, over."

"Copy One, see you in a bit. Oh, and ah, bring back some cold beer, would you?"

He laughed and took off as soon as Three and Four reported in. One gave them the lowdown, and they went into orbit and waited. I welcomed them after they checked in with us and told them we were going to hunker down here and wait for the bad guys.

Then I went upriver to the most eastern part of our position and sat down next to Lt Tomanaha, our Artillery Forward Controller. He was Japanese-American and also Amish. A strange bird. We talked for a while, sitting on the river bottom with our asses in the water to cool off. The water was ninety degrees, but it was cooler than the air.

I was sitting with my rifle barrel across my legs when suddenly an NVA soldier jumped down from the river bank into the water. On his way down he opened up on me and Tomanaha with his AK-47. It was slow-motion, just like in the movies. I could see the muzzle flashing, the spent cartridges falling, the grimace on his face, everything in super-slow-motion.

I turned to the left. Bullets were hitting there, sand getting in my eyes. I turned to the right, same thing. To my horror bullets hit between my legs – all around me. I knew I was hit and probably mortally because I didn't feel anything.

Lt Tomanaha opened up on the bad guy on automatic. I could see the gunner firing as he stood in the river, Tomanaha's bullets splashing all around him.

I pulled the emergency release on my rucksack, got up and ran in a panic back down the shallow river. I ran past the Captain. He reached out and grabbed my leg with his good arm, and I went down, face-first in the river.

He pulled me in with his good arm and pulled me right up to his face.

I was in hysterics for the first time in my life. I screamed at him crazily. "We need to get out of here! NOW. WE NEED TO GET THE FUCK OUT OF HERE NOW!"

He back-handed, me and then slapped me again. It brought me back.

I moaned to him, "We got to get out of here, Captain."

He looked at me sternly. "We will. Now go back and get your radio. Move it!"

I started to moan some more but he slapped me two more times and yelled: "GO GET YOUR RADIO – NOW!"

That worked. I got a grip from the slapping. Slowly, I got up and walked real carefully back to where my radio was, hugging the river bank as I moved toward it.

Two guys came with me and poured fire into the clump of trees the NVA gunner had come out of.

I snatched my radio and rifle and made it back to safety, sitting down next to the Captain, mentally spinning like a top.

It took me ten minutes to calm down. Captain Dunagan pointed out that maybe I should have the choppers do something about that clump of trees where the gunner had come from.

"Good idea Captain," I keyed the radio and called up to Blue Ghost Three. "Blue Ghost Three, this is Ashcan Five-zero Juliet. We are getting fire from a position, which I will mark with smoke. I need you to snuff it out, over."

"Roger, Ashcan, rolling in. Pop the smoke."

I picked a purple smoke grenade and pulled the safety pin on it. I got as close as I dared to the clump of trees and threw the grenade.

It fell ten meters short. That was okay. I ran over to my radio and called up to Three. He saw the smoke. I adjusted him ten meters south.

I sat down close to the Captain, Brian and the mule and we watched the Cobra roll in.

The Cobra fired three rockets at the clump of trees.

Instead of homing in on the target, all three rockets took off in different directions and one of them headed right for us.

We only had a chance to roll over onto our sides and hope for the best. There was a deafening explosion as we (the Captain, Brian, the mule and I) were all blown away from each other.

The rocket landed in between us, but luckily hit the mud and plowed in quite a way before it ignited. The blast hurt, though. It rocked my entire body, rattled my teeth and rang my bell but good.

It took quite a while for my hearing to return. Finally, I heard Blue Ghost Three frantically calling on the radio. He'd seen the whole thing and was screaming for someone to answer.

After I did a survey and astonishingly found that none of us were hurt by the rocket, I called up to him: "Alright Blue Ghost Three, we are all okay. It shook us up bad, but no one hurt. Over."

"Oh my God, Ashcan, I cannot believe that happened. I am so sorry. There is something wrong with my launcher. Are you sure no one is hurt? That looked bad. Tell me the truth. Over."

I understood. I knew he must have freaked out, and I knew it was some kind of mechanical problem. "No sweat three. Honest, no one injured. Just rang our bells pretty good. Over."

"Unbelievable, Ashcan. It looked horrible from up here. I mean that rocket landed right in the middle of you guys. Hard to believe no one got hurt. Over."

I thought about that for a second; "Yeah, that is actually good news and bad news at the same time, over."

"Uh, roger Ashcan. Okay, I need to go back and get this fixed. One and Two are five minutes out; I am going to diddy back to Chu Lai, over."

"Roger Three. No sweat man. Out"

Blue Ghost One came back on the line after he went into orbit. He apologized again for the rocket screw-up and wanted to make sure I knew that it never happens. He was very apologetic, kind of like buying a new Mercedes from the Beverly Hills dealership and having all the wheels fall off, then getting an apology from the manager.

I asked him if his group had ever been in a situation like this, and he said no, they had not. I pointed out that we were in such a severe situation that we were all new to this type of fighting and that mistakes were allowed, as long as no one was killed.

He chilled a bit, but promised nothing but the best of service from now on. I told him it was cool because we weren't paying for it anyhow. I finally got a laugh out of him.

I couldn't blame them for anything. This was a new situation. We were in circumstances none of us were really trained for. The Cobra was new and it had to wring out its problems. But I was still glad to have those guys with us, they were professionals, and they were saving our asses.

I found out later that Blue Ghost One was a major in the Army, which meant he had lots of hours in a chopper. They didn't trust new expensive equipment to greenies, so we were dealing with seasoned warriors with new, un-tested equipment. I'd still take them over anyone else.

We lolled in the hot sun for another hour or so without incident. Kirby's guys shot at a few NVA on the south side as

Vietnam – The Teenage Wasteland

they were trying to get close to our position. Other than that it was quiet.

It was getting on to around two o'clock, and it was hotter than ever.

A call came out from the north side of the river. "Heads up, incoming NVA."

A call came up from the south side. "Incoming NVA".

They were hitting us from both sides. This was it – the final push. I was more concerned about the south side. I knew Blue Ghost would handle the north.

I climbed up the south bank of the river with Sgt. Kirby. We all picked up targets and started dropping them. Blue Ghost was working the north side with the rest of our guys.

The south side was under control so I jumped over to the other bank. I saw something I thought was pretty spectacular. Blue Ghost One had come right down on the deck, his skids just two feet off of the ground, shooting his mini gun, rockets and cannon at the NVA point-blank. He was kicking his rudder back and forth, swinging in position, just spraying ordnance as he hovered there.

He started backing up and yelled "Cover me!"

We all opened up on the enemy while Blue Ghost One backed up over our heads, still spraying rockets and using his mini-gun. We dropped all of the rest of the NVA, and things quieted down, except for the sound of choppers.

I called up to Blue Ghost. He didn't answer. He was in orbit. I called again. I called two more times until he finally answered.

"You okay Blue Ghost One? That was a little crazy there. Everything okay? Over."

He sounded strained. "Uh, Ashcan, I lost my canopy, got shot up pretty good, I need to go back and change it out. Will be back ASAP, over." With that, he just took off.

I figured his canopy must be really torn up after he went in there at ground level and point blank range. Blue Ghost Three and Four came in three minutes later and Blue Ghost Two took off after One.

We settled in, spent a little time mopping up any NVA possums still lying out there.

I didn't find out until just three years ago what actually happened when Blue Ghost One went down to deck level and fired all his ordnance point-blank at the NVA. He took a lot of machine-gun and AK fire and his canopy was blown out. But he also lost his gunner who was sitting in the front, killed instantly. Blue Ghost One didn't tell us on-the-ground troops because he didn't want to give us any bad news.

I was really sorry to hear about the gunner being killed. Now I understood why Blue Ghosts' tone changed when I talked to him on the radio right after. The normally enthusiastic Major was very subdued.

Blue Ghost One came back an hour later with a new canopy and new gunner. All four choppers stayed on station.

Blue Ghost One radioed me around three thirty in the afternoon. "Uh, Ashcan, the bad guys are probably getting ready for another attack. They've got a major staging area north of you, think it would be a good idea to get an air strike on it to give us all some relief, what say?"

"Uh, Good idea Blue Ghost. Air strikes are hard to come by these days, but I'll call it in. Over."

"I already called it in. Over." He was terse. He had a score to settle.

Back in Chu Lai at the Marine Air Base, four pilots raced to their F-4 Phantom jet-fighter/bombers, incredible machines that could carry eight thousand pounds of bombs, and fly supersonic to your position, loiter for around twenty minutes, do pin-point bombing and chew up the landscape with their twenty millimeter cannons.

The pilots jumped in their steeds, loaded with five-hundred pound bombs and napalm, drove to the end of the runway, got the safety pins pulled off of the bombs and guns by the safety

Vietnam – The Teenage Wasteland

officer, ran up the after-burners and flew straight to our location faster than the speed of sound.

Just fifteen minutes after I spoke to Blue Ghost One, four sonic booms sounded, followed by the morbid screeching of air brakes. My radio sprang to life.

"Ashcan five-zero, this is Pegasus One, you copy, over?"

"Pegasus One, this is Ashcan Five-zero Juliet, loud and clear. Over." Finally, an air strike. Thank god.

"Roger, we are in orbit over your local, copy your orange panel 'F'. Roger?"

"Roger, Pegasus. We need the ordnance six hundred meters from our orange panel on azimuth south to north; ah your entrance is one-seven-seven out to three-three-seven to the north, copy?"

"Copy Ashcan, I am going to make a dummy run and check it out, standby, over."

It was a tough approach, seeing that the target was in the wood line, tight up against the hill. It meant the jets had to fly over us from the south, drop their bombs, pull up hard and to the right and then come back around.

Pegasus One rolled in and made the run. He came in right above us, over the target, pulled up and rolled out to the east as he made his way back to orbit. He didn't call back to me right away; he just went back into orbit.

It was five minutes before he called back to me. "Uh Ashcan, that's a negative on strike. Two problems with it: First, cannot bomb across friendlies. Second, cannot bomb within kilometer of friendlies. We cannot do this strike. Over."

I was a little stunned. I mean, what the hell was he talking about? I picked up the handset and called back to him.

"Uh, what do you mean you cannot do the strike, over?"

"Uh, Roger, it's against regulations for the two reasons I gave you. I'm sorry, over."

Blue Ghost One jumped in. "Pegasus, this is Blue Ghost One. It is not a matter of regulations. You have to do the strike. Our guys are surrounded by beau-coup bad guys. They've already had several big rushes from NVA from target area. If you don't do the strike they may not survive the day. Copy?"

"Uh, roger, copy Blue Ghost. Regulations are regulations. We cannot do the strike, over."

Blue Ghost was pissed: "Bullshit, Pegasus, who gives a shit about regulations. Help the boys on the ground. They need your help. Knock it off. Copy?"

There was a long lag. Finally Pegasus came back: "Negative, strike is off-regulations, cannot be done. We can drop bombs somewhere else if you want, over."

I heard Blue Ghost start to really let Pegasus have it, but he broke off for a second and I jumped in. "This is Ashcan, Pegasus, ah, negative on dropping bombs elsewhere. We don't need your kind of help. Take your bombs, drop them in the ocean. Go back and write yourself up for denying us an air strike. Copy?"

"Roger, out," was all he could say. And with that the Phantoms took off back east headed for Chu-Lai.

It was real quiet. Captain Dunagan and the guys were looking at me as if to say "what the hell was that?"

Blue Ghost chimed in, "Marines are pussies. They lack ... confidence, over."

Dunagan laughed. I laughed and answered him, "Roger that."

When a major incident occurs, there are always looky-loos, bystanders staring at the action and some help if they can – you know, like when a building burns or when there's a big car wreck. It was no different with our situation. An army company was trapped, surrounded, being attacked and whittled down, and some aircraft were over the scene having a look, to see if there was anything they could do.

Luckily for us, there happened to be an Air Force forward observer orbiting our position in his observation plane. He

Vietnam – The Teenage Wasteland

called down to me: "Uh, Ashcan, this is Helix two-zero, a local Foxtrot Oscar (FO = Forward Observer), I think I can get some "flyboys" (Air Force) down from Da Nang for you. Wait one, copy?"

"Uh, roger Helix. Thanks. Over."

I put down the handset and rubbed my temples.

Captain Dunagan gave me one of his "I'm in pain" looks.

I looked at him and said, "Good, I hope he can get some Air Force guys down here. They won't let us down. Then we get the fuck out of here."

The Captain nodded.

Blue Ghost One called down to me. "Hey Ashcan, we don't need Marines. The Army takes care of its own. We'll handle them from here. Copy? Over."

"Roger Ghost. I'm completely happy with you guys, over."

"Go ahead and get some shut-eye down there. I'll stand watch, over."

"Thanks, Ghost. Appreciate it."

I put down the handset and looked at the Captain, who was back reading the map.

"Got any ideas, Cap?"

"I dunno, I think we can get out of here if bombers are sent in to help us. Putting napalm in the tree line to the north there would definitely relieve the pressure, and they probably have several hundred they are willing to throw at us. So if we wasted the rest of them we could fight our way out to the south-east. Let me look some more."

My radio came to life, it was Colonel Uphill. "Ashcan five-zero, this is Eagle, over."

"Go ahead, Eagle."

"I have Charley Company coming in from the south down a stream to hook up to you. Keep an eye open for them. ETA ten minutes, over."

"Copy Eagle, be advised the bad guys have our radios. Copy?"

"Ah, Roger. Out."

I threw down the handset. "Idiot! Why didn't he just advertise it? The Colonel knew the NVA had our radios"

Dunagan shook his head in disgust.

The 2nd Platoon of Charley Company, led by Lt. James Hamm eased up to the river bed not far from where Alpha Company was surrounded. There were twenty in the platoon, all stripped down to their canteens and bandoliers. Easing into the river bed, they spread out and moved up on both sides.

They approached the "U' shaped bend in the river, we were just a little ways around and beyond it.

The platoon point-man turned around and signaled, showing a snaking bend with his wrist but also pointing straight ahead, across the peninsular of land, directly at our position as the crow flies.

Lt Hamm motioned for Robert Henderson to climb up the river bank and take a better look across the short peninsula of land directly north of our position.

He then grabbed the radio handset from his RTO and made a call. "Ashcan five-zero, this is Beaver five-two, over."

I picked up the handset. "Go, Beaver."

"Uh, roger, we are at your local, across the peninsula to your north. Get your men up and ready to go, we will escort you out. Copy."

"Roger Beaver. Give me two minutes. Copy?"

I turned around and the Captain got up and said, "Get them up and ready. Let's move them out of here."

I got everyone up.

Pointing to five of the closest guys I told them we were moving out across the peninsula.

I went to the top of the river bank and looked west, out across the short peninsular of land the river snaked around as it made its "U" turn on the valley floor while I called up to Blue Ghost;

"Blue Ghost, did you copy all of that?"

"Roger Ashcan. So did the whole world"

"Roger, get ready to give us cover. Copy?"

"Roger, we're on it."

I looked back across the peninsula. Nothing there. I called Charley Company. "Okay Beaver, we are ready. Give me a sign, over."

"Roger Ashcan, one of my men will hold up a grenade launcher, head for it."

Just then a brown arm popped up and it held a grenade launcher.

I told the first five guys to head for it. They got up and moved out, followed closely by me, the Captain and the Mule.

All of a sudden, all hell broke loose. There was AK-47 fire all around us. The five guys in front went down. I went down.

I lifted my head a little and looked around. All I could see was the Captain behind me and in front I saw the boots of Robert Laubaucher, one of the first five guys to head out. I yanked on one of his boots and called to him to pull back.

There was no response.

I got up and looked at him; the back of his head was missing. I looked at the other guys in the group of five, and two others were also dead. Of the five, Robert Laubaucher, Tyree Caldwell, and Donald Priest Jr. died right there.

Another man from Recon platoon also died and in the mad, crazy fight to survive, the Mule ditched the heavy scrambler.

The survivors crawled back into the river bed and sat down.

The Captain then went back up on the river bank and returned with the scrambler and dumped it at my feet. "You can't let them have this." He had gone back up to where the scrambler was and fetched it and brought it down. He did it so the NVA did not get our cipher. I personally didn't give a shit at that moment, but now that I look at it, he made a good move because it would have cost the lives of a great number of men if the cipher had fallen into the wrong hands.

The 2nd Platoon of Charley Company, led by Lt. James Hamm was wiped out in that attack. Seven men killed in an instant with another eight severely wounded.

It was Sargent Kirby's platoon that was decimated by that attack. He was now down to four only troops.

I was completely discouraged. Yet more people had been killed trying to save us. We were surrounded by a far superior force and utterly doomed. Anyone else coming to try and bail us out was going to get killed along with us. I had to end it and end it now.

Dunagan was sitting down rubbing his face. He was done. It was over and we were going to die. I picked up the radio handset. I made the call, speaking in truncated sentences. "This is Ashcan Five-Zero Juliet. Listen up everyone. Do not try to save us. Do not send anyone else. Any attempt to help us will result in disaster. Stay away from us for your own good. Stay away. Out."

Blue Ghost called to ask what happened.

I told him, "Charlie Company tried to hook up to us. We both got ambushed. We lost more men. Charlie Company took a lot of casualties. We're in big trouble, Ghost. Copy?"

"I know you are Ashcan. I know you are. Just hang in there buddy, we'll get you out. Roger?"

"Rog."

I put the handset down and looked at the Captain. He looked at me. We both knew that our time had come. We had come along way, had fought well, done everything we were supposed to and more, but now we were hopelessly trapped. I sat back and a cold, darkness took over my being. I was really, really scared. And it was unlike any time before; this time it was a deep terror and it was starting to paralyze me. It was a panic growing inside me, and it began to take over.

At that moment, Helix came on the radio: "Ashcan five-zero, Helix Two Zero, Over."

I picked up the handset: "Go ahead, Helix."

"Introducing four flyboys from Da Nang."

I heard four sonic booms followed by the screeching of Phantom jet air brakes. I looked up and saw the sleek dark shapes of the Phantoms as they glided into orbit around us at three thousand feet.

"Ashcan five-zero, this is General Richard Armstrong, and I don't care what radio procedure I am breaking, and I don't care what North Vietnamese are listening, you can even have my address you little pricks. I'm at fifty-five, Air Lane Street in Da Nang. I invite you little pricks to come up and visit me, any time. Ashcan, I have been fully appraised as to your situation and I'm here to see to it that you make it out of there. I'm shocked and horrified those Marine pilots failed to help you in your time of need. They have a confidence problem, afraid they couldn't pull off the kind of strike you need. Well, we have confidence. We are all Generals and flew together in World War Two. Our call name then was Tiger Sharks. I am sure you've heard of us. So don't fear: the 366th Tactical Fighter Wing is here. How can we help you down there, Son?"

I was so depressed I didn't think it possible but the General's introduction put a big smile on my face. I also realized that the four most likely volunteered for the mission. They probably heard about our predicament and told other pilots to stand down as they were going to come out and help us. Four Generals! What service from the Air Force! I picked up the handset with my new lease on life: "Uh, Tiger Shark, I am sure glad to have you up there, Sir. Uh, we need some close support. You have to enter the run at one hundred seventy-seven degrees and exit at three-thirty-seven. Your target is five hundred meters north, north-west from my orange "F" panel. That puts the bomb run right across our position, copy?"

"Copy son, we can handle it. We're good and you don't need to worry about us dropping short ones. We aren't like those candy-assed Marine babies. You put a smoke grenade in your right rear pocket and I'll put a five-hundred pounder in your left rear pocket. Copy?"

I laughed. "Copy!"

"Alright, I'm going to do a dummy run here…."

He flew in low on a recon run to look at the strike before dropping bombs. He came in hot, at four hundred knots and peeled off to the right drawing a lot of fire.

"Alright Ashcan, I can do the strike." My heart lifted. Uh, Ashcan, throw a smoke as far as you can at the intended target and direct me from the smoke. Copy?"

I grabbed a green smoke and threw it as far as I could, which was thirty five meters."

"Tiger Shark, smoke is out there. Put first bomb four hundred and fifty meters past the smoke on azimuth three-four-two. Over."

"Roger Ashcan, I'm on the run…"

He was about a mile out when I saw a little black dot appear underneath the Phantom. Then the parasols popped out the ass-end of the bomb and it dropped straight at us.

Tiger Shark One got on the radio talking to his other pilots. "After you drop, do a knife-edge over the tree line. I caught a lot of bullets going through there. Like flying through a hailstorm. Copy?"

"Two."

"Three."

"Four."

They dropped a total of sixteen, five-hundred pound bombs on the NVA staging area. The bombs were walked in deeper and deeper into the wood line, killing NVA and scattering the rest of them all over the woods. Then they buttered the area with deadly napalm.

When all the bombs had been used, the pilots rolled in, one after the other, shooting their twenty millimeter Vulcan cannon as if to let the NVA know they were even willing to pull out their snub-nosed .38s if needed, to get them off of our backs.

The strike was done and the tree line was ablaze. The pilots went back into orbit. Tiger Shark One called back down to me, "Alright Ashcan, we are bingo and Winchester and need to RTB. I hope we helped you guys and seeing that I am a

General I am ordering all of you up to Da Nang for a steak dinner next week. Copy?"

"That's a roger One. Only I'm buying. Over."

"Negative Ashcan, I do the buying, I make more money than you do."

The pilots left orbit and gunned their steeds, heading north. The General made one last call: "You guys get out of that mess, you hear? We are proud of you men down there and know you will do us proud. God bless you all. We'll pray for you on our way back. See you in Da Nang. Out."

Tears welled up in my eyes. I was proud of the people who flew the planes and choppers. They had been lawyers or executives in offices back in the states. They were teachers or insurance adjusters before the war started or they were lifers like the Generals but they were all heroes, each and every one of them. They cared for us and went out of their way to help us out. I was proud to have served with them.

When the last vestiges of sound from the jets had faded away, Blue Ghost One came back on the line. "Ashcan, the strike was effective and took out that staging area to the north. Now we need to plow a corridor to the south so you guys can get out of there. Get your men to the south side of the river while we work them over out there, and drive them to you. Copy?"

"Copy Ghost, give me a few, over."

"Roger, standing by."

I sat down with Captain Dunagan and he pulled out his map. We were working on a strategy to get out of the river bed and head east when I heard the popping of several mortar tubes.

Someone called it out, "incoming!"

For the next ten minutes it literally rained mortars on our position and with accuracy. They landed all over the place. There were calls for medic from every point of the compass. The attack felt like it lasted for an hour before it ended, but it was only ten minutes. I remember laying there, the acrid smell of cordite mixed with dust hanging in the air like smoke from a funeral pyre.

I was covered with dirt and burnt vegetation, dust and cordite. I looked around at the rest of the guys. They were in apathy and had given up. They were done. The mortar attack all but finished them off. It seemed like everyone was bleeding but they didn't even care about that anymore.

I started to order the men back up on the river banks. Donnie waved me off: "Let them come and finish us off. I can't take this anymore. I'm done."

It took a lot of hard work to rally the troops but I finally got them back into a defense posture. It took a lot of yelling, kicks in the ass and pleading, but I got them back at it.

I went back to my radio and looked at my watch. It was five-fifteen. It was going to be dark in another two hours and then they were going to come get us. The NVA weren't going to dick with us any longer. They suffered immense casualties trying to finish us off as we threw everything but the proverbial kitchen sink back at them. But I was sure they now had orders to finish us and be done with it. They would come in right after dark and mop us up.

Such thoughts chilled me to the bone. I looked at the Captain. He was beyond pain, in another place where it didn't hurt, half alive and half in the grave. It was painful to see a magnificent man crushed by such injuries.

I looked around at the other men. They knew the end was near and looked scared and resentful at the same time. As they started back at me there was a combination of fear and resentment. The cause of the fear was obvious; they had seen their friends die horrible, excruciating deaths and knew the same fate awaited them. The resentment was toward the leadership. They were not leaders; they were followers and had now followed their leaders to their imminent deaths. The Captain and I had let them down and now they resented it.

It pissed me off because I had only just become a leader, but now leadership had been thrust upon me, I knew the men did not have the determination or wherewithal to get themselves out of the mess we found ourselves in. It was up to me, and it was up to the Captain – but at that moment he was out of the game. Now I was the man, by default. Okay, so be it. I was not going to let another man die. We were getting out and we were getting out now.

I decided to use the most powerful weapon I had in my arsenal, the only real weapon I had left – communication. I picked up the radio handset and cast our fates to the wind. I didn't care about protocol, about being a good subordinate or about anything else. I just wanted the men to live. I keyed the handset: "Eagle, this is Ashcan, Five-Zero Juliet. Over." My voice was succinct and terse.

The Captain picked up on something in my voice, came out of his reverie and looked over at me, interested.

[Freeze the action here. I want to make a point: This is one of those real important life lessons for me, probably THE most important life lesson. Call it an epiphany if you wish, but I learned it right at that point in the battle, and I learned it big time. When you are in a corner and the knife is up to your throat, you have to make a decision. And that decision is to live or die. It is an active decision. It is a "do I want to live now or do I want to die now?" kind of decision. Believe me, it is the EXACT question you ask yourself under those kinds of circumstances. Sometime people go "Ah to hell with it. I'm going to die right here." And that is exactly what happens. In that situation, at that point in time, I had to make a conscious decision to live and that is when I called Colonel Uphill. After you've decided to live you have to *do* something. I called the only lifeline available and decided to do whatever I had to do to slap it into action. Sometimes you never know what is going to happen, but as long as you are there and want to live, you communicate and something happens.]

"Ashcan Five-Zero Juliet, this is Eagle, go ahead, over." The Colonel came back to me right away. He was in the Command Bunker listening to us, probably pacing back and forth, wondering what to do. He wasn't about to call us because he didn't have anything to offer by way of help. I knew I had him by the ass.

I acted like I was a customer of his, and actually I was, because he was the leader of our outfit, and he was supposed to lead. So where was the leadership? I was being short changed. Well, I was going to have a talk with management about the matter and force the issue. "Eagle, we just got the piss mortared out of us and took on more casualties. We are almost done. It will be dark in less than two hours and then we will be history. Do you copy the situation, over?"

Dunagan was real interested now. He was looking at me with a mixture of surprise and amusement. I gave him the smallest wink.

"Ashcan, I am appraised of your situation, and we are doing everything we can to get you boys out of this mess, copy?"

I snapped back at him. "Negative, Eagle. If I thought you were doing everything you could, I wouldn't be calling you. I don't think anyone there has a clue what to do. I think you're just waiting to hear our final call but that's not going to happen. You are going to come up with a plan for us, and it is going to be in the next ten minutes. I don't care if you come out here on your chopper and start shooting at these bastards with your .45, but you need to do something, and it needs to happen now. You are the Colonel of this battalion, so what is the plan? Over"

I snapped the key of the radio and looked at the Captain, who was now smiling. I knew it hurt him to smile, but I'd just done what he wanted to do for the last several hours but couldn't, and it made him real happy.

Uphill came back, trying to placate me. "Alright, calm down son, we are all working on it right now. We will get you out of there, over."

"Cut the crap Eagle, my life is less than two hours from being over. I want a plan and I want it now. Copy Eagle?"

Dunagan slapped his thigh and actually chuckled.

There was a long lag. I knew the wheels were turning. Finally, Uphill came back: "Ashcan, we want to see this through. Just need to give us some time. We have to work this out. Over."

More empty talk. Now I was genuinely pissed. "Eagle, you've had plenty of time to work out a plan; you just haven't done it yet. We are out of time, I repeat, out of time. I want a plan now. So let's get smart. What is the plan? Over."

Uphill finally exploded. "I don't know Ashcan. I ... I ... just don't know. I'll... I'll ... I'll call every firebase that can reach you and have them pour artillery all around your location until nothing is left of the valley. By God, I'll bring more smoke on that valley than you ever heard of ..."

When Uphill claimed he was going to "bring smoke" into the valley, a bright light went off in Captain Dunagan's head. He grabbed the handset from me, keyed it and called to Uphill.

"Eagle, this is Ashcan. Smoke is a great idea. Have the firebases bombard the area with smoke rounds. It will give us cover to get the hell out of here and connect up to Charley Company. Do you copy?"

Uphill came back, excited, "Yes, yes Ashcan, that's an excellent idea. I'll put the calls in now. The arty should be to you in less than five minutes. Get your men together and get them ready to go, over."

"Roger Eagle, out."

Dunagan was back in control. He ordered me to get all the men in groups of five and to make sure they had a compass in each group, and that they knew to go south. The smoke would be so thick they would not be able to see ten feet. We could steer ourselves south using the compasses.

I gathered up the men and put them together in groups of five, making sure they all had compasses. The wounded would be carried on make-shift litters that had already been constructed by Doc Ballenger.

Another big decision had to be made. We had 12 dead bodies lying around the landscape. There were also still a lot of NVA in the area and especially to the south. The dead were going to be used as bait by the NVA because that's what they do. We made an active decision not to lose anyone because they had to care for a body. That was it. The dead would be left behind.

There were also three machine guns that no one claimed. I shot them in the receiver and buried them in the silt in the river.

I didn't know it then, but I found out later that most of the arty companies were out of regular smoke rounds. They only had White Phosphorous (WP or Willy-P) rounds left. They are very dangerous because they land, explode and spread phosphorous fragments that burn at seventeen hundred degrees Fahrenheit and water does not extinguish them. You're hit by the stuff it just burns through your skin.

Just then the first smoke round came in and landed right in the river, then another on the north river bank. Then more. They were landing all around us – ten of them, twenty of them, then thirty.

The smoke became thick enough to cloak us and the Captain yelled to move out.

I got everyone started and then called on my radio for cease fire on the artillery but the rounds just kept coming. We were dodging rounds landing all around us. White-hot phosphorous landed on all of us. You had to be fast to brush it off; otherwise it started to burn through your clothing and then your skin. I don't have to tell you that it hurt like hell.

Everyone had taken off except me, Brian and the Captain. As soon as he saw all the men had taken off, he gave us the nod and we took off through the smoke.

The NVA was wise to our ruse and lay down a withering base of rifle-fire through the smoke. It was a gauntlet we had to run – the final attempt by the enemy to carry out their orders to finish us.

I was giddy and trying to move as fast as I could as I felt the bullets going past me, inches away, but somehow I felt invincible. It was not going to end for me in the smoke. We had figured out the perfect escape and no bullets were going to get me, not now. I was too close.

One thing we didn't count on was the massive amount of burning phosphorous in the field. It was hot out there; around two hundred degrees and the oxygen was almost gone, used up by the burning phosphorous. Each step required more and more energy. We were quickly running out of oxygen, if we didn't get out of the smoke soon, we would expire from a lack of breathable air.

Just when it got its absolute worst and my legs were leaden, we popped out of the smoke and into Charley Company's waiting arms. We ran right to them and collapsed, our burning lungs begging for air.

Dunagan found Captain Brownlee and they shook hands. I shook hands with Brownlee's RTO. We watched the stragglers coming in. I did a head count and came up with twenty-nine.

Dunagan came over to me and asked me how many had arrived. I told him twenty-nine. He said it was "not enough. We left with forty-five" and with that he took off into the smoke.

Just then a wounded man came out of the smoke and collapsed at my feet. I asked some guys from Charley Company to help him out because I planned on taking off after the Captain.

Before I got back into the smoke, Captain Dunagan suddenly popped out of it with a man over his shoulder.

Dunagan dropped Bob Tullos, from Recon, at my feet and disappeared back into the smoke.

Bob Tullos lifted up his right leg and proudly pointed at it. "I'm going home," he declared. His foot was chopped off at the ankle, pouring blood. I grabbed his leg and tied it off with the lacing from his pant leg, and then I helped him over to Charley Company's medic.

I turned around looking for the Captain. He was still in the smoke and the bullets were still flying. I had to get him out of there. I ran into the smoke and almost bumped into him. He had another man over his shoulder that he carried all the way to Charlie Company defense line. He dumped the injured man off there and headed back towards the smoke.

I intercepted him. "Captain, you need to go check on the men that made it through. They need a leader. I'll go back and look for more, okay?"

"Tom, we have people in there. We left the river bed with forty-five men, we have only thirty three. There are thirteen men unaccounted for. Look hard, okay?"

I assured him I would.

I went into back the smoke. It was eerie in there. I heard gunfire close by. An NVA soldier suddenly popped into view and I shot him before he could bring his AK up at me. I looked around some more and called out for anyone. No one answered. I went back towards Charlie Company. The Captain saw me.

"No one else, Cap."

"You sure?"

"Absolutely."

He wasn't convinced. He looked back into the smoke, and then we heard someone yell from deep in the smoke. "Help me. H-e-e-lllp me."

Dunagan ran back towards the smoke.

Vietnam – The Teenage Wasteland

I stopped him. "Captain, if it was one of ours they'd have used a name. That's the NVA trying to call us back in there."

"You can't be sure," the Captain replied. He seemed anxious to go back into the smoke.

"No more Captain. It's done."

He was not convinced.

I urged him. "Captain, they'd call my name or someone else's name. It's the NVA trying to sucker us back in there. Don't fall for it."

At that moment, Captain Brownlee called Dunagan over. "Eagle wants you on the radio." He held up the hand set.

Dunagan went to the radio but turned to me and said, "Stay there and wait for more. If you hear anyone call out a name, go get them."

"I promise, Cap."

I could hear jet fighters on station. I called to them and asked them what they were packing. They told me they had napalm only. I nodded to myself. Just what the doctor ordered. "Drop napalm on that area in the river. Waste everything to the north of it. Copy"

"Roger, Ashcan."

They rolled in and dropped their canisters.

When the napalm went off Dunagan yelled at me, "Who ordered that air strike?"

I told him I did.

He was livid. "We don't know if there are any survivors in there, Tom. You could be killing our men god dam it."

"Not anymore Captain. It is finished, done. I burned the bridge."

He just glared at me, really pissed. He then turned and looked at Captain Brownlee, but he just shrugged his shoulders like it wasn't his business.

A chopper came in and took some of our wounded out. Eagle called me and told me another chopper was coming in and to put Dunagan on it, no fail. I assured him I would.

The second chopper landed and I turned to Dunagan. "That chopper is for you, Sir."

He waved me off. "Tell Uphill I am not going back and to go fuck himself. And you too!"

"Captain, that chopper has orders to stay on the ground until you are on it. Please get on it, go get fixed up and then return. Charley Company will get us back."

He ignored me and continued talking with the survivors.

I walked up to him. "Captain, that chopper isn't going to leave without you. You're endangering our lives and the lives of the chopper crew by being stubborn. Get on the fucking chopper or I will relieve you of command for endangering lives and refusing direct orders from the colonel."

He glared at me. I had him and he saw my resolve. He turned around and got on the chopper. I put the handset to my mouth and called the chopper pilot. "Viper Seven, this is Ashcan five-zero. The package is aboard, please take it on to Chu Lai Medical and drop it off there along with the rest of the wounded. Over."

"Roger Ashcan, out."

And with that, the chopper took off.

Dunagan never so much as looked at me. I knew he hated me, but that was too bad.

I went and found Lt Waltz as he was the only officer we had left in the group. He looked like shit, covered with mud and blood; he was not looking too good at all. I grabbed him by the shoulders and said, "Dave, you have command of the company. What are your orders?"

Dave looked straight through me as if I wasn't there. He'd lost just about his entire platoon. His best friends were lying dead on the battlefield and he was in shock over it. He was not in shape to lead the company right then. I patted him on the back.

Walking over to the Captain of Charley Company, I addressed him. "Hi, Captain, I'm Specialist 4th Class, Tom Martiniano, Captain Dunagan's Radio Man. We have thirty-three men who can still fight but no officers left. I'm taking command of the company. We'll follow you, and I suggest we get out of this location before they stage another attack."

"Yeah, we're moving out now. Get your guys together and spread them out. Put a good man on the slack position and have him keep his eyes open. Get ready to move out. We're going to high ground for the night."

My guys were all lying down, lolling in the grass. I got them up and moving by telling them we needed to get out of there because there might be another attack. That made them move.

I then heard the sounds of Cobra choppers and realized that Blue Ghost was still on station. It was getting to be twilight and they needed to get out of there. I keyed the mike: "Blue Ghost, Ashcan, over."

"Ashcan! Did you guys make it?"

"Ah, Roger, for the most part, we lost some on the way over, but the majority are safely in the hands of Charley Company. Copy?"

"Copy and thank God. I was worried about you guys. The smoke was a great idea. Who came up with that?"

"The Captain. He may be severely wounded, but he still had the wheels working. Over."

"Roger. That was brilliant. You guys on the move now?"

"Roger, we're going to logger for the night with Charley, over."

"Rog Ashcan."

I needed to cut Blue Ghost loose. He sounded burnt out. They'd done a bang-up job, but they had been in the choppers for eleven hours and had to be fried. I wanted to thank him too and the rest of the Blue Ghost gang. "Uh Blue Ghost, this is Ashcan. I have no words for you guys. You saved our lives down here and I can only say that your dedication to the ground troops will not be forgotten. I stand in awe of you and will never forget you guys. Copy?"

"Copy and thanks Ashcan. I am glad we helped get you out of that mess. I'm sorry we couldn't save everyone. But we all did our best."

"Just so you know, Blue Ghost, you saved our lives, so understand that. As a team we kicked butt. The KIA for the bad guys is estimated at around one thousand to fifteen hundred. I think you guys did the lions share. Copy?"

"Whoo!"

"Alright, listen, you guys RTB, it's getting dark and I know your mother is worried. Thanks again buddy, you guys are the best. Next time we get in trouble, we'll call you."

"Please don't call us, please! Just kidding. Good luck and – hey – look us up on the beach next week for a burger and beer, copy?"

"Good idea, get some cold ones ready and I'll be there. God Bless, Blue Ghost. Out."

With that, Blue Ghost One and Two departed the area and headed back to base.

All of a sudden it was quiet. No jets, no choppers, no nothing. Just the quiet sounds of the jungle hunkering down for the night. I didn't like the feeling of silence from the sky. It made me feel alone, unarmed and vulnerable.

If there is any question whether the helicopters made a difference in Vietnam, trust me, they did. It was a bad feeling not hearing the sound of their rotors in the near distance. When you had them above, you knew you had a bad-assed big brother ready and more than willing to rain steel from the sky to help you out.

We made it to a small hill that night. I tried to get the scrambler up and running but it had taken two rounds and was junk.

Uphill called me and wanted to know our strength. Because security was still a big issue with our radios in the hands of the enemy, I told him cryptically how many we had left, and again, he told me he was sorry. Well, who wasn't?

Vietnam – The Teenage Wasteland

We all ate for the first time in three days. God I was so starved that even cold C-Rations tasted good. So we ate and then slept like babies. Charlie Company stood watch for us and let us catch up on the sleep we so horribly needed.

The next morning the Colonel called me and ordered Alpha back to the Hill, which was now three klicks away. I told Captain Brownlee that we'd be able to make it ourselves. I shook hands with him, and we went our separate ways.

I walked point, with Lt Waltz right behind me. We skirted as much thick vegetation as possible. We ran across a few scattered NVA scouting patrols, but we hid, avoiding any contact with the enemy and pressed on to the hill.

After seeing more NVA, we stopped and I decided I needed gunships and asked for Blue Ghost back but they were up north helping the 101st Airborne and were not available so they were sending me the Firebirds.

I remembered the last time I used them. We received more casualties from them than the NVA. However, they were better than nothing.

They came on station and I gave them clear orders. "Firebird, I want you to just hang loose and patrol. We are pretty spread out down here so do not – repeat – do not engage without clearing it with me, copy?"

"Copy Ashcan. Where are you, over?"

"Uh, understand, Firebird, that the bad guys have our radios. I cannot give you a location over the radio. You are just going to have to be good with your eyes. Copy?"

"Copy Ashcan. We'll look hard. Over."

So we moved out again. We arrived in an open area and I could see the gunships with their tiger teeth painted on the nose of the craft as they circled the area.

It took us an hour and a half to walk a klick. We moved with stealth, stopped, looked and listened, and then we walked a little more, stopped and so forth. It was taking forever because we were so paranoid.

At one point we took a break. It was another fiercely hot day. Lt Waltz and a machine gunner named Lamont, and I rested up against a clump of small trees with the rest of the guys spread out from there in the shade.

Firebird One came around a grove of trees a hundred meters in front of us just twenty feet off of the ground. I waved at him. The door gunner opened up on us with a mini-gun and the ground erupted at our feet.

Not again! Are these guys blind or what? I jumped up and saw the chopper slam on the brakes and start to turn into us. I had to do something fast. We had little cover and were easy targets for them. I brought my rifle up, and opened up on the gunship, full automatic. I dumped a whole magazine into the chopper.

The chopper turned back left and went around the grove of trees. I knew he was going to do a missile attack on us.

I called to Lamont. "Set up the pig, if he comes around those trees, bring him down. That's an order!"

I picked up my handset. "Firebird, Firebird, this is Ashcan Five-zero, break off attack NOW. Do you copy?"

"Negative Ashcan, we received ground fire. I lost my windscreen to ground fire. Copy?"

"That was me, you idiot. Your door gunner opened up on us and I returned fire. Do not come around – I have ordered my guys to shoot you down, do not engage, copy?"

He came at us on a missile run. I stood up with the handset to my mouth and looked straight at the chopper.

"It's me you're sighting in on. Do not shoot, you will be brought down. Over."

He hovered for a minute and then turned his side to us just a hundred feet away, looking us over.

The door gunner waved at us cheerfully and I flipped him off.

The gunship left us and went back on patrol.

I looked at the rest of the guys: "Everyone okay?"

They all nodded. Avery laughed incredulously. "You tried to shoot him down?"

"Fucking-A. He was going to kill us."

He just shook his head. He was not sure what he saw. After the last three days he thought he'd seen everything, but this – Americans trying to kill Americans was just an overload for him.

I called to Firebird; they were two for two in trying to kill us that month. "Firebird, you are dismissed. We do not need your kind of help here. Return to Base and write yourself up. Over."

The pilot called back to me to make a case of it "Uh, Ashcan, my gunner said you guys fired first, that's why he shot at you."

That pissed me off even more. "Hey, fuck you Firebird that's not the way it went down and you know it. Get the fuck out of here, you are relieved. Out" (When you say "Out" that means "conversation ended).

So Firebird took off.

Eagle called me and asked me if I wanted some other gunships.

My response: "Negative Eagle. We'll go the rest of the way ourselves. We're coming in, ETA thirty minutes. Over."

"Copy Ashcan. We'll open the wire for you. Which side are you coming up?"

Again, he was blowing it. His security was the pits.

"Uh, I'll let you know, Eagle. Out."

I turned around and told the guys we were done with fucking around. We were going to march straight to the hill and take our chances. The longer we stayed out the greater the danger. I told them we were going in a straight line to the hill, across open area – no more screwing around. This caused a litany of responses from the guys. Some wanted to wait until dark and others wanted to wait for some help. I finally pointed out it was not a democracy and ordered them to get moving and they did.

We went the rest of the way to the Hill without incident and walked to the top. Colonel Uphill was there to greet us. He hugged me and then hugged Waltz. It was over.

My adrenaline shut down. All the events of the last four days came crashing in on me like a flood from a broken dam. The grief was so overwhelming it forced me to the ground.

I was crying for a few minutes, and then the grief turned into rage. I turned around and threw my rifle over the side of the Hill. Then I took off my rucksack and threw it over the Hill too, radio and all. This upset Uphill and he came over to console me.

"Okay, Tom. I know you went through some bad times out there, but your company will get built back up and you guys will be back as big and bad as ever before."

I cut him off. "No way Colonel, I am NEVER going back out there. I quit. I don't care if you send me to jail. I am DONE. NEVER going back out there, NEVER. Now get away from me."

Uphill walked away rather than confront me, which was probably very smart of him – because I don't lose it that often, but when I do, I'm impossible to deal with and everything just escalates. The best thing to do is let me unwind and chill out by myself.

A few other officers came to see me and asked if I was going to help build the company back up. I looked at them like they were from Mars and told them, "Fuck you; I am not going back out there, find someone else."

After that they led me to an outside jail of sorts and locked me up in a pen about the size of a dog run, made of cyclone fencing material. Just as well, I was ready for jail. It was better than lying out in the bush, rotting like so many my friends were right now.

I sat there and thought about all the dead men we'd left behind out there somewhere, the Valley of Death. That sucked.

Vietnam – The Teenage Wasteland

The remaining thirty-two of my guys from Alpha Company camped near me on the Hill for the night. They stuck together, more from not knowing where to go or what to do, waiting for someone to give them the word. For now, they were a decimated company and out of commission.

I woke up the next morning with the sound of a chopper coming in. To my total chagrin two recruiters moved in on us like sharks when there's blood in the water. They wanted to know if we wanted out of the infantry and if we did, they would get us out if we re-upped for four more years.

I told the rest of the guys not to listen to them. I told them that the vultures were lying scumbags and they were just playing on our frayed nerves and fear, and they'd all end up back in the infantry in Vietnam for another two tours.

The recruiters, both Lieutenants, told me to shut up and I told them to go fuck themselves.

They pulled the guys away from my cage and worked them over one-by-one. At the end of the day they walked off with fifteen men.

Fuck them. So there were seventeen of us left. Jessie and Kirby, Joe Rutherford, Holloway and other good guys stayed. To hell with the rest of them – they could have four more years of shit. Not me.

Then I thought; "Holy shit, between the NVA and the recruiters, our hundred and ten man company had been reduced to seventeen men in four days," But what did I care? I was going to prison and I was happy about it.

18

LAMAR PLAIN

On May 15, 1969 the Commander of Americal Division put out an official TAC-E (Tactical Emergency). This is done only when a unit is under severe attack and needs help. Other infantry divisions then offer their services and help handle the situation.

Americal (my division) was the biggest Division in Vietnam but for some unfortunate reason it had fewer helicopter gunship resources than any other division. By 15 May, Americal found itself in the sticky situation of having only a few birds that could fly. What few they had before 12 May, were either destroyed or badly shot up in the three days that followed (May 12 to May 14).

Americal had lost a total of seventy five men in those few days with another two hundred twenty wounded and out of action.

A lot of their aircraft lay in the bush, destroyed by enemy anti-aircraft artillery. Most of the rest were damaged and out of action.

And there was something new – it was the first time in the history of the Americal Division, in Vietnam, that NVA forces

Vietnam – The Teenage Wasteland

were engaging American forces in broad daylight, out in the open. This, above all else, meant something to the Americal top Brass. The NVA were brazen because they now had troops in big numbers and that meant they were going to continue to attack and attack with renewed vigor. Army Intelligence figured this was just the start of a major enemy offensive in our AO.

With the 1st of the 46th out of commission, B Battery Artillery on LZ Pro all but destroyed and their attack choppers out of commission, Americal had a serious situation: They would not be able to engage an aggressive NVA force of any real size and survive it. Thus the TAC-E was called and help came-a-running.

The TAC-E kicked off the operation known as Lamar Plain which lasted from May 15th, 1969 to August 15th, 1969.

The 101st Airborne Division volunteered some of their vast resources and choppered in two battalions of infantry to our AO. The two battalions were the 501st and 502nd infantry battalions. Our Brigade became attached to and under the control of the 101st. They were our new bosses.

The 501st and 502nd went straight out into the bush on May 16 to clean up the rest of the insurgents and their troops immediately met heavy resistance. In the first day they lost five men KIA and a score of severely injured.

A pilot from the 101st Airborne Air Cavalry's B Troop, 1/17 Air Cavalry reported the following details of the start of Lamar Plain, from "a bird's eye view". This account shows what the chopper pilots from the 101st saw and ran into on the days following 15 May 1969. The article is written by John Hayes titled "Recon Zone Alpha" (Recon Zone Alpha was the 101st Airborne Divisions name for "The Valley of Death"):

"The Americal Division's area of operations (A/O) was the largest and, in some ways, the most difficult in South Vietnam. Although Americal was numerically one of the largest U.S. divisions, it lacked the helicopter assets of the 101st Airborne Division. The terrain offered several advantages to the enemy.

In extreme northern I Corps, the villages and friendly population hugged the thin coastal strip; anyone in the mountains was the enemy. In the area west of Tam Ky, the terrain was gently rolling with open areas and friendly villages interspersed with low jungle. This afforded the Northern Vietnamese Army (NVA) rapid movement, easy resupply, and some protection when in or near friendly villages.

"*The A/O for the 1st Brigade would be roughly an oblong shaped area from east of Tam Ky to the village of Tien Phouc toward the west. Most of this landscape consisted of a valley formed by a lone mountain on the west (later called Recon Zone Alpha), a river meandering north and south near Phouc to the west, and low ridges forming the north and south boundaries. Helicopter crews said this place was called "Death Valley." FSB Professional was located on a small rise on the valley floor, with higher ridges to the north and south. Enemy pressure on the landing zone was so great that resupply was in danger of being cut off. Several days earlier, a CH-47 Chinook had been destroyed by recoilless rifle fire while it hovered over the helipad - in daylight. The day before the alert was issued; a company-sized infantry team had left FSB Professional on foot to sweep the immediate area. Only a handful of the team members had returned; the opposition had been so fierce that the dead and wounded had been left behind. It was thought that grunts had run into the main body of the 2nd North Vietnamese Army (NVA) Regiment. The S-2 (military intelligence) officer believed that the NVA regiment was reinforced with an anti aircraft battalion equipped with 12.7mm machine guns. Roughly equivalent to American .50-caliber M-2 machine guns, these weapons were sometimes referred to as ".51's."*

"*The first mission of the brigade aero-scouts was to find the site where the infantry team had been lost, locate the enemy, and look for American survivors. Probing the foothills northwest of FSB Professional, the brigade scouts in their small LOHs began investigating trails and hooches made of*

Vietnam – The Teenage Wasteland

bamboo and thatch, experiencing sporadic automatic-weapons fire at every turn. The mission was different from what they had experienced up north. Up north it was rare for only one or two weapons to open up; troops were more likely to run into a heavy volume of disciplined fire. Here, however, it seemed that the NVA gunners on the ground were trying to swat gnats away—a few bursts of fire and perhaps the pests would fly away. One NVA gunner would fire from a hut, another from some nearby trail, and yet two more from a tree line. It was obvious that enemy troops did not perceive any real threat from the little choppers buzzing overhead.

"On the first day, the white team operated alone; the Cobras and the FACs were not yet available to the scouts. The scouts had to be content with returning fire, dropping a few fragmentation or white phosphorus grenades, marking their maps and waiting for tomorrow.

"The Americal Division had only one air cavalry troop (F Troop, 8th Cavalry "Blueghost") and very limited gunship support. The 2nd NVA Regiment was unaccustomed to the tactics and sheer numbers of helicopters it would face in the days to come. By the second day of the mission, the full weight of the 101st's Air Cav, the ARA (aerial rocket artillery) and close air support was being brought to bear on the NVA. On the third day the brigade Aero-scouts found what they had been looking for. A scout pilot had noticed a series of dark spots on the ground in a low area dominated by several small hills. When the pilot began working the area, he encountered a large volume of fire from the surrounding hills, and the accompanying ARA gunships made strike after strike. The enemy here was now more disciplined and much heavier than the scouts had experienced in the previous two days. When the birds ran low on fuel and munitions, a FAC arrived with F-4s (Phantom fighter-bombers) to continue the fight. The cycle was repeated several times, alternating Cobras and F-4s, until the enemy action had ceased. At that point the scouts were able to examine the target area closely. Each dark spot *marked a fallen American soldier, the dark spots around each body caused by blood that had soaked the ground and turned dark as it dried. And each body had several bamboo poles thrust into it at odd angles. The scouts had found the wounded that had been left behind, and there were no survivors.*

Although their makeup was different, the size of the two opposing forces was similar enough that neither side could maneuver for a decisive advantage. For every company-sized flanking movement performed by one opponent, a successful countermove was devised by the other. For several days this deadly fandango continued without letup. The helicopter crews as well as the infantry were beginning to feel the pressure of sustained combat. By the end of the first week of the battle, only one OH-6 and two Cobras were flyable. Of all the aircraft of an Air Cav troop, an ARA (Aerial Rockets Artillery) battery and a scout section, all but three were shot down or were so badly damaged that they could not fly for a 24-hour period. It was rumored that the "ground-pounders" had lost 75 killed in action, and it was easy for those who were there to believe it.

"The main problem was the .51s. Their fire was devastating to unarmored troops and thin-skinned aircraft. Their heavy staccato hammering made all other battlefield noise seem like whispers. A team of .51s (two, three, four, even more) and supporting small arms would stop an infantry advance cold.

"The initial helicopter losses were a result of poor tactics. Pink teams and unprotected white teams were simply outgunned by the anti-aircraft the enemy had deployed in and around Death Valley. Recon flights that normally required a team of two helicopters were now performed by a team of five or six aircraft. After the tactics were changed (by the middle of the second week), helicopter losses dropped significantly.

"The Air Cav operated in heavy teams of two or three Cobras covering the scouts, with a Huey high overhead to act as a recovery bird if someone was shot down. The brigade

Vietnam – The Teenage Wasteland

aero-scout teams were even heavier; each mission consisted of two LOHs (Light Observation Helicopters) low, two ARA Cobras, a FAC and two F-4s on station. There was no more hovering or following footprints for the scouts. From 3,000 feet, the LOHs would dive for the jungle as fast as possible. This would put them in the "dead man's zone" for the least amount of time. (From a distance of 50 to 1,500 feet, automatic weapons were very effective against helicopters; when the LOHs were operating against .51s, the danger zone was increased to 3,000 feet.) The LOHs would keep their speed up as they made a run over a target area. Inevitably they would draw heavy fire from dozens of AK-47s and as many as six or seven .51s. The gunners and observers would drop as many white phosphorus grenades as possible to mark the targets, while trying to simultaneously suppress the enemy with M-16, M-60 and mini gun fire. After a marking run by the scouts, the Cobras would roll in with rockets and 40mm grenades. Usually the Cobras would expend their ammunition and the enemy positions would be pounded by ground artillery.

"Although the U.S. and NVA forces were numerically somewhat similar, the fire support and logistical backup afforded the American forces made for a vast difference between the 1st Brigade and the 2nd NVA Regiment. By the third week of the battle, the 2nd Regiment began trying to break contact, in an effort to fade away into the jungle. The regiment had broken up into company and platoon-sized elements and dispersed. The primary goal of the U.S. Air Cav and Aero-scout units at that point was to find these elements so the infantry could finish their destruction. There were reports of a complete NVA hospital to the south of the A/O, and it was thought that the remnants of the 2nd Regiment would try to evade in that direction or to the west, toward Laos. For days, scout teams and patrols scoured the hills north, south and west of Death Valley. Although there was frequent contact with the enemy, the NVA troops encountered

were generally isolated stragglers or small, disorganized units. Had the 2nd Regiment successfully evaded the 1st Brigade, either linking up with the hospital to the south or, more likely, reaching Laos in the west? To most of the brass, it seemed likely."

(The 2nd NVA Division was finally found by the choppers of the 1/17th and the was destroyed by the ARA Cobras, the F-4s and the ground troops of both the Americal and the 101st Airborne, as fully described in later chapters.

Vietnam – The Teenage Wasteland

19

MAY 16 1969
A NEW START

On May 16th I learned something disturbing. At end of the day on May 14, Captain Dunagan flew back to LZ Pro instead of going to Chu Lai, where he was ordered to go. At LZ Pro, Dunagan jumped off the chopper and punched out Colonel Uphill.

After being sent on to Chu Lai, Captain Dunagan wrote us a letter saying he was sorry so many of his men had died and wished he was with us. He felt he would be back soon – but he was sent to Japan for surgery, then off to America, never to return to Vietnam.

What disturbed me was why Dunagan punched out Uphill. It was weird. I wondered about it for quite some time. I fell asleep again wondering about it.

I woke up just before dinner and a smiling face was outside my cage. It was the Captain from Delta Company. He was a large man, around 6'1" and a good 180 pounds with a round jovial face and a standard military crew-cut of light brown hair. His eyes told his entire story. They said that he was a happy man and he was compassionate but he was also one person you did not want to mess with. His name was Captain Roberts. He reminded me of Captain Dunagan.

He brought dinner for both of us and was eating with me when he told me he was assigned to Alpha Company by Division and wanted to know if I would help him put the company back together. I told him the same thing I told the Colonel – I was going to jail and that was the end of it.

He told me some good news, that Lt Tomanaha and five other Alpha and recon men had walked up to Bravo Company perimeter and convinced them that they were Americans. That was brave of Lt Tomanaha because he was Japanese and from a distance could have been mistaken for Vietnamese. Six more survivors was very good news and it definitely raised my spirits. Our Medic Richard Bellanger was there too. I was blown away. They were folded right back into the company and hunkered down with Alpha on LZ Pro.

Captain Roberts stayed with me for three hours peeling me like an onion. I told him everything and he consoled me. Finally, he found my button and pushed it – the "please help me" button. It worked like a charm. At the end of the three hours I was out of the cage and was Captain Roberts' new RTO.

The next day we received about forty new men from Chu Lai. They were cooks, clerks, truck drivers and so on. They were really pissed they had been pulled from the safety of the rear and brought to an infantry unit.

None-the-less the Captain, Sergeant Milton and I trained them by re-acquainting them with the M-16, rockets, machine guns and so on. By the end of the third day, we had a company of around eighty-six men but only one Lieutenant for a platoon leader. It was a rag-tag bunch, but it was what we had.

Our first duty was to go back out and pick up the dead men we left behind. They had been out there under the burning sun for seven days. But the area was still too hot to go into. The NVA knew we would be back for the bodies and would be using them as bait.

Vietnam – The Teenage Wasteland

It was really dangerous for us to be out in the bush with a brand new, un-experienced company, so we had to be careful not to get into any fights. We still had a ways to go to train the new guys to a level anything like our old company.

We left the LZ every day and went out on day-long patrols no further than one or two clicks. The new guys were freaked out about being in the bush, but doing our daily short trips helped them acclimate.

And LZ Professional was still under siege. Any aircraft that approached LZ Pro was hammered by three .51 caliber machine guns, positioned 120 degrees away from each other and about two miles out. No chopper could get near us. The idea was to starve us out.

One day we boarded a big Chinook helicopter on the lower pad, and he caught a round in the front rotor bearing. The front rotor froze as its bearing melted, the driveshaft snapped and the front of the chopper dropped to the ground. Everyone jumped out as the rear of the chopper still hovered.

The friction from the freeze-up in the front rotor bearing caused a grease fire which spread to the rest of the chopper and destroyed it totally. It was made out of magnesium which is the same thing old fashioned flash-bulbs are made of. So the chopper burned hot and burned thoroughly. One couldn't look directly at it while it burned; it was like looking at the sun. Later, when we looked at the remains, all you could see were the two turbine hubs, the two rotor hubs and the barrels of two machine guns. Everything else was fine ash.

After the Chinook went down, we figured we were screwed. No water, no ammo, no food again, and probably for a long time. It was the no-water that was the most dangerous in the heat.

Another Chinook headed in with a 5,000 gallon water blivet. The blivets were made of rubber, are round and huge like a swimming pool. I saw the Chinook coming in and thought I'd help him with some air cover from the .50 on top of my bunker. The Chinook came in and started taking fire. I gave him cover fire, but I didn't know where the gun was that was hammering him. The next thing I knew bullets were hitting around me. I bailed off the bunker.

I was on the ground hiding when the Chaplain, Colonel Francis Murphy came up and said "Let me show you how a real man handles this." He climbed up on the .50 and opened fire. Rounds hit all around him and he jumped off the gun.

He hid next to me, behind the bunker, looked at me and said, "Why are you letting a man of God fire machine guns?"

That was funny. He was a funny guy. I looked at him and said, "I thought God made you do that."

He shook his head and said, "No! The Devil made me do it."

The water didn't make it. The chopper dropped the blivet but it rolled down the hill and exploded like a huge tidal-wave, washing down the hillside.

I sat behind the bunker and thought a little longer, when I noticed a skid mark on the ground. It was from an incoming bullet. Then I looked at my bunker where the overhang was supported by some four by fours. There was a bullet crease in one and a hole in another. I sighted down the skid in the ground and looked at where it came from. Then I did the same with the crease in the four by four. They all pointed to the same place. "Gotcha!" I murmured, excitedly.

I ran into my bunker and got my map. I looked again along the creases and saw the coordinates for where one of the .51's was. I called for an air strike. The Colonel came out to see me.

"Whatcha got, there son?" I showed him.

He got excited. "By god, I think you got it, son."

We called in the air strike and told them to carry napalm only. The NVA gun emplacements had hiding holes by them, but napalm gas went in the holes and fried them on the spot.

The F-4's arrived fifteen minutes later, and I told them the coordinates, but I wanted to pin it down exactly, so told them I was going to mark it for them with my .50 when they were ready for their run and to watch my tracers.

Number One rolled in and told me he was on his bomb run. I looked over my shoulder and saw him rolling in. I opened up and laid my tracers right in where the enemy .51 was.

The enemy started to return fire, but then saw the F-4 coming at him and focused his aim on the jet. I could see green tracers coming from the other enemy 51's, but they could not catch a Phantom doing three-fifty knots.

The F-4 laid the napalm right on him. I told Two to roll in and drop another one on him just for good luck. He did and the .51 was silenced for good.

I called to my crew to move my .50 to the south side of the hill. While they were moving it, I ran ahead of them to the south side of the hill and I looked for skid marks and creases, found them, and did it again on the other side.

I want to tell you that duking it out with another .51 caliber machine gun is not for the faint of heart. As soon as he saw me setting up, he opened up on me because they knew I was going to find them. Those half-inch bolognas passing your ear at three times the speed of sound is not what I call fun.

I checked my map, laid the tracers in and the F-4s fried them with napalm.

Then we got the third one the same day. I got my Bronze star that day. The whole hill was happy with me because the Chinooks were able to land. I was getting to be a celebrity on that hill.

We got our food, water and ammo and kept it coming until the NVA got new .51's to harass us – but we handled them in the same fashion. Their master plan of starving us out was not going to work.

We left the hill a few days later and went to find our MIAs. The chopper and air strikes in ".50 Caliber Valley" as the airmen called it, or the Valley of Death as we called it, had cleared the way for us to sneak in there and get our dead.

We were informed that the bodies were still bait, not only for the choppers, but for us, so we moved in very carefully. I still didn't know the operational status of our new company or if they could fight at all. We would soon find out.

We snuck in and picked up what was left of the bodies, which was not much. We put them in body bags and onto a chopper ferrying them to Graves Registration for their ride home in the metal boxes.

We went on with a new attitude but just did patrols around the base at LZ Professional. We ran into only a little contact.

The 101st Airborne battalions were still involved in heavy fighting. They were losing choppers left, right and center. Americal was out of choppers and the landscape in our AO was becoming a junkyard of metal carcasses.

But the little skirmishes we were getting into were just the thing to break in the new troops in our company, and I felt less and less nervous about them.

At some point, a few days later, my right foot started to pain me. I had not removed my boots for several days because wet nursing new troops in the field freaked me out so I slept with my boots on, ready for action at a moment's notice.

It really started to hurt so I went to the medic. We tried to get my boot off, but it wouldn't come off. The boot and the sock were glued to my foot by mung. The medic reported it to Captain Roberts.

Captain Roberts was not happy about me having to leave the field. He asked me to hang in there one more day because he didn't want to mark our position with a chopper coming in. So I hung in there one more day, but by noon of the next day I couldn't walk. He called a chopper to come get me.

When I got off of the chopper at the Hill I noticed a bunch of brass bunched around near the chopper pad. I spied the Division Commander's chopper there and then I saw the Division Commander, a two-star general. Then there was the Brigade commander – a full-bird colonel, our colonel and then our major, Major Burns.

I walked towards the medical area when Major Burns called to me. I know I looked a fright with my facial hair, my

Vietnam – The Teenage Wasteland

clothes were a mess with mud and blood stains on them and because of my foot I had a god-awful limp.

The Major came towards me and yelled at me, "Troop! Go get cleaned up and make yourself look like a real soldier".

I knew he did it only because the Division Commander was present but for some reason his statement to me pissed me off like no other statement since, in or out of the Army.

I stopped and looked at him. I saw the other senior officers looking at me and I said to the Major: "With all due respect Sir, I look more like a soldier than anyone on this hill." And I was sure they knew exactly what I meant.

The Major was about to finish me off when the Division Commander came running at me and said, "You are right, son, you do look more like a soldier than anyone here. Sit down," as he helped me to the ground.

I thanked him as I took the weight of my foot.

"What company are you from, son?" The Division Commander asked.

"Alpha Company, Sir."

"Oh Alpha, did you know Captain Dunagan?"

"Yes Sir, I was his radio man."

He looked at me for a moment and seemed to lose his train of thought. Then he said, "Of course. Now, what's the limping all about, here?"

"My foot is rotting, I'm afraid."

The General turned to his aide, a Lt. Colonel and said "Go get my doctor, bring him here right now.

The Colonel took off running and the General said to me: "We'll get you fixed up right away and back into the fight."

The Colonel and the General's doctor came-a-running and the doctor sat down next to me and asked me which foot was hurting. I pointed to it and told him we couldn't get my boot off. Other medical types showed up with a stretcher and the doctor told them to take me into the examination bunker. They picked me up, deposited me on the stretcher and carried me off.

The General yelled "Take care of him. He's Dunagan's RTO!"

We got to the exam room and the doctor looked at the situation. He used a scalpel and cut my boot and sock off in thin little strips. When he was done, my foot was red and raw with no skin on it. I had a real bad case of "Trench Foot" and the doctor told me that if I had waited one more day to come in I would have lost the foot.

He went to his refrigerator and pulled out a jar and handed it to me. I looked at the contents of the jar. It looked like a dark black and green Vaseline type of salve.

The doctor gave me instructions: "Take this outside and find a place where there are no other people nearby and put it on the raw areas of your foot."

"Why don't you put it on, doc? I don't want to do it," I whined.

The doc laughed. "No way, you are the only person in the world that is going to be able to apply this. If I did, I would be in danger of losing my life. No, go on out there and put it on. You have to put it on three times a day. So go on now!"

I found a crutch and hopped outside to a place where there were no people. I sat down on the edge of a sandbagged roof and took a gob of the salve on my fingertips.

"What's the big deal?" I wondered, and with that I smeared it on the top of my foot from the toes to the ankle.

I screamed like a little girl and at the top of my lungs. It felt like someone was blowtorching to the top of my foot. I kept screaming until I passed out.

I came to a few seconds later as the fire on my foot waned. I was soaked with sweat. It took me another two hours to get up the nerve to put the rest of it on, but I finally did it.

I hopped back over to where the Doctor was, and he laughed at me and assured me that the fact that it hurt so much showed it was working.

I nodded at him, he was probably right.

Vietnam – The Teenage Wasteland

"I could hear you screaming from inside my office." He was very amused. I wasn't.

That night I woke up when Charley-Charley chopper took off from the exec pad. I looked out to where Alpha Company was and they were popping flares. I went into the Radio Center and asked what was going on.

I found out that a brand new guy that had only been with the company for two days got turned around and confused in his foxhole when on guard duty at two in the morning, and opened up on the position next to him when they were changing guard. He killed George "Hobie" Noe, who had only been with the company for a month but was an upcoming star. He also severely wounded Lamont Prior, a vet from May 14th.

That it happened really disturbed me and it meant the company was not up to speed; we had a lot more work to do to bring it up to par.

The salve worked excellently and I was pretty much healed after five days. The Doc gave me the thumbs up to return to duty, and I flew out to the company where I resumed command of the radios.

The next day, Captain Roberts confessed to me that he had only been the temporary CO of Alpha Company and he was now to assume command of Bravo Company. He said the new Captain of Alpha would arrive tomorrow.

It kind of pissed me off because I felt comfortable with Captain Roberts, and now I had to break in a new one as well as the company. The company was not yet up to speed and needed more time under a good Captain. You just never knew what you were going to get when you got a new CO. I was concerned.

The next day a chopper came out to us and picked up Captain Roberts. He hugged me and told me to take care. The new CO would be out later in the day. So we spent half of the day without a CO.

Just before dark, Charley-Charley came out with our new CO. His name was Captain Krupp. He was a tall man, with dark curly hair and looked a little anemic.

After the introductions he told me he had orders from Uphill to take us to the nearest high ground and park for the night. We took off and walked for an hour and stayed on a local hill.

Captain Krupp followed me around while I saw everyone, got them settled in for the night and had them set up night-defense positions. As I moved around the camp I watched him. He seemed real tentative, timid. It bothered me right away. He was putting on airs and wasn't sincere. I grew more and more worried.

The next day we moved from our night position to another high ground. The Colonel was letting us settle in with the new CO before we got into any contact. We made it to our new position by noon and settled in.

The CO and I had lunch and then he asked if he could talk to me in private. We walked to a part of the hill where we were alone.

As he began to address me I could see he was embarrassed. He looked around and then confided in me. "I'm afraid, Tom. I don't know what to do out here. I've never been in combat before. I'm sorry, but I know this is a rough area, I don't want to screw things up and get a bunch of people killed."

I smiled at him, happy that he was a man who knew his limitations and an honest one at that. I respected him for telling me the truth that he was afraid, rather than trying to live the lie and get people injured or killed as a result. "Don't worry Captain; I think I know how to handle this diplomatically. As I know how to run the company under any conditions, you wear the bars and I'll call the shots."

He smiled in relief: "I was hoping you would say that. Thanks Tom, that's what we'll do, then."

He lasted another three days and then asked to go back to battalion to "debrief". He never came back. We sat on a hill

Vietnam – The Teenage Wasteland

for hours awaiting his return. Finally, Uphill called and told us to put Lt. DeLuna on as the new CO until he found another one. It was just as well, no sense having a CO that did not want to be there.

Colonel Uphill threw me a bone at the same time. He told me I had been promoted to Sergeant. That was good news because it meant more pay.

Three days later we got another Captain. His name was Winslow. He was a fiery little guy – a miniature version of H. Ross Perrot. He told me straight up that we were infantry, and we were going to charge out there and kill the enemy AND we were going to do it without the help of choppers or other air support. This took me somewhat aback so I asked him why. He told me that it just wasted the tax payers' money to use jets and choppers all the time. He asked me if I knew how much an air strike cost. I asked him: "Who gives a hairy shit?" He told me to shape up, or he was going to get another RTO.

I thought, my God, another loony.

Two days later I went head to head with him. He marched us into a blind canyon that was barren of trees or any other kind of cover or hiding places. Before we went in there I told him we shouldn't. It was a bad place to get caught in.

His response was: "Well, the NVA know that, and they know no one is stupid enough to march a company in there, so that is why we are going in. Besides, if they do ambush us there, we will defeat them. After all, we ARE looking for them."

After this harangue I knew for sure he was an idiot, and you know what? We did get ambushed in that canyon. We had one person killed immediately and another two severely wounded.

The first platoon was pinned down by a machine gun. The Captain and I were pinned down by another machine gun as we took whatever cover we could find. I got on the radio and called for helicopter gunships.

Captain Winslow told me to belay the order, and that we were going to stage a counter-attack. It was just plain insanity, and I tried to tell him we were going to take a bunch of casualties if we tried a counter. The best thing to do was withdraw from the ambush and call gunships on the dinks and then, and only then, go after them. That way we'd take fewer casualties.

Nope, he ordered me to coordinate the counter-attack and get it going now!

No way was I going to do that and told him so. I took off under a hail of bullets and ran to another place I could take cover fifty feet away. I changed the radio frequency and called for the choppers.

Captain Winslow yelled over to me to not call in the choppers.

I yelled back to him that he should come across and stop me. And, as I thought, he was too chicken to come.

The choppers came in and hosed down the bad guys while I pulled our guys out of the canyon. It took twenty minutes to get us all out of there, and it was a miracle we didn't get more killed.

But we did suffer a number of going-home wounded, seven to be exact, three of them veterans from before May 14. A lot of hard won experience was lost that day.

After we pulled out, the Captain came over and yelled at me for fifteen minutes on how I disobeyed a direct order under a combat situation, and that I was going to jail for a long time and so on.

I finally wheeled on him and screamed, "Shut the fuck up!" He wrote me off at that point, I could see it in his eyes.

That night, we arrived at our night logger and I set up the scrambler to talk to the Battalion Commander. The Captain yanked the handset out of my hand and ordered me to go check the perimeter. While I was gone, he complained to the Colonel about how I'd disobeyed him and so on. He didn't know that I was the fair-haired boy in the battalion and that it wasn't going to work.

When I came back from doing my rounds he told me the Colonel wanted to talk to me. I picked up the handset and the Colonel asked me my version of what went gone down. I told him everything. He told me he was not happy with me but that I did make the right decision and told me to put the CO back on the radio.

I handed the handset to the CO, and he spoke with Uphill. This is all I heard: "Yes Sir? Yes, Sir…but Sir… but…. No Sir… but… but… yes Sir, yes, Sir, yes Sir. No Sir, yes Sir"

Then he looked at me, defeated and said, "Colonel wants to talk to you." And he handed me the phone.

I keyed the mike "Yes, Sir?"

"Tom, this Captain is out of there, and we have a new CO coming out in a few days. I am coming out in fifteen minutes and relieving Captain Winslow of command. I'll put DeLuna back on temporarily. However, you are going to be demoted for your blatant refusal of legal orders from a senior officer in a combat situation. You created a sticky mess, and I am going to try to smooth it over. You lost one stripe, try to get it back soon. See you shortly."

Even though demoted, I was still elated. We got rid of an idiot before he got us all killed. I put the handset down and never said a word to Winslow until the Colonel arrived.

The Colonel finally arrived and took the CO back with him. Lt. De Luna and I both sighed in relief. Then we sat down and played three-handed hearts.

It had been two weeks since the May 14th incident. DeLuna was still the temporary CO. I guess there weren't many takers for the job because of our reputation as a massacred company.

That day I got a call to get my gear ready and turn the radio over to someone else. A chopper was coming out to get me and I'd be gone a couple of days. I thought I was getting busted out of the field and was a little grief stricken as I turned the radio over to my friend Jessie.

When I arrived at the Hill, Colonel Uphill briefed me. There was an enquiry at Chu Lai regarding 14 May.

Uphill and I took a chopper to Chu Lai. I was fitted for a Class A uniform and we went to the inquiry. I waited two days for my turn to be interrogated by the board. I was finally called to go in.

I entered the room. There was a board of one General, two full colonels, a bunch of Lt Colonels, a few majors and a lot of Captains. I had not seen any of them before, except the General and the Colonel to his left. The General was the Americal Commander and the Colonel was the 196th Brigade Commander.

On the wall behind them was a very large map of the AO and a lot of arrows and stickers and notations in grease pen.

They walked me through the incidents that took place from May 10th to May 15th. It took about six hours. They were very thorough and asked me very specific questions about this and that and what exactly did Captain Dunagan say about this or that to Uphill or anyone else in Battalion.

They seemed very interested in the Marines refusing to drop bombs for us and asked me how I felt about it.

I told them I thought the Marines were good, but those particular pilots were disgusting. I got a grunt back from the General on that point.

Then the General asked me all about Captain Dunagan's actions on May 14th and finally what I thought should be done about it.

I told him I thought the Captain should be put up for a Medal of Honor.

The General smiled but then frowned when he asked me if I had heard that Captain Dunagan flew back to LZ Professional on the 14th of May and punched Colonel Uphill.

I told him I heard a rumor about that.

He asked me "Do you know why your Captain did that?"

Vietnam – The Teenage Wasteland

"Not really, Sir." I replied.

The General straightened up and steeled himself a bit. "Just so you know, your company was ordered into the NVA's staging area – the very area from which they attacked LZ Professional. It seems your company was deemed, ah, expendable."

I was stunned but it made sense. But then it pissed me off. I looked at the General and said, "My god, had they told us where we were going and why, we would have treated the situation much differently. We would have used whatever support we had differently. Why didn't they tell us?"

"My thoughts exactly, son," he said dryly.

Finally we got near the end, and the General said he had a few more questions for me. He wanted me to listen to a tape recording and nodded to a Captain standing on the right of the panel to turn on a tape recorder.

I was in horror when I heard my voice from May 14th talking to Colonel Uphill.

"Negative, Eagle. If I would have thought you were doing everything you could, I wouldn't be calling you. I don't think anyone there has a clue as to what to do and I think you are just waiting to hear our final call. But that is not going to happen. You are going to come up with a plan for us and it is going to be in the next ten minutes. I don't care if you come out here on your chopper and start shooting at these bastards with your .45, but you need to do something and it needs to happen now. You are the Colonel of this battalion and you need to do some colonel-ing. So what is the plan?"

The General nodded again and the Captain turned off the recorder.

I was so embarrassed I shrunk in my chair.

The General looked at me sternly and spoke clearly and evenly and the words rang in my ears. "What on earth possessed you to talk to a senior officer like that?"

I knew I was dead meat. I mean, you just can't be a corporal and talk to a colonel like that. It is a huge offense, especially in a combat situation. I had nowhere else to look for an answer except in my soul and it came out of my mouth involuntarily. "I didn't want any more of my friends to die," and with that I broke up a bit, doing all I could to the stifle the sobs that were welling up from somewhere deep inside.

I wiped away the tears that had escaped and looked up at the General. He was a picture of compassion. The tape was played to make me squirm a little and see what my answer was, and I guess I hit the nail on the head because I noticed the other senior officers were smiling kindly too.

Finally, the general said. "I understand, Son. I do. Good answer."

All I could do was gently nod my head by way of reply.

The General straightened up, looked at me with curiosity and spoke again. "One more question, son. From all accounts, most men in Alpha dumped their rucksacks by the morning of 14 May. It seems you were the only one in the entire company who kept their radio. It is understood, when men are fighting for their lives, they tend to shed the packs that slow them down. But my question is this, why did you not dump yours?"

To me it was a no-brainer. I answered him immediately. "Uh, without a radio we were dead meat. I never dump my radio. It was our only lifeline, Sir."

The General smiled, right answer again. "And that's why you are going to get a Silver Star. This board will recommend the Congressional Medal of Honor for Captain Dunagan and you are going to get a Silver Star. I will catch up with you later, Son. You and Captain Dunagan and the rest of Alpha Company performed outstandingly and made the United States Army proud. You defended yourselves in an outstanding manner against such a superiorly numbered enemy, while also inflicting maximum casualties on them. I want you to tell the survivors in Alpha that I salute them and that I am proud of them all."

With that I was dismissed.

Vietnam – The Teenage Wasteland

I went outside and saw Lt David Waltz there. He still looked haggard, but he was cleaned up. I asked how he was doing.

Tears welled up in his eyes. "Tom, I lost them. They are dead, and I am alive."

I hugged him.

After a few moments and just before he was called in, he asked if we were in trouble. I told him it was just the opposite, we were the heroes. He looked at me astonished and when I told him I got a Silver Star looked surprised.

But that is the way the Army works. A situation where an entire company is massacred is a real flap because so many dead and wounded makes the Army look bad. The press has a bit of a field day with it, and the Army can't afford bad press about heavy losses on the battlefield, especially in light of the growing animosity towards the war back home.

So in the Vietnam War, the Department of Defense learned the fine art of public relations. People at home were tired of weekly statistics showing figures representing dead teenage sons. It was better to give them some "good" news. So the DOD handled situations such as an entire company being wiped out with some public relations.

There were only two solutions for a disaster in the field. The first solution was to bust everyone up and down the line, condemn the officers concerned and appease the American public that way. But it was very costly because there was already a shortage of officers.

So the second solution was invoked. You laud everyone involved and promote as many as possible and make it into a heroic event and amaze and dazzle one and all with the war story. That is what we call military PR.

I was personally in favor of the second solution because it certainly saved me a lot of trouble. And we didn't need to lose any more officers.

We waited until the inquiry was over, and the General called Dave Waltz and me back in to the inquiry room. We had a quick little ceremony where he pinned Silver Stars on us. He took them back after the pictures were done because they only had two of them and would need them later. He said ours would be sent to us in the mail and we were dismissed.

Neither Dave nor I saw our Silver Stars after that. They were never mailed to us and whenever we inquired about them we never got an answer. But we didn't care, we saw each other get them and that was enough.

Dave went back to Echo Company and I went back to Alpha and debriefed to one and all, and told them Dunagan was going to get a CMH and what the General said about Alpha Company. Everyone was proud.

The day I came back was sort of fun. We celebrated and partied hard.

The next morning the new CO arrived, a Captain named Thornton, a wiry little guy around five foot-seven, balding, with intense eyes. He looked experienced and sharp. I liked him right away.

He introduced himself to me and asked if I was his RTO. I told him I was, and he told me he'd heard a lot about me and he was proud to have me as his RTO.

I had already warmed to him when he told me he had been the CO of an infantry unit in the Mekong Delta, down in the south. But, he said, it was a lot different there and wanted me to teach him everything there was to know about this place, and promised me he was a fast learner and would listen to everything there was to learn. I was real happy. He was smart.

We also received a new Battalion Commander that day. Uphill didn't survive the TAC-E and found himself back in the states commanding a desk.

The new commander mustered us up and introduced himself as Colonel Coventry, calling himself "The Old Bull". He was in his early forties, a little overweight with two pearl handled six-shooters hanging low from his hips. He

Vietnam – The Teenage Wasteland

flamboyantly announced to one and all that he was a cowboy and told us all a story, a joke we'd all heard before.

"Gentlemen, my name is Colonel Coventry and I am your new Battalion Commander. I am proud to be a professional. I am different to your last commander, and I will explain that to you with a little anecdote. There is the story of an old bull and a young bull. One day they were on a hilltop looking down at the cows below. The young bull said to the old bull 'hey let's run down there and fuck all those cows.' The old bull replied, "No, no, no, we're going to walk down there slowly and screw all of those cows one at a time." And that is why I call myself the 'Old Bull'. So we're going to change the way we do things around here to avoid another catastrophe like 14 May."

He went on, ranting and raving about how things were going to change, but I was too pissed off to hear the rest of it. I just bit my tongue and sat there pretending to listen. I wanted to punch his lights out and shove those fancy six-guns up his ass. What a pretentious dick. Had he been there he wouldn't have survived 14 May and he would have changed not one thing about the way it went down. What a dick.

We went out to the field and after another week or so the company was in the groove.

The new Captain was working out just fine. At first, I ran the company and he would ask me why I did this and why I did that and sometimes he would add improvements. By the end of the first week, he had a good grip and took full command, and we were working like Mutt and Jeff. Things were beautiful.

Finally, on the 4th week after 14 May the 101st Air Cavalry choppers found the rest of the 2nd NVA Division. They were holed up right under our noses on Hill 56 about six klicks to our south. The brass decided that it was time to evict the NVA from our AO and destroy what was left of the 2nd NVA division, once and for all.

Our Battalion, now ready for combat, and the 502nd from the 101st were to mount an attack on the NVA position, which we called Recon Zone Alpha.

We loaded onto choppers and flew out to the foot of Hill 56 and together with the 502nd, set out to destroy the NVA.

The 1/17th Air Cavalry mounted air strikes, directed artillery and choppers in on the 2nd NVA Division, and pounded the mountain ahead of us with devastating firepower.

The Marines joined in by placing a regiment behind the hill in a horseshoe ambush to cut off any retreating NVA.

Once the 1/17th Air Cavalry decided they had chopped up the 2nd NVA's hill enough, the infantry moved up that mountain.

It was a horrible go because it rained most of the time, turning the slopes into a muddy vertical quagmire that was near impossible to negotiate. You would climb up fifty feet and slide back forty feet.

We were supposed to take the mountain in one or two days but because of the rain it took us five. Not only was it rough going up that muddy slope, but the remnants of the 2nd NVA were there in high numbers and willing to fight to the death.

The amazing thing was that we took surprisingly light casualties in those five days.

When we finally made it to the top the NVA decided to make their last stand. We were all behind trees shooting at them, and they were shooting at us and we were stuck there in a stalemate. The clouds were down on the mountain so any kind of air support was out of the equation and we weren't going to retreat. The NVA had plenty of ammo and were going to fight to the end, so it was locked up good. It was a bad situation for us to be in though, because we were burning ammo at an alarming rate so something had to give, fast.

I looked over at the Captain and he looked at me and he shrugged his shoulders.

Vietnam – The Teenage Wasteland

Bullets were flying in both directions. It was so intense that the tree I was standing behind sounded like there was a woodpecker pecking at it.

Captain Thornton looked at me again and then got a crazy kind of look in his eyes. With all the intention he could muster, he screamed CHARRRRGGGGEE! at the top of his lungs as he broke from behind his tree and took off running toward the NVA.

It was as if an invisible, giant hand pulled me around the tree and pushed me forward. The next thing I knew I was charging towards the NVA firing at anything that moved.

The rest of the company broke forward as well. We all charged the NVA screaming at the top of our lungs.

What an adrenaline rush it was. It was, without a doubt, the craziest thing I have ever done. It was a magical moment. I felt invincible, and I was finally going to defeat the people that had chopped up my company so utterly. We were now the victors.

The NVA freaked. They never expected us to charge them, never thought we would do such a thing and now they were dying wholesale. They broke, turned and ran for their lives.

It was a killing frenzy. We shot them down as they ran. I was running over dead bodies. We were still shooting them as they ran down the other side of the mountain. But when they finally disappeared into the brush the Captain called to halt.

I sat down to catch my breath. A few minutes later we heard them run into the Marines. The gunfire was intense. It lasted three minutes, and then it was quiet.

The Captain and I looked at each other quizzically because that fight sounded too short.

We went back up to the top and spent the next day stripping the dead of their weapons, searched for and discovered caches of ammo and weapons, blew them up, blew up bunkers and headed back down the mountain.

We were picked up by choppers the next day and flown back to the LZ Pro. The 2nd NVA Division was history.

It was peaceful for the first time in what seemed like an age. I watched the sun go down in a spectacular display of colors.

That was a night we partied hard. We had decimated the rest of the NVA and that was cause for much celebration.

That night I was called to TOC. There was a Marine Colonel there with Colonel Coventry. I reported in with Captain Thornton.

The Marine Colonel wheeled on me and asked me if I was the RTO of Alpha.

I told him I was.

He yelled at me. "You cost the lives of seven Marines by your negligence. You were supposed to inform us when the NVA were headed in our direction. You didn't call us did you?"

I was a little dumfounded. "Uh, no Sir."

He charged at me. "I lost seven killed and twenty three wounded and out of action because of you. What the fuck is your problem, soldier?"

I was confused. I tried to handle it, but I was in too much shock. "We, ah, were… ah… talking to each other on the, ah, radio, weren't you guys listening?"

He exploded. "Where was the call?? Why didn't you call us? We were overrun you fucking idiot!"

Now I was pissed, and that brought me out of shock. I attacked him back because he was trying to blame me for his own incompetence. "Bullshit, Sir! Your guys were supposed to be monitoring our frequency and when we made our final attack we were a little too busy fighting NVA to call, but there were calls to other platoons when we were chasing them. Besides, what did the Marines think all that gunfire was that was coming at them, fireworks?"

His jaw dropped open at my insolence and that gave me time for another shot.

"Besides, they should have been on alert, and when the NVA came running at them, they should have been able to handle it. I'm willing to bet they were smoking dope and fucking around rather than tuning into the action. If they had their shit together they would have been able to defend themselves no matter what the situation. Those NVA were running for their lives. It should have been an easy kill. You're just looking at the Army as a scapegoat instead of looking at your incompetent officers, Sir."

He went ballistic. "You little prick. I'm gonna have you court martialed. I'm gonna have your fucking head. I'm gonna rip your fucking eyes out and puke in your skull."

With that he wheeled and was gone.

My Colonel asked me what had happened out there. I told him again. The Marines should have been listening to the radio. They should have understood the NVA was coming at them. I mean, what did they need a call from me saying: All of that yelling and screaming and gunfire and radio chatter about the NVA running means it is happening? I told the Colonel it was bullshit, they had some kind of severe breakdown in their own units.

He nodded his head and said, "I've never had success working with the Marines."

The Captain and me were dismissed and went back to our company.

I was in my seventh month in Vietnam and wondered what the remaining five would bring me. I thought about life and figured I needed to be cool and just get through the last five months of my tour in one piece. I decided too, that we were going to get through those months as a company, with no more men killed. We had cleaned out the NVA from our sector – for now. It would take months for them to get their shit together enough to mount another offensive. By that time I'd be back home. My spirits rose, things were looking up.

I never heard from the Marine Colonel again. He backed down and worked on handling his obvious internal problems, I'm sure.

I went on R&R a week later. I needed a break.

20

REST AND RECOUPERATION

R& R was a treat. I went to Sydney, Australia for a week and got myself properly laid. I really, really, really had a good time. Forgot all about Vietnam and got lost in a woman I met and almost got married! She was wonderful and genuinely loved me. We made plans to meet each other after the war and get married and all that. How magical she was, just like her country. Magic.

But when I went back to Vietnam I broke off all contact with her and never talked to her again. I just didn't want to hurt her by getting myself killed, couldn't even face the thought of putting her through that so told myself I had to move on.

I actually started to worry about the company the last day of R&R and became anxious about getting back. I got on the plane and made it back to Chu Lai.

I hooked up with First Sergeant Thomas Alt (nicknamed "Top" for Top Sergeant) and he took me to the chopper that was going out to my company on a re-supply run.

As we walked the two hundred yards or so to the chopper pad, I noticed he was kind of quiet and walking close to me.

Vietnam – The Teenage Wasteland

"Top, I know my way to the pad, you know. You don't have to take me."

He just nodded and said nothing as we walked on.

I got within thirty yards of the chopper when all of a sudden my legs turned to rubber and I collapsed on the sand. An overwhelming surge of grief came over me and I started crying.

Top kneeled down and held me in his arms.

"I can't go back out there, Top. I can't. I can't."

He was real gentle with me. "I know, Son, I know how you feel." Somehow he knew this was going to happen.

I looked at him. "Does this happen to everyone?"

He nodded. "Just about everyone. You'll be fine. All you need to do is get to your company and you'll be fine. They need you."

I stood up and walked the rest of the way to the chopper. My legs were stiff and felt like they were made of lead.

I was shocked it happened. But according to Top it happened almost every time someone came back from R&R. It was just an odd thing and there was no real explanation for it.

As soon as I was on the chopper I was back to normal.

We took off and set out to join up with Alpha.

I was the only person on the chopper except for the crew. I sat on crates of food, mail, ammo and other crap.

After a while the chopper started spiraling down to an LZ on the side of a hill. I saw guys down there as the chopper started to land.

But there was something wrong with their uniforms. They were khaki. Holy shit! NVA. No one else noticed.

I charged a round in my M-16 and opened up on them. The door gunner woke up and opened up as well. The pilot gunned it and got us out of there, just as bullets started to hit the ship.

It really pissed me off. The pilot landed in the wrong spot and almost killed us all.

I went up to the pilot and yelled at him over the noise of the rotors, but he just glared at me so I gave him a butt stock upside the head and went and sat down again.

The chopper finally landed where Alpha Company was, for real, and I got off. I threw the finger at the pilot as I left and walked up to the CP. The Captain jumped up and shook my hand.

"Welcome back, Tom."

"Thanks, Captain. It's good to be back."

"What happened over there?" He said, pointing a few klicks away. "He land in the wrong place?"

"Yeah, and it was loaded with NVA, going through last night's garbage you guys left behind."

The Captain was amused. "I heard an M-16 go off first, that you?"

"Yeah. I had to wake everyone up. Luckily the NVA were just as surprised as us. What an idiot of a pilot."

The Captain shook his head and told Jessie to throw some artillery over there to see if we could get a few more.

For the next few months we walked the AO and cleaned up the last vestiges of NVA and peace reigned throughout. Through August and September we were pretty much on a camping trip. It was quiet.

Only one thing happened, I was struck by lightning one night. It hurt real good, but I survived it.

I had obtained an air mattress and slept on it every night because it stormed so much in the wet seasons and the air mattress kept me dry. One night, though, I woke up in the middle of the night during an intense thunder storm, floating in a small pond of water. I was getting wet, so I stood up and put the air mattress over my head. The lighting was landing all around us. It was a pretty ferocious storm and the downpour was almost biblical. I lit a smoke and puffed on it while I watched the storm from under my make shift mattress roof.

There was a blinding light and the next thing I remember was waking up in Sergeant Martin's lean-to.

Vietnam – The Teenage Wasteland

I could see through the flashes of lightening that he was trying to say something to me, but I couldn't hear anything. But I could feel millions of needles pricking me all over my body.

Finally, I started to hear the Sarge, he was asking me if I was okay. I thought I'd answered him a hundred times that I was fine, but I realized I wasn't saying anything. I nodded and he chilled.

After the storm subsided to a continuous rain, they wanted to send me off in a chopper. I declined and said I was okay. I felt fine, except my head hurt.

The Sarge told me the storm had woke him up and he was watching me standing there smoking when a bolt came down and hit a tree twenty feet in front of me, the bolt went along the ground, between my legs and hit another tree behind me. He said I did a back flip and landed on my head.

I think it was a good thing that I was wet and standing in water because all that moisture kept me from being burned. I was lucky.

We kept patrolling and kept kicking up patrols of NVA and blasting them. For the most part, there was just enough action to keep us alert and alive.

21

BEING SHORT IS ALSO A SHORT FUSE

It was around September 20th. I had less than a month to go. I was now officially "short" which meant I had only a short time left on my tour. That was the time period when religion and superstition kicked in.

I was scheduled to rotate back to the States on October 15th so I was getting a little uptight but I knew I could eke it out. However, people were walking on eggshells around me because I had a very short temper. I would allow no mistakes, large or small, because I didn't want to make it that close to the end of my tour and then be killed because of someone else's screw-up.

People grew to dislike me during that period because I was not happy with them screwing up and I let them know it rather loudly. I had too much to lose at that point and was pitiless on them.

The incidents of contact with NVA were increasing. At the end of September, we were on patrol in the range across from LZ Pro. There was rumor of a battalion of bad guys in our vicinity. We had just climbed a three thousand foot mountain and camped there for the night. We were in triple canopy jungle and there was no moon. That night, you could not see your hand in front of your face.

Vietnam – The Teenage Wasteland

I had the first shift of guard on the radio, calling around to positions every fifteen minutes asking how things were (sitrep). I finished my shift, turned the next shift over to Jessie, lay down in my lean-to, turned on my small, hand-held transistor radio with the volume down low, pressed it real tight to my ear and listened to the Rolling Stones on the Armed Forces Radio Network.

It was nice and quiet and peaceful, and I started dreaming of home. I started to get elated about the idea of going home because I had less than thirty days to go, and if I was careful I would make it.

I was just drifting off into a very peaceful sleep when Jessie woke me.

"Tom, wake up, we got movement on the trails."

I sat up. "What's happening?"

"There are three flashlights three klicks down the trail, headed our way."

"Okay, keep an eye on them and let me know if more show up." I turned over and lay back down again to get more sleep; I could get another forty-five minutes before they arrived. Three flashlights – usually there are three or four men between flashlights. Could be just a patrol, but what if it was the battalion we were looking for. Nah, they wouldn't move at night. I closed my eyes and was drifting off again when Jessie came back.

"Tom, now we got fifteen flashlights on the trail moving up to us. What do you want to do? Should I wake the Captain?"

I got up. Fifteen lights. That was the battalion. Goddam! "I'll handle it. Let him sleep, he needs it."

That trail led right up to our position. In fact, the trail went right through our perimeter.

Waking up the entire side of the perimeter that the trail ran up to, I put them on red alert and had them set up Claymore mines all down the sides of the trail. There were enough of them placed to take out a platoon. And set up two machine guns right on the trail. I had a meat grinder ready for whoever came up this trail to our position.

I went over and woke up Lt Milliken. He was our new Forward Artillery Observer. The guy was a real clod, a "milk drinker", a sissy boy. He wore horn-rimmed glasses and was what we now call a nerd. How he made it through OCS was anyone's guess.

I told him we had Dinks on the trail headed for us. I asked him if he had laid in the DTs before dark. He said he hadn't, the idiot.

DTs are Designated (artillery) Targets that one lays in around the company at night. Should you get an attack at night you can call artillery boys and have them drop rounds on DT One or DT Two and adjust the fire from there. The cannons are set on these DTs with rounds in the barrels so all they have to do is fire.

It really pissed me off that he hadn't done the DTs. I told him to get the coordinates of the trail three kilometers down from us. I wanted all cannons available to pour fire in there and march it up the trail. The Dinks would run from it and right into our waiting arms.

All of a sudden, there was a blinding light. Lt Milliken had turned on his flashlight and pointed it at the map. He might as well have stood up with a spot light screaming our location at the top of his lungs.

I stomped his flashlight into the ground and it went out. "Milliken, what the fuck is your problem? Didn't they teach you in school how to read a map at night? You use your poncho for cover, and you use a red lens. Now do it right. We need those coordinates right the fuck now."

He got out his poncho and put it over his head and used my flashlight with the red lens. Then uncovered his poncho and almost yelled out to me, "I've got the coordinates."

The flashlight shone in my face. I kicked it out of his hand and turned it off. "You got a real serious problem, jackass.

Vietnam – The Teenage Wasteland

Keep the noise down and the light down or we are going to get fried. Understand?"

"Yes," was his answer.

"Alright, now call the arty in. Let's get this moving."

"Okay."

I crawled over to the radios and asked Bob the situation. He told me there were twenty five flashlights on the trail. They were two klicks and closing.

Okay, the balloon was up. There were at least a hundred dinks on the trail. It was the battalion. I needed the arty.

I crawled back to Milliken. He started yelling on the radio "Redleg, Redleg, this is Red Dawg Seven, over."

I grabbed him by the shirt front. "Why in the fuck are you screaming?"

"I can't reach Redleg."

"Do you have your long whip antenna up?" I asked.

"Uh no, I forgot."

"You idiot, use my radio. I set up my long whip antenna. Never mind, I'll call it in. I don't trust you. Give me the numbers, I'll call it in."

He just stood there, saying nothing.

I put my radio on the artillery frequency. "Redleg, fire mission, over."

"This is Redleg, go."

"Uh Redleg, I need all cannons on coordinates (and Milliken read them off to me), repeat all cannons. We have battalion size unit coming up that trail. I want all cannons on those coordinates. Then walk the arty up the trail. Do you Copy? Over."

"Copy Ashcan, do you want smoke first?"

"Negative, use Hotel Echo, (High Explosive rounds) copy that?"

"Copy Ashcan, wait one.... Round out"

We listened for the rounds. Nothing. Then suddenly there were four explosions right above us in the trees. The goddamn rounds landed in the trees right above us, and it was raining red-hot shrapnel on the company. Milliken gave them our coordinates. On purpose, or was he just a real fucking idiot? I heard the call of "medic" all over the place. Jessie told me the flashlights on the trail had disappeared.

"Go get the guys to shut up Jessie, the NVA will move in on us."

He dashed off to quiet the men.

I got on the radio. "Redleg, cease fire, repeat cease fire. Rounds landed on us. Out."

Someone was screaming. It was Lt Milliken. He was screaming "I'm sorry, God I'm sorry."

I homed in on his voice and grabbed him and told him to shut the fuck up.

He freaked. It was dark and he couldn't see me so started screaming at the top of his lungs, "Don't kill me, please don't kill me." He kept screaming and tore away from me.

I tripped over a rucksack and while I was on the ground found a machete.

Milliken was still screaming, only louder and louder. I grabbed the machete. He had to be silenced. I got up and swung it in the direction of his voice.

He heard it just miss his ear.

I'd just swung the machete again when someone tackled me while another man tackled Milliken and punched his lights out. The man on me was the Captain. He punched me in the forehead and dragged me over to a tree. He got a piece of rope and tied me to it.

Then he tied Milliken to a tree across from me and gagged him.

The Captain came back to me and asked me to debrief him. I told him.

"Why didn't you wake me up?"

"I wanted you to sleep, you haven't been sleeping enough."

"These guys might attack us, and if they do we're fucked. We have several wounded with us now."

Vietnam – The Teenage Wasteland

It was a serious situation. The NVA were going to do something, we just didn't know what. I was in a pickle myself because I tried to kill an officer. But I was still operational and they needed me.

"Cut me loose Captain."

"No, you're going to stay here like this all night," he whispered.

"Cut me loose if they attack."

"I will, but for now I'm leaving you right here."

The night wore on and we waited for the attack. It didn't come. I didn't sleep. I just rested there.

The sun finally came up and light filtered through the trees. The Captain came to see me.

"You okay, Tom?"

Yeah, I'm fine. Cut me loose."

The Captain looked over at Milliken, who was wild eyed and crazy looking. "What about him?"

"He's gonzo, look at him."

"You know, if I were an asshole I could get you in a lot of trouble for what you tried to do to him."

I smiled. "Nobody saw anything, Captain."

He smiled and cut me loose.

As I pulled the rope off of my wrists the Captain looked at me thoughtfully, and then he said, "Uh Tom, I've been thinking. You have had a long time in the field and you've been through a lot. I think, after we get the wounded out of here, I'm going to send you to the rear and let you spend your last days there. You've paid your dues man. Time to go."

At first I was insulted, but as I thought about it, I realized he was right. I was fried. I was hanging by a thread and wound too tight and was going to cause a mess someday. It was for the best. "Cool, Captain. It's for the best."

The Captain sighed with relief. "Who you want to turn the radio over to?"

"Jessie Spencer. He's a good man, Captain. I trained him myself."

"Okay then, turn it over to him."

Jessie Spencer was a black dude from Louisville. I loved him like a brother, and we were best of friends. I put him on as RTO because I knew he had good sense and could think with how to call in air support. Battalion didn't approve of him being on the radio, at first, because "Blacks talk differently and are hard to understand." I called their bluff and played the NAACP card, and they let him in the secret circle of white radio men. I trained Jessie. He was the man for the job.

I turned the radio, the codes and everything to do with the job over to Jessie, and then I called in Charley-Charley to come and get me. I told them, "Come and pick up a short-timer."

When the chopper came, I jumped in and never returned to the field. I spent the next three weeks driving a jeep and picking up stuff for Top and the XO. Then I went home.

PART THREE

ARE WE THERE YET?

22

RE-ENTRY

When I stepped onto the plane for home I was vividly alive and aware I had drastically changed since I arrived in country the year before. I was a new person, and for the better. I was honestly happy. Not because I had killed people and not because I had a good tenure, but because I had endured the worst possible circumstances and lived to tell the tale. That is happy stuff.

However, an unexpected nightmare started when I arrived in the United States. Had I known what was in store for me, I would have stayed in Vietnam where things were simple and crystal clear.

We took off from Cam Rhan Bay on October 16, 1969 on a Flying Tiger Airways jet airliner. The plane felt like it took forever to roll down the dammed runway and when it finally did get in the air, we all cheered and applauded. We knew we were done with the war. However, we still had to get home and combat vets tend to be superstitious types and learned to take nothing for granted.

The flight took 24 hours what with all of the stops in Japan, Alaska and so on but we finally broke through the clouds somewhere above the state of Washington heading for Ft Lewis and the runway there.

Vietnam – The Teenage Wasteland

As soon as the front wheel of the DC 8 touched the tarmac a huge cheer broke out from all 200 veterans on board, and we hugged and clapped each other on the back. We had finally done it! We were on home turf. No one was going to shoot at us now. No one was going to try to hurt us or kill us. We were home.

The plane came to a stop at a remote section of the airport with the left wing almost touching a fence that separated the airport from the public.

As we stepped off of the plane we were immediately confronted by forty or so hippies all festooned with signs that cried: "baby killers", "murderers", "killers" and so on.

As I stepped onto American soil I ceremoniously kissed the ground.

While getting back to me feet, I heard a voice on the other side of the fence say to me, "How 'bout you kiss my ass, baby killer."

I walked to the fence and looked over the crowd for the smart ass. All were yelling and some were trying to spit on me while others were pushing on the fence trying to get at me.

I looked for an opening in the fence but not seeing one, I walked away shaking my head. Nice welcome home. And it bothered me. All of a sudden my elation at being home was tarnished by some idiots the other side of a fence.

As I processed into Ft Lewis, I asked one Captain there, our hospitality guide, why in the world they parked the plane next to that fence. He had no answer.

I wondered, after having my obligatory steak dinner, if the rest of my time home was going to be like that, what with rampant war protests going on across the States.

They treated us well at Ft Lewis, we watched a movie, hung out talking to each other and showing off the goods we bought on our layover in Japan.

The next day, the officers at Ft Lewis decided it was okay for us to talk to civilians so I was allowed to call home. There was no answer. I had to catch my plane to Detroit in a few hours and my parents were nowhere to be found. I tried my brother. No answer. Where the hell was everyone? I finally boarded my plane not knowing if anyone was going to greet me at the airport.

I landed in Minneapolis four hours later and I tried home again during the half-hour layover. No parents, no brother. I got hold of my aunt and told her I was home. She told me my mom and dad were visiting friends for the weekend but should be home by now, and she would call them and tell them to meet me. She took my flight info and welcomed me back, telling me she was proud of me and was glad I was home.

I received totally mixed looks from people in the airport and on the plane. Some people smiled and were real nice to me while many of my fellow countrymen looked at me like I was vermin.

Finally landed in Detroit and my parents were there to meet me but I had to take the wheel on the drive home from the airport because my dad didn't drive and mom was too shaken up to drive. It was hard. I drove at a steady forty five miles an hour and stayed in one lane on a freeway where people were zipping around like race car drivers at speeds in excess of the seventy five mile an hour speed limit. People honked at me and flipped me the bird, but I just couldn't go any faster. I felt I was now in real danger, driving on a freeway with a bunch of people who thought they were at Daytona. Understand also that a year in Vietnam was like ten. I'd come back a different person, one that had literally forgotten how to drive.

My dad looked at me at one point and asked me if I was okay. My only response was, "Why is everyone in such a hurry?" This upset him and I think it made him think there was something wrong with me.

We finally made it home and when we got there, I was in for a real treat. I sensed there was something wrong, my parents were very edgy, and I didn't feel as welcome as I thought I would be.

Vietnam – The Teenage Wasteland

Before I left for Vietnam, I told both my parents that I was going to be a clerk. I never let them catch onto the fact I was in the infantry and was in danger most of the 365 days I was there. When I wrote letters home, I wrote of happy days working with files, but I had filled my brother in on the real scoop.

When I stepped off the airplane in Detroit with all my medals showing, my dad, a WW II vet, pointed to them and said I didn't get a silver star, bronze star, purple heart and Combat Infantry Badge for being a clerk. I said that was true, I had been in combat the whole time and that I had lied to them. My mom just about fainted.

Mom and I made a deal before I went to Vietnam. I would send my pay home, and she would put it in a savings account for me. So I put $600 per month into my savings account the whole time I was overseas. That's around $7,000 I had in the bank when I got home.

In my last two months in Vietnam I dreamt of that money and spent it a hundred times over. I spent it on college, then on useless stuff. I invested it, loaned it out, and used it to start a new business and so on. I finally settled on the idea of buying a Corvette. I was going to buy a nice red Corvette. Then, in my mind, I drove that Corvette with a thousand different beautiful girls all over Detroit. I still have fond dreams of that car.

I woke up the next morning at around noon. My parents were already up, and I took my shower, shaved, dressed and all that.

I walked into the living room. "Alright, let's go to the bank."

Mom looked at me. "What for?" she asked. My parents were poor people who'd had a lot of bad luck with money. They just made it by from day to day on a minimum of money.

"We're going to get my money out of the bank, and I'm going to buy a new car," I said enthusiastically.

"I think you should leave the money in the bank and use it for college when you get out of the Army," mom countered.

I came back with, "That's not going to happen. I've thought about nothing else for months, I'm going to buy a car. So let's go!"

My dad lowered his paper and announced, "Your mom and I decided you're going to leave that money in the bank." My dad was born and raised in Italy until the age of fourteen. He was used to giving commands and everyone obeying.

It was not going to work that way this time. I was too hot for him. "Nope, we're going to the bank now, and we're getting that money out and I'm going shopping for a car."

I looked over at my mom. She looked like a heart attack was coming on. I looked over at my dad, who was still glaring at me from his last command, but his eyes averted mine and he looked back down at his newspaper.

I was a little taken back by this. "What's going on here?" I asked.

Mom burst into tears and dad just looked at the newspaper on his lap. All of a sudden it hit me. They'd been at a friend's house the weekend I was coming home. They'd given me a less than warm reception upon arriving home. And then there was that edginess. They spent my money!

"Did you spend that money?" I demanded.

Dad looked scared for the first time in my life. Mom was about to have a nervous breakdown. I looked at them and my world exploded. That money was all I had. I had gone without for a whole year and struggled with saving that money. It was all I had in my life that meant anything, and they just spent it like it was not a problem.

"Did you spend all of it or is there some left?"

Dad steeled himself. "All of it. Every penny."

Grabbing my coat, I left the house. It was the best thing to do at that point because I was really hurt.

I walked over to my best friend's house. Tony would be good to talk to. He always had a sensible point of view.

Vietnam – The Teenage Wasteland

The walk did me good. I chilled out a little on the way and when I got to Tony's house, I was warmly greeted by his mom, Mrs. Geshel. Tony wasn't there, but I visited with his mom for an hour and had a good time chatting. She waited on me hand and foot and treated me like an American hero. She would have given me her house that day if I had asked for it. Her appreciation and kind words brought me back to reality. At that time I thought the whole world was just crazy, but being with her made me realize it was just a few crazy people that made it seem that way.

Talking to Tony's mom chilled me out enough to be able to think again. I thanked her and left.

I went home and talked to my parents. I asked them if they had good credit. They said they did. So we went car shopping.

I found a nice 1969 Ford Galaxy LTD. Payments were $125 a month, a piece of cake on my Army salary. It was a good substitute and gave all concerned a chance at redemption. I realized that at that time I still had parents but someday I wouldn't, and would feel bad about it all, so I gave them a break for now, but they had to make it up to me at some point in the future. That was for sure.

Later that day my brother showed up. He took me to a bar, and we drank ourselves silly and had a good time.

The following Friday my friends had a party for me at Tony's house. When I arrived all of my friends were there.

I saw one of my close friends, Eddie, who was asleep in a chair over in the corner. I went to wake him up but Tony cautioned me, "I wouldn't wake him up, Tom."

"Why not?" I asked.

Tony was a little sheepish, "He's in a nod."

"What the fuck is a *nod*?" I asked

Tony looked at me cautiously. "He's on Horse."

"Heroin?" I was shocked.

Tony nodded.

My head reeled. My good buddy Eddie was on heroin, and I was not to wake him. I looked at the rest of my friends and they all looked at me as if they were waiting for me to blow a gasket. God dammed right I was going to blow a gasket.

I reached down and grabbed the front legs of Eddie's chair and shook them. His eyes opened up and he gave me an evil glare for rousing him from his reverie.

I looked at him. "Hi Eddy, I'm back. Are you glad to see me?"

He started to bitch at me for disturbing his peaceful buzz, so I turned his chair over and slapped him a few times. The guys pulled me off him and told me to knock it off.

I looked at them. "Who else?" I demanded.

Tony tried to placate me.

"We knew this was going to flip you out, so we didn't invite Eddie. He came anyway, because he wanted to see you."

"Aw, bullshit. Who else?"

Tony took me outside so I did not disturb the party. I challenged him, "You? You on Heroin?"

"No, not me."

"Who else?" I demanded.

Tony looked me in the eyes.

"Greg and Mickey. And Eddie, Tom Hughes and Mike. That's all."

"That's all?" I bellowed. I turn my back a year and you let these guys get hooked? What the fuck, man?" I was pissed.

Tony told me it was probably better if I left the party. I did. I was not happy and I didn't want to hurt anyone, but I was going to get down to the bottom of this at some point.

After that night no one called me. I talked to Tony a few times and he told me that people were saying that I had changed and was not myself and they did not want to hang with me. They all felt the war had ruined me.

I was stunned. My friends. I lost all of my friends because I got pissed about some of them being on heroin. What happened? Had I changed? I guess.

Vietnam – The Teenage Wasteland

I tried to visit some of my friends for the remainder of my month home, but they all seemed like they had something else to do or were "busy" or whatever. I decided the friendships were over.

Before I left for Vietnam we were all hippies and against the war. I was drafted and had a choice of going to Vietnam or leaving for Canada never to see my friends again.

I went to war so that I could keep my friends, but it seems like I crossed the line with them and they now figured I was part of the other side.

I would have made out better if I'd gone to Canada. Nixon would have let me back in a few years later, and I would have still had friends and loved ones. So I lost all the way around.

I spent the last six months of my two-year hitch serving Uncle Sam in Killeen, Texas – otherwise known as Fort Hood. That was probably the lowest point of my life. Fort Hood was probably the most industrious drug outlet in the United States.

When I first got there, everyone had the weekend off, but I stayed behind in the barracks. Some guys came and got me and asked if I was interested in spending time with them.

I went to their barracks and they lit up a joint. It was passed around. When it arrived with me I took a toke. It was tobacco. What were these guys up to?

I looked at the leader whose name was Jerry and passed the joint back to him.

He looked at me and asked, "What do you think of that weed?" All the other guys were looking at me intensely.

"I didn't know Bugler made weed."

Jerry smiled large. "Okay, you're cool."

"What is this that all about?" I asked.

Jerry shrugged. "If you would've said it was good weed, we would've killed you. We all thought you were a narc."

I thought they were dorks, but two nights later a Lieutenant was found in a dumpster with his throat cut. He was a narc.

In the six months I was at Fort Hood I did a lot of drugs which was a mistake.

In that time I did a military funeral for my cousin, who was also one of my best friends at home. He'd arrived back from Vietnam and got in a car wreck at Fort Riley, Kansas and got himself killed. I was asked to bring the body home. Another mistake.

I took my cousin Alfie's body to Detroit. We set up the funeral. My job was to stand at "Parade Rest" for two days while his body was shown. All the time I was standing there people whispered at me as they left the casket. I got around twenty "baby killer" and another fifteen "murderer" and maybe ten other sordid comments.

It was a good lesson in self-control because I wanted to beat a few asses, but I maintained my cool, mainly and only because my family were there. My brother caught one asshole doing it, took the guy outside and ripped him a new one. He came and asked me if others were doing it. I told him not to worry about it, I was used to it.

The real 'fun' occurred when we went to the cemetery.

The night before, the funeral home director told me the cemetery was on strike. He said, "we will not have a funeral there."

I told him not to worry; just to arrange it and we will go in and have the ceremony without fail. He was not so sure, but I told him that it was going to happen. The deceased was an Italian and it was a military funeral so there would be close to a thousand people there, so it had to happen.

I told Alfie's parents that the cemetery was on strike, but that we were going to muscle our way in there and they were very grateful.

Seven guys from Alfie's unit came up from Kansas. They came for the twenty-one gun salute. I briefed them that night, and we worked out a plan of attack. There's nothing like combat veterans.

The next day we took off. The word had spread that we were going to crash the cemetery and have the funeral no

Vietnam – The Teenage Wasteland

matter what. At least two hundred cars were in that procession. Italians love a good confrontation.

Off we went to the cemetery. I was in the lead car with the casket. The GIs were behind me in another limo with the family behind them. We rolled up to the gate and sure enough, seven burly grave diggers stopped us with the outstretched palms of their hands. They all had signs calling for better wages and benefits.

I got out of the car and walked up to the one who looked to be in charge and lit a cigarette. "Good morning bubba. Got a military funeral, here. We're coming in."

Bubba shook his head. "No one comes in today. We're on strike so no funerals."

I looked at him and his buddies; they were all tuned into the conversation, turned and looked at the line of cars that stretched all the way to the horizon. Then I looked back at Bubba.

I tried to be as placating as possible. "You don't understand; this is a military funeral. This guy here fought so that you could have the right to be on strike. We are coming in and you are going to accommodate us."

The other six thugs moved in closer to me.

Bubba got himself a new nerve and blocked my view of the cars. He tried so hard to be professional. "Sir, we are on strike here. No one crosses the picket line, not you, not anyone else. Please turn your cars around and go back to the funeral home or find another cemetery."

I took another puff of my cigarette and threw it on the ground, looked back up at Bubba and felt sorry for him. He was going to lose this one. He had really tried to be tough and stand his ground. But no one was going to be able to deny military precision and force.

I turned around and waved to the limo. The soldiers from Fort Riley jumped out, opened up the trunk of the limo and pulled out their M-16's. They all ran in formation to where I was, and stood next to me, at port arms, rifles ready.

I gave them a command and they charged rounds into their rifles. They looked mean.

I turned around and looked at Bubba and his buddies and they looked worried.

Standing at stiff military attention, I announced: "Gentlemen, all of us are fresh from the killing fields, and we have certain deep feelings about fallen comrades. Now, things are about to get ugly. There is going to be a funeral so you can step aside or we will do what we do best. Take your pick."

Bubba smiled at the cheek of it all. He looked at the other men. They were scared. He looked back at me and smiled. "I'm not going to allow it. Sorry, son."

I nodded at the vets and they turned to Bubba in military precision and brought their rifles up to the ready position, slipped the safeties off and glared at Bubba.

Bubba tried to glare at them and then decided not to call our bluff. He looked at me again and sized me up. Then he let his shoulders sag. "Well, I guess there is going to be one funeral today. Take the casket into the mausoleum and we'll bury him tomorrow."

"Thank you gentlemen, you've done a service for your country." I motioned the cars to proceed, and they went through the gates. Hundreds of pictures were taken of us as the cars entered the grounds. It was a good day.

The only other thing that happened was when I folded up the American flag that had draped the casket. Taps was playing and the twenty-one gun salute was going on. It was a very emotional moment. I presented the flag to the mother on behalf of the President of the United States. She took it and threw it in my face, screaming, "I don't want your fucking flag, I want my son back." I was shocked to my toes. She apologized up and down afterwards, but I was still pretty rattled. Italians!

I finally left the Army on May 25, 1970. It was the happiest day of my life. But at the same time, I felt I had lost two years of my life and my future was going to be peppered with fallout from Vietnam, not all the time but just enough to make my life miserable.

23

LIFE AFTER

Life can only be understood backwards, but it must be lived forwards.
— Soren Kierkengaard

Before I was drafted I had a great job, was attending college, had a great fiancé and a future in professional drag racing. It was the last time I was in control of my life.

The draft was the worst thing that could have happened. I lost it all. My fiancé left me even before I arrived in Vietnam. My job was available to me when I got out of the Army, but I could tell I was not really wanted when I went to get it back. "We'll have to fire someone to give you your job back" was the only welcome I got. To hell with it, I went and got another job, another girl and started a new life.

The only other trouble I ever got into was military related.

My dad, being the President of the VFW chapter in our part of the city, wanted me to be in the Veteran's Day parade in Benton Harbor, Michigan.

I declined, but my mom begged me to go because Dad would be so proud to have me there, and it would mean so much to him, yadda, yadda, yadda.

So I went. It was another big mistake.

Vietnam – The Teenage Wasteland

The night before the parade was all drinking and telling war stories with my dad and other veterans. It was fun but to tell the truth, I couldn't be bothered about the parade.

I went to bed drunk and got up the next day with a hangover. We got up early and put on our uniforms. I put on my uniform with all of my medals and gear, and we went off to do the parade.

There was some concern because I was the only Vietnam vet in the parade. The guys voiced their concerns that there might be trouble because of it. I agreed. However, my dad was not to be denied. He told everyone that this was Benton Harbor, a small city and mainly redneck, so there was no need for alarm.

I was to be part of the twenty-one gun salute, so I was given an M-1 with blanks in it. The blanks were already loaded so we were ready to do it without fumbling with the magazines which were a bit testy on those particular rifles. We took off and marched along the five mile route.

In the second mile some sixteen year-old kid on a bicycle rode next to the parade. He was looking through the ranks, as if trying to find something.

He finally saw me and pointed at me and yelled at the top of his lungs: "Baby killer! There's a baby killer in the parade. Right here! Baby killer!"

The men just in front turned to take a look at me to see if I was okay.

We moved on but the kid kept riding back and forth on the side of the parade yelling that I was a baby killer.

Finally, around the third mile or so the kid got up the nerve and drove his bicycle through the ranks, right up to me and shouted at my face "baby killer, baby killer, baby killer" as he slowly peddled by.

The cops came and grabbed him, took him off to the side and told him to knock it off as we marched on.

Fifteen minutes later the kid came back, turned right down my rank, yelling "baby killer" again, but this time he spat on me too. I mean, a real phlegmy gob of spit.

That was it. I watched him from that point on. I slipped the safety off of my rifle. The kid was going to learn a lesson.

The parade was held up, we were standing still and the kid came back at that point. He kept his distance because he knew he'd pissed me off with the spit so he pulled up and stopped next to my rank. He said, with an evil sneer, "You are a baby killer aren't you?"

I smiled at him and said, "Yes, yes, I am." And with that I drew the rifle up, pointed at him and pulled the trigger.

The report was deafening as the kid flew off his bike and landed hard on the ground.

The men around me tackled me and the police moved in and cuffed me after they kicked me a few good ones. I was picked up and thrown into a police car. Oh, it was a monumental flap. The rest of the parade was canceled and the police moved the vets out of the area.

A short while later I was in the police station being interrogated by the head inspector. He was furious. "What is your problem soldier?" He growled.

I told him everything that happened.

He got cutesy with me: "You know, that kid is in the hospital, not expected to live."

"Cut the shit, I used a blank." I sneered back at him.

The detective smiled. "You're a fuck-up, aren't you?"

I pointed to my medals. "Not according to Uncle Sam."

He sneered at me, got up and brought the father of the boy in. The father had a nasty scowl on his face and before pressing assault charges on me, wanted to confront me so asked me what happened.

I told him everything from start to finish. When I got done I added, "Look, I'm sorry if the boy got hurt, but he seemed old enough to be responsible for his own actions, and he paid for it. I am not a baby killer by any stretch of the

Vietnam – The Teenage Wasteland

imagination. I took great care while in Nam not to harm civilians. I'm highly decorated and I'm proud of my service. I ignored your son until he spat on my uniform. That was the final straw."

The father was taken aback. "He spat on you?"

I pointed to it. "Yes, Sir."

The father was humbled. He asked the detective if he could bring his son in.

The detective looked at me.

"I'm cool," I said.

The detective nodded and the father took off and brought his son in.

The kid had a bandage on his head from landing on the ground. The report from the rifle scared the shit out of him, and he threw himself off the bike and onto the ground, hitting his head.

I jumped in before anyone else, "Sorry about your head, kid."

He smiled sheepishly.

The father addressed his son. "Jeffery, did you spit on this man?"

Jeffery nodded his head as he looked at his feet.

The father's shoulders sagged. "What on earth is wrong with you, boy?"

I chimed in again. "It's not his fault. He watches the news and sees all the crap on TV. He is about 2 years from being eligible for the draft. He just needs to picture himself in a similar situation and think about what he is doing."

Jeffery jumped in, "I'm not going to go to that stupid war."

"I hope not, son. I was drafted, forced to go. If I'd been asked, given a choice, I would never have gone. I hope you don't go. It is not a nice place. But just for the record son, I only killed the enemy."

The kid got a tear in his eye. "I… uh.. Sorry."

The father stood up. "Sorry detective and sorry to you, Tom. I'm taking Jeffery home and we are going to have a nice long talk. I'm dropping all charges."

With that he and his son walked out of the police station.

The detective turned to me. "I'm not done with you yet. We still have serious a problem of you discharging a firearm within City Limits. I can still get you for that and throw in a charge for mayhem. Do you know how much commotion you caused?"

I looked at the detective. He was a pitiful cop in a pitiful little town. I called his bluff. "You know what? Do what you're going to do and let's get it done. I don't want to play games anymore."

He smiled. "Okay, Mister Attitude. You know what? All Vietnam Veterans are crazy. I think you guys are walking time bombs. I think today's little demonstration from you is just a sign of bigger things to come."

I got tired of him. "Whatever."

He gave it some thought. He couldn't rattle me and he didn't want to play anymore games either so took a breath and let it out. "Okay. I am releasing you back to your father. Get out of my town and don't come back. You hear?"

"That's punishment? I am glad to leave this little shit hole," I taunted him.

With that he took me to the booking room. They gave me my personal belongings and the detective talked to my father who was looking at me like he didn't know who I was.

I walked out with dad and we got into a car with two of his buddies. My dad explained that he had to get me out of town, so we'd be going home.

They all nodded like it made sense, but the truth is they were going to miss out on their partying and those guys loved to party.

I told them to just drive me to the next little town and let me out. I would take a bus home. They all brightened up on that and agreed it was a good idea.

Vietnam – The Teenage Wasteland

As we were riding along, one of my dad's friends, Pat asked me, "So what happened in there?"

I told them, "Well the father had the kid apologize to me. The kid is alright; banged his head on the ground and he feels like an idiot now. The father was a nice guy. The detective was a dickhead and told me never to come back to his fair city. I'm going home tonight. I'm sorry I messed up your parade."

Things went all quiet at that and it was a long silence.

I was thinking how sorry I was for screwing up their parade as the silence continued.

Bill Tuttle, one of dad's best friends, was in the front seat. I was looking at him and saw his shoulders begin to shake, head down, then Bill burst out laughing. "Best fucking thing I ever seen." Everyone in the car burst out laughing and the event thereby became another story for everyone to muse on later.

I never went back to Benton Harbor, never needed and or wanted to. I wanted to get away from the stigma of the "Vietnam Veteran." It was a horrible time and you didn't want to be walking around with your uniform on for fear of being spat on, or chastised or even harmed.

All I really wanted to do at that point was go back to the Army and hang out with the guys there and be part of something again. But that was no good, if I went back into the Army, I'd be part of something ugly again – like combat – so that was out.

I got a job a few months later selling furniture in a suburb in Detroit. They hired me because there was a campaign going on to "hire a vet". I guess it was because vets weren't able to find work or something. Another black eye for us.

I'd been back from Vietnam about nine months and got to know everyone in the neighborhood of the furniture store. There was a titty-bar right next door to us, and I ate lunch there a lot. I got to know all of the girls and became friends with the bouncer.

One day I was standing in the front window of the furniture store looking out at the construction going on across the street when I heard yelling from next door. I looked over and saw some dude in a white shirt running for the parking lot at full speed. Then I heard three gunshots. The guy in the white shirt went down. I ran outside and saw the bouncer standing in front of the bar taking aim on the guy.

I yelled, "Hey, what the fuck?"

The bouncer, his name Nick, looked at me dumbly, then at his gun and then at the guy lying in the parking lot, and back to his gun. Then he started to say something to me but didn't finish, instead he took off running down the street.

I ran over to the guy in the white shirt. He was bleeding but good. I asked him to lie still because there was already a god-awful amount of blood on him and on the ground. He fought me while I tried to see where he was hurt. He was freaked.

He tried to take off on me, but I tackled him and then sat on his chest. He bucked me off, and tried to run again, and I tackled him again. This time I punched him in the forehead.

I'm only five-foot seven and weighed around 135 pounds. The guy in the white shirt was around six-foot two and a good two hundred pounds. I couldn't wrestle with him, so I gave him a good shot to the forehead, and he went out.

I straightened out his left leg and was rewarded with a lot of squirting blood in my face, on my shirt, all over me.

White shirt was lucky I was combat trained, because I knew he was within minutes of dying. He had a hole in the femoral artery of his left leg and his life was now oozing away by the second.

I looked around and was fortunate to find a stick lying right next to us. I pulled my tie off and made a tourniquet; put it above the wound and tightened it. I looked at my watch and started timing when to let go of the stick to let some blood flow, so he would keep his leg. I was sure someone had called the cops and EMT but he was running out of blood and it was just a matter of time before I had to tighten the tourniquet for good, meaning he would lose his leg.

I kept the rhythm up on tightening, loosening, waiting for EMT, when white shirt came to. He was still freaked and started bucking me again, trying to throw me off so he could run.

I yelled at him to stay calm, but he was in panic mode and tried to throw me off. The tourniquet came loose and he was sprayed blood all over me again. I was dripping in blood. I gave him another shot to the forehead and he went out.

I'd just gotten the tourniquet back on when I felt something really hard press into the side of my right temple. It pressed so hard my head was bent as far left as it could go. Then I saw the cop out of the corner of my eye and his shotgun against my head and another cop appeared in front of me, also wielding a shot gun.

Without moving an inch, the cop to the side ordered me to get off the man. I told the cop I had a tourniquet on him and could not get off. The pressure on my right temple was killing me as the cop pressed harder.

The cop in front came in for a closer look and then he looked at the cop that had the gun to my temple and nodded to him. The gun came off me.

I resumed the procedure, let go of the tourniquet again and blood squirted and then I tightened it. I yelled out that we needed an ambulance

The cop in front told me it had arrived already. I realized I'd been so focused on what I was doing that I hadn't heard the cops or the ambulance sirens.

The EMT arrived on the scene and I told them what the deal was.

They asked me if I was medically trained.

I responded: "On-the-job, Vietnam."

The EMT guy smiled and told me I'd done an excellent job. He took over and they rushed the guy to the hospital.

I was standing there with blood all over me. The two cops took my statement.

One cop apologized for putting the gun on me so hard. "Understand," he explained, "we were responding to a report of a shooting, when we rolled in the parking lot, all we saw was one guy punching another and both were covered with blood."

"I get the picture, must've looked real bad."

They took my name and shook my hand.

The EMT gave me my tie back before they left. It was gold when I put it on that morning, now it was brownish red.

My boss came and saw me and said, "Uh, I think you need to go home and clean up. In fact, take the rest of the day off."

I went to the backroom and cleaned up as much as I could and left. I felt good. I finally used something from what I had learned in the Army and put it to good use and saved someone's life.

Two weeks later I received a commendation from the Fire Department for saving the guys life and leg. That was cool, his leg made it.

Life went on. It was a struggle. I missed the action but I was not going back to it. Life was boring. I had a good girl, but I didn't want to get married. I could not picture myself settling down and having kids. So we finally parted.

Eventually, I handled my Vietnam nightmares and many other negative thoughts and moods I'd inherited from my stint in Vietnam. I also did a program to rid me of the terrible side effects of Agent Orange – side effects that in my opinion ended up the lives of Kern Dunagan, Dave Waltz and Jessie in the last few years. The effects of Agent Orange are a very controversial and covered up situation that is really another story altogether.

I got married, had four kids and now I'm getting ready to retire.

Vietnam – The Teenage Wasteland

If anyone wants to know how I rid myself of the terrible nightmares, bad moods and effects of Agent Orange they should email or write to me and I will tell them.

I finally got onto the internet about seven years ago, located the Americal Division and found their locator. I discovered that several had been looking for me for a couple of years. One was looking for whoever knew Kern Dunagan and left his number. It was Kern's brother.

We hit it off real well and became friends. He asked me to do a write up of how Kern got his Congressional Medal of Honor. (I was surprised to learn that the Congressional Medal of Honor started with the Civil War in 1861, and to this date, only slightly more than 3,400 have been awarded). I did the write-up and sent it to Kern Dunagan's brother. He was thrilled and told me I should write a book.

I found John Miner, who was one of my best friends in Vietnam. He was living in Oklahoma. Then I got hold of Jessie Spencer. We all met up in San Francisco and hung together for a couple of days. It was a love-fest. We really enjoyed hanging out together.

Then I went to a candlelight vigil that is held in Fort Knox, Kentucky every year to remember fallen friends from the 1st of the 46th.

I went to the vigil in 2001 because the Army decided to dedicate a leadership school on the base there to Kern Dunagan. I had supplied a lot of the facts from the Medal of Honor incident and so was invited and attended the dedication.

It was a good trip because I met a lot more of the guys from Alpha and Charlie Company. Many who tried to help us out that day on May 14th, 1969. It was good to meet them.

We were treated like celebrities when we arrived. I was assigned a Captain, actually the then Captain of Alpha Company, 1st of the 46th Infantry, to be my aide, should I need anything.

The dedication was spectacular and Kern Dunagan was honored properly. We went on a tour of the facilities, and were invited to eat in the mess hall with the troops. The food was good and the guys there all too happy to talk to us.

I met with Kern's wife and kids, and it was real fun being with them. The kids all wanted to know stories about their dad and were really excited to hear anecdotes about him. They said, "yep, that's him!"

24

AN ICE DIP

It wasn't until around the year 2001 that I dug in and tried to understand what the Vietnam War was really all about. I had a lot of questions. Questions like: Were we fighting on behalf of the USA to battle communism out there? I think not, because if communism was the real issue why didn't we go ninety miles across the water from Florida and fight it in our own backyard – Cuba?

Then were we fighting for oil or something similar? Well, no, oil was never found there, so I guess not.

So I decided to take my own experiences and add to them with some in-depth study utilizing the internet and many dusty library books. I leapt into it and after years, I finally came to my own conclusion about what the war was about.

It all started during World War II. The French had been occupied by Germany and the occupation took a great toll on the country. The French were robbed of their valuables – anything that would bring fair market value was stolen by the occupying Nazis and sold. Not to mention the huge amount of real estate destroyed by the Nazis and the liberating English and American forces. In the end, the French were left with little of worth.

Before the war, France's biggest exports to the world were wine and cars. The French factories were destroyed and some of her vineyards went uncared for during the occupation.

When the war ended, the French expected help from the allies in the form of relief, financing or loans to help them rebuild their country.

However, England was in ruins and it too was trying to borrow money to rebuild, not to mention the fortune it already owed, borrowed to fund its six year long war effort so it had nothing to give the French.

The Americans spent all their relief money establishing their own landed prize – Germany. The United States poured millions of dollars into the country getting it rebuilt and functioning, leaving France out in the cold.

The French were pretty miffed by the whole thing and decided to strike out on their own. They needed money badly, to finance the rebuilding of their nation as quickly as possible.

By 1946, just a year after WWII ended, the world heard of French soldiers in Vietnam. What in the world was a war-torn nation like France doing in Vietnam? Their Public Relations answer: "We are fighting communism along with the United States. We are doing our part and stopping it here before it spreads like a cancer."

Good answer. It positioned them with the conquering heroes, the USA, and also gave them the perfect cover, fighting communism, which was now in vogue around the world.

But what were they really doing in Vietnam? Did anyone really believe they had the kind of money it took to support an idealistic venture like fighting communism? That they really had that kind of money to spare just a year after the greatest catastrophe their country had ever experienced? Fighting communism made no money. There was no profit in it, so why were the French in South-East Asia, half a globe away, fighting for a cause that produced no profit?

Actually the French invaded Vietnam way back in 1860 and took advantage of Vietnam's assets such as rice, rubber and a very valuable commodity that few knew of, except the crafty French.

Vietnam – The Teenage Wasteland

There is a piece of real estate high in the mountains that spans the eastern part of Laos, the north-eastern third of Thailand, and the north and mainly western sections of Burma. It is called The Golden Triangle, more than one million square miles of poppy fields and heroin factories that supplied two-thirds of the world with opium. We're talking about a major money-making operation that had gone on for more than hundred years. The French stumbled on it in 1860, and were fast to move in with troops and seize the opportunity.

However the Golden Triangle had its own military, and a formidable one at that. It had millions of dollars to buy any government protection it needed. So it was self-sufficient.

The only Achilles heel the Golden Triangle had was its shipping lines. The only ports close enough to be usable for shipping opium were Haiphong Harbor (Hanoi) and Saigon harbor. All others were thousands of miles away across treacherous lands. On the other hand, the Triangles' mountain routes to Hanoi and Saigon were exposed and could be taken over and controlled easily by a small army. The French somehow realized this was the quickest and easiest way to make big money fast and moved in on these lines before anyone else found out about it.

The French took up positions in Hanoi and along the supply routes of the Golden Triangle. The Vietnamese were outraged, but there was little they could do about it because the French PR message was that they were fighting the horrible communists that threatened to take over Vietnam.

The Vietnamese had nowhere to turn for help. What were they going to say to the rest of the world? "Please help, the French took over our opium trade lines". No, that would simply have made the situation worse. It would have invited in the rest of the world, and a huge war would have broken out in the tiny country.

Also, one could ask: "How come the communists wanted to take over that lowly section of the world called Vietnam, one of the poorest countries on the globe?" The answer is the same: The Chinese saw an opportunity to grab control of Golden Triangle supply lines; they wanted that action and tried to corral it in the name of establishing Communism.

Meanwhile, the French sent opium by the boat-load to Marseilles, France. Marseilles became the opium outlet for the world. Huge manufacturing plants were established, turning opium into heroin and supplying the rest of Europe and the United States with heroin and opium during the 1950's and early 1960's.

Remember the movie The French Connection? Remember when "Popeye" Doyle found the world's largest supply line of opium running from Marseilles to New York? The French had established a major artery of the addictive drug that ran right into the heart of the United States. If you ever wonder why there is so much friction between the United States and France that is half the reason. The French were making many hundreds of millions of dollars a year at the expense of American citizens whose lives were being enslaved by that highly addictive drug. The other half of their beef with us is that we took the opium away from them.

By 1956 the lords of Golden Triangle had built up enough forces in Vietnam to throw the French out of the country, which is what Ho Chi Minh did. The French were being defeated at every turn in the country and were finally forced to leave, having lost the supply line to the "communist forces".

During this French occupation of Vietnam, the hierarchy of our own CIA observed and watched closely. They knew about the opium trade and when they saw the French were defeated and ready to pull they decided that much money could not be ignored.

The CIA moved in on Vietnam, first in 1945 when seven OSS officers, led by Lt. Col. A. Peter Dewey, parachuted into Saigon to "gather intelligence".

Ten days later Ho Chi Minh delivered his famous "Declaration of Independence" (independent from Japan and

Vietnam – The Teenage Wasteland

France) speech to half a million Vietnamese. The French rejected Ho Chi Minh and his declaration, and shelled Hanoi from the harbor, killing 6,000 citizens. The OSS stayed in Hanoi while the French started losing their grip on the country even though the French had been steadily building up forces to combat Ho Chi Minh and his revolutionaries.

Meantime the OSS, cum CIA had designs on the lucrative opium trade, and "stood by" in Saigon as the French finally fell in 1955 and departed Vietnam with their tails tucked between their legs.

How come the French failed all of a sudden when they'd held that country under their rule for more than a hundred years? There are two interesting "coincidences": 1) Ho Chi Minh returned to Vietnam after being exiled for 30 years and was avowed to make Vietnam independent and 2) The CIA had arrived in the area.

Once the French were gone, the CIA moved more troops into the area and took over the opium routes, sending the drug back to the USA.

This was not the USA. It was agents of the CIA who were profiting from bringing the dope home and selling it to dealers in the USA, who in turn, distributed it on the streets.

The CIA established an air-cargo system "Air America" to ferry the heroin out of the Triangle to Vietnam. The CIA also purchased "Flying Tiger Airlines", which was the main airline carrier to ferry American troops to and from Vietnam. On each trip back from Vietnam, the DC-8 passenger planes, filled with elated troops going back home, had hundreds of pounds of heroin in their holds.

The planes would disgorge its troops in Seattle or Oakland and then the plane would be towed to a hanger owned by the CIA and the drugs would be removed from the plane. No one questioned why in the world the CIA, our intelligence agency purchased an entire airline. That's what's wrong with America. No one asks questions.

Undaunted, the Golden Triangle finally funded North Vietnam with as much money as it needed to get rid of the Yanks, and it did.

But it wasn't the Vietnamese or the lords of the Golden Triangle that threw us out. It was the voice of the American people. The people know when evil is afoot. The citizens of the USA protested the war from the beginning and especially near the end. They knew something evil was going on and they wanted no part of it. It was the American citizen who ended the action and got us out of Vietnam – no one else.

When you think that 58,000 unsuspecting teenagers gave their lives (not to mentioned hundreds of thousands injured) so that the CIA could make money from other teenagers becoming addicted in the streets of the USA, you have to wonder what kind of people these guys were.

And the question remains, how many Americans died on the streets of America due to heroin and opium addiction? One might guess it was twice as many as died in the war.

But this was not perpetrated by the CIA itself. This plan was carried out by just a few rouge agents at the top of the CIA who made their millions and left the United States. Some were found and handled in a manner only the CIA can, while others got off free.

The CIA became a spinning conspiracy of cut-throat rogue agents that turned our intelligence community into a mafia-style money-making operation. Those who stood in the way of their money were simply eliminated.

When Nixon resigned his presidency and Gerald Ford took over as president, he ordered George Bush recalled from his post as Ambassador to China to become Director of the CIA and put the place back together so that it would serve the USA and not destroy it.

This story may be a little hard to swallow, but the facts are the facts. There are criminals everywhere and they try to get away with stuff like this. I think the only reason the CIA got away with their scheme for so long was the magnitude of it. It

Vietnam – The Teenage Wasteland

was hard to see the forest for all the trees, a principle used by the CIA in Vietnam. They made it look like they were leading the way, fighting oppression while they were robbing the indigents of their valuable opium trade.

Had I not seen it with my own eyes and first-hand I might not have believed it. I was sent on a patrol one day, to guard a government agent, who was wearing unmarked fatigues and carried a little snub-nosed .38.

We were flown to a village ten miles from the LZ and were told by the agent to guard the perimeter around a house.

The agent went into the house and started shouting in Vietnamese, "where is it?" Then we heard screaming.

I went to the door to see what was happening and what I saw floored me. The agent had a Vietnamese man tied to a chair and the agent was beating the man to death.

The agent saw me standing there and yelled at me to go back outside. I didn't move at first because I wasn't sure what I was supposed to do, so the agent pulled his little .38, pointed it at me and screamed, "Get back to your post, soldier."

That did it, and I went back outside. Then I heard some more screaming and beating and then he finally beat the man to death.

The agent then came outside and ordered us to look in the bushes around the house for anything unusual, like a piece of cloth on a bush, and to let him know when we found it. It was then that I knew that he was looking for drugs.

One of the guys (Smith) did find a piece of cloth tied to a bush. He called me over and showed it to me. I shook my head and decided to not tell the agent. We pulled the cloth off of the bush and Smith hid it in his pocket. We reported back to the agent that we found nothing.

With that, he went back inside the house, tied an old woman to a chair and started punching her as hard as he could in the face, screaming in Vietnamese, "Where is it!"

She was screaming in pain and the rest of the village started screaming at us. I figured this was getting out of hand

and that two things were going on. One, the village was about to have an uprising and two, you just don't beat old ladies to death. I'd had it.

I went in and put my rifle up and slipped it to automatic: "Alright, knock it off and get the fuck out of here."

He pulled his snub-nose and aimed it at me, "You get the fuck out of here or you'll get them same."

By this time the rest of the guys in the patrol came up to the porch and had their guns aimed at him. They were backing me up. I said to them: "He beat the man to death and now he's beating the woman to death."

The Agent screamed back at us: "These people are Viet Cong. I'm trying to find out where the enemy is and you people are cutting across intelligence gathering that could save thousands of lives. Now get out of here and get back to your posts."

I countered, "If what you say is true, then let's call the chopper and take her back to the rear and have her interrogated there."

He screamed at me, "Just do your job and get back to your posts!"

By that time the whole village had erupted and started to become violent.

The agent got rattled at the uprising and walked back outside. "Call the fucking chopper back in. You guys are fuck-ups. I'm going to get you all court-martialed."

I called the chopper on my radio and while we waited we covered him with our rifles.

He sneered at us saying: "You think you're going to get away with this. I'm a federal agent of the United States. You're all in big trouble." And so on. He was a little weasel of a coward and I will never forget his red hair and freckled lily-white skin.

The chopper came, and as it was descending to our position, he told me to tell the chopper to just pick him up and that we were to walk home. So we did walk home. I didn't care if we were in trouble.

When we had finally walked the ten klicks back, the Captain told me I was in deep shit and that I should never have caused trouble. He said, "That guy was CIA. They run this place."

I never heard another word. Never got into trouble, but I learned to hate the CIA after that.

That was an example of what the CIA was doing there. I saw it with my own eyes.

25

IN THE END

So was it hard being a Vietnam Vet? Ya, a little I guess. I think the government owes all Infantry soldiers of any war a lot more than they get. I feel like anyone who has been in combat deserves a lot more than they get from the country they defended. I disagree that I should have the same benefits as someone who served peacefully in Germany during the same time I was crawling around in rice paddies getting my ass shot up. I feel quite strongly about that. I also feel that a mechanic on a ship off the coast of Vietnam shouldn't have the same benefits as I have. There's an imbalance there. I would have traded jobs in a heartbeat with some clerk in the rear area who got to drink and have fun every night while we were getting shot at. Why should he get the same benefits?

But that's the way it has been since Americans fought in the war of 1812. Infantry always got the short end of the stick.

I feel better and more of a person due to my experiences, and that makes me more of a rounded individual. Think of it: someone has been to hell and back and then makes a life for himself and is a good citizen.

My friends from Alpha Company all have good jobs, good families and are living good lives. I am proud of them all. We meet at reunions and talk about this and that and we have a good time. They're like brothers that I lost touch with and now we're back together.

Vietnam – The Teenage Wasteland

Unfortunately Captain Dunagan died well before his time in 1992 of Melanoma, skin cancer, also known as Agent Orange as far as I'm concerned. It had to be a horrible death and not one he deserved for sure. I will always miss him.

Dave Waltz died August 29th, 2001, just days before 9/11. I'm glad he missed that. He died of complications of Agent Orange (Diabetes, Hepatitis C etc.).

Jessie Spencer, my brother of another mother, died of Lou Gehrig's disease in 2003. Agent Orange struck again. I miss him so much it aches.

After all has been said and done, how did my life turn out? I think well. I eventually handled my aversion to marriage and raised four good kids.

Lisa is the CEO of a major software company in Los Angeles with a husband and three beautiful kids.

Jason is an aspiring actor. He will make it someday, I'm sure.

Jeremy has his own custom furniture shop. He lives in Hollywood and hangs out with some of the Hollywood elite.

My daughter Leia is the baby and is an executive at another company.

I love my kids and they love me and I couldn't ask for more. None did drugs, never have, and they are honest, hardworking people. I am so proud of them.

I have to take a little credit. It all started on May 14th when I saw the GI floating face down in the river. I knew something was terribly wrong with the way man treated man, and I swore that my children would never, ever, ever have to go through what I went through. And I work to make sure of it.

War is not needed to shape us. We can learn to deal with people and treat each other without the cruelty I witnessed over in Vietnam. There are other, more positive solutions, we just need to find them and work hard to make this a happy and safe world to live in.

AFTERWORD

Thank you to all of you who have purchased this book so far. I have garnered a lot of reviews, mostly good; some harsh and some banal. But they are all treasured because they are written by people who care.

This was not an easy book to write. It was a very emotional trip for me and it was full of pain and heartache.

But ever since Teenage Wasteland was published I have been accused, by only a few, of painting myself as some kind of hero. I read the book over and I can see how some could get that. I am sorry that it came across this way as I had no intention of doing so. But I also want to point out that after comparing my tour in Vietnam to others tours in Vietnam, I can safely say that my tour was a lot more vivid than most and lot of responsibility did fall onto my shoulders. I actually, at first, wrote this in order to honor Captain Dunagan for his heroism. I have to tell you that being as close as I was to this kind of heroism is both an honor and privilege. And you can't help but get some of that rubbed off onto yourself.

I learned a lot about life from my exploits in Vietnam and also from writing this book and looking back at the tumultuous time that shaped my life and turned me into who I am now. I am pretty happy how I turned out. Not too many were as fortunate. There are only a small handful of guys left from the original Alpha Company. Agent Orange has claimed most of the remaining thirty-eight. It's a hard thing to confront that the Grim Reaper is chasing you down wearing an Orange cape. I know my days are numbered.

Anyhow, a man who used to run part of the CIA read my book and raves about it. He said it should be read by Congress and the Senate before any laws get passed in this country

Vietnam – The Teenage Wasteland

again. I thought that he made quite a leap there from reading my book, and while this is not a response I was trying to elicit with this book, in circumspect I tend to agree. I was trying to paint war as a horrible thing. I was hoping to get the message across to today's young men to avoid going to war. I try to discourage every young man I meet, from going to war. It is just something that they don't need. Nobody needs war. And if my book has discouraged one young man from going off to war, then I am happy.

I understand why veterans are committing suicide in high numbers at this writing. They are not being handled correctly. There are lots of things we can't talk about to others ONLY because it would be unsocial to do so.

I talked to a very troubled Vietnam Veteran who was nice to a young girl of about seven years of age in Vietnam. He would give her candy and treats. He singled her out because she was cute. One day he stepped into her village and found her hanging from the entrance marquee, dead. Pinned to her was a sign from the NVA saying that she was hung for collaborating with the enemy. He didn't kill her, but who is going to convince him otherwise? I was the first one to put him out of his misery by agreeing with him. It was his fault she died. And then I asked him what he was going to do to make up the damage there. He ended up supporting a program that cleaned up Agent Orange toxicity in Vietnam. He has since been living life without this grief hanging over him like a dark cloud.

The point is what are these soldiers going to do with stuff like that? People they talk to just don't listen to them. If people did listen to them they would find out what is killing these vets from the inside out.

Afghan and Iraqi veterans have seen horrible things they cannot get rid of. They are tainted. They see dead mangled children's bodies and it sears into their brain like an atomic branding iron. They can't say to their parents, "Did you ever see a ten-year-old kid with his intestines hanging out of his body?" If he said that to his wife she would tell him to quit being silly; and by the way, when does he get a raise at work?

I knew a WWII Vet who was a tanker under Patton. He had a real rough time with life after the war. After twenty years of marriage after the war was over, he was out on the front porch smoking a cigarette, looking at the moon, and his wife stepped out onto the porch. After a bit he said "I didn't bother me too much if they were dead, but if they were so hungry why did their stomachs look so swollen." He flicked his cigarette into the street and went inside. His wife never said a word to him and the man died a few years later, still in turmoil by what he saw.

The point is that I saw war, and I saw how ugly it is. And what I have learned is that Honor, Bravery and all of that macho stuff does not supplant the idea of a peaceful world. If we spent as much time and energy helping one another then war would become pointless.

If my book helps steer this world into more peace, then I have accomplished something.

Tom Martiniano

Vietnam – The Teenage Wasteland

Made in the USA
Lexington, KY
09 July 2017